Engaging Children's Minds:
The Project Approach
Second Edition

Engaging Children's Minds:
The Project Approach

Second Edition

by
Lilian G. Katz
University of Illinois at Urbana-Champaign

Sylvia C. Chard
University of Alberta

Ablex Publishing Corporation
Stamford, Connecticut

Printed in the United States of America

Library of Congress Cataloguing-in-Publication Data

Katz, Lilian.
  Engaging children's minds : the project approach / Lilian G. Katz and Sylvia C. Chard.—2nd ed.
    p. cm.
  Includes bibliographical references and index.
  ISBN 1-56750-500-7 (cloth) — ISBN 1-56750-501-5 (pbk.)
  1. Project method in teaching. 2. Early childhood education. I. Chard, Sylvia C. II. Title

LB1027.43.K38   2000
371.3'6—dc21   99–055602

Ablex Publishing Corporation
100 Prospect Street
P.O. Box 811
Stamford, Connecticut 06904-0811

Contents

Acknowledgments   **vii**

Foreword to the First Edition   **ix**
     by Mary B. Lane

Preface to the First Edition   **xi**

Preface to the Second Edition   **xv**

Chapter 1. Introduction to the Project Approach   **1**

Chapter 2. Principles of Practice in the Early Years   **21**

Chapter 3. Project Work in Action   **55**

Chapter 4. Phases and Features of the Project Approach   **69**

Chapter 5. Issues in Selecting Topics for Projects   **83**

Chapter 6. Teacher Planning   **91**

Chapter 7. Phase I: Getting Projects Started   **105**

Chapter 8. Phase II: Projects in Progress   **115**

Chapter 9. Phase III: Concluding Projects   **129**

Chapter 10. Drawing in the Context of a Project   **137**

Chapter 11. The Project Approach in Perspective   **159**

Appendix A. Houses: How Are They Built?   **165**

Appendix B. Guidelines for a Project on Seedpods   **171**

Appendix C. Dramatic Play in the Hospital   **173**

Appendix D. Instructions for Children: How to Make your Own Book   **177**

Appendix E. Project Webs for Going Shopping, Weather, and a   **179**
     Construction Site

Appendix F. School Bus Webs for Younger and Older Children   **181**

Appendix G. Zoom Web on Homes   **183**

Appendix H. A Walk Around the School   **185**

Appendix I. Project Web for "How We Get Our Fish"   **191** vi

References   **193**
Author Index   **201**
Subject Index   **205**

Acknowledgments

As always, we owe thanks to many. We have benefited greatly from our work with teachers around the world and in our own classes at the University of Illinois and the University of Alberta, respectively, and from the work of those teachers and colleagues we refer to throughout the book.

Very special thanks are due to our colleagues on the staff at the Child Study Centre of the University of Alberta, Canada, and to the staff at the Valeska-Hinton Early Childhood Center in Peoria, Illinois. From these educators we have gained much insight into the daily opportunities and concerns involved in implementing the project approach. We are especially indebted also to Dr. Judy Helm, Sallee Beneke, and Kathy Steinheimer for sharing their experiences of using the project approach and how to document the children's experiences.

The constant support and encouragement of the staff of the ERIC Clearinghouse on Elementary and Early Childhood Education at the University of Illinois, and their hard work of supporting the PROJECTS-L listserv and publishing the Project Approach Catalogs 1 and 2, and Beneke's *Rearview Mirror: Reflections on a Preschool Car Project* (1998) are gratefully acknowledged.

We continue to be grateful to our husbands, Boris and David, for their unfailing encouragement, support, patience, and interest in our work.

Foreword to the First Edition

To attempt a foreword to *Engaging Children's Minds: The Project Approach* is a humbling experience. In these days, when the pendulum has swung so far toward mechanistic trivia in the educational process, this book offers a refreshing approach. In our desire to make education uniform in this country, we have almost forgotten the true aims of education, especially as they concern our youngest citizens. The conclusions of the authors that "compelling evidence to support our views is needed" is far too modest, for Katz and Chard have not been content to introduce the *project method*. They have presented a method for teaching young children in such a way that the outcomes result in enriched human beings, socially, intellectually, and emotionally.

The plan is buttressed by sound and thorough research in many interrelated areas: normative and dynamic dimensions of development, learning theory, motivation, and communication. At a time when the United States appears to be losing the essential characteristics of appropriate early childhood curriculum, the *project approach* could be an effective deterrent to the "first-grade push" in kindergarten and throughout the primary grades. Katz and Chard's approach is both innovative and resourceful.

The emphasis placed on the development of social competence of young children by suggesting that they learn by interacting with their own firsthand experiences and with their real environment is not a new idea. However, this book is a much-needed reminder that workbooks, patterns, and cutting and tracing lines is largely a waste of children's time. More importantly, such activities are teaching the 5-year-old that school is a dull place, having little in common with real life. It is not accidental that many children's zest for "going to school" at 5 years has been replaced, at age 8 or 10, with boredom and with children separating school hours from after-school hours "when we can really live."

Engaging Children's Minds: The Project Approach offers the inexperienced teacher all of the examples needed to trigger the imagination. This is further strengthened by the presentation of various steps in implementing the project from beginning to conclusion.

If I may be allowed a personal note: I began teaching when the ideas of progressive education were flourishing. Teaching in those days was exciting and challenging, for *the teacher's mind had to be engaged along with the children's*. The outcomes of such collaboration were unpredictable and therefore the process of learning was inherently attractive to young minds. The young seek novelty. They respond to the new and innovative. There's no better way, also, for keeping the mature mind growing. Therefore, my response to this book is: it's about time! We need to get back in touch with the reality of the young children we teach. How auspicious that this book is appearing now, authored by such prestigious individuals as Katz and Chard!

Mary B. Lane
Professor Emeritus, San Francisco State University

Preface to the First Edition

A class of first graders settled down for the morning assignment. Each child was to trace the outline of a maple leaf around a template onto green or yellow construction paper. They were then to cut out the leaf, draw a face on it, glue a popsicle stick to it, and use it as a puppet in a play intended to celebrate autumn and its colorful leaves.

In another class, each kindergartner has cut from a ditto sheet six small, square drawings depicting the story of the *Three Little Pigs*. Their assignment was to paste each of the six pictures on construction paper according to the order of the story. Most seemed to place their pictures in the correct order, though several placed them upside down. Many seemed more absorbed in the properties of the glue than the story sequence.

The activities described are not unusual. They reflect the prevailing views of their teachers that young children should be provided a mixture of creative and reading-readiness activities. Although the children in both classes pursued their activities with moderate interest, one of the girls cutting out her maple leaf turned to her neighbor and said, "You know what? This is really dumb. But my Mum will love it!" We can only speculate about the basis of her evaluation of the task.

To be sure, young children's judgments of appropriate activities are not a reliable guide to educational planning. However, it seems to us that current practice in the early years of schooling is too heavily dominated by the kinds of mindless—though harmless—activities described in the observations above. We suggest that young children should have activities that engage their minds fully in the quest for knowledge, understanding, and skill. Specifically, it is our view that the project approach described in this book provides a context in which all aspects of children's minds can be engaged, challenged, and enriched.

While most of our teaching experience has been in the United States and Great Britain, we have also worked with colleagues in other parts of the world. Although each country—indeed, each locality—has unique problems and conditions, many concerns are universal. Our experience suggests that the project approach to early childhood education can be implemented in virtually all localities.

In the descriptions and explanations of project work that follow, we have attempted to take into account the diverse conditions and varied situations in which teachers work. However, because the application of the project approach has a longer history and is most extensive in Great Britain than elsewhere, many of the examples are drawn from there. Nevertheless, we have attempted to select examples that readers can adapt in their own situations. References to underlying principles relevant to the project approach are included to help teachers judge for themselves how to adapt the approach to situations that are different from those we know best.

A NOTE ABOUT TERMS AND CONTEXTS

Early Childhood Settings

This book is addressed to teachers who work in settings known by a variety of names: preschools, childcare centers, nursery schools, playgroups, prekindergartens, basic schools, kindergartens, or infant, primary, and elementary schools. Whatever the settings are called, they serve the developmental and educational needs of children between the ages of 4 and 8 years, give or take a year on either side.

Project Work

In some countries, project work is referred to as theme or topic work. Others refer to a project as a unit. Some teachers combine project work with a learning-center approach. Although the meanings of these terms vary somewhat, they all emphasize the part of the curriculum that encourages children to apply their emerging skills in informal, open-ended activities that are intended to improve their understandings of the world they live in.

Terminology

Writing for a diverse readership requires difficult compromises with respect to terminology. For example, the term *early childhood education* is not as commonly used in Britain as in other English-speaking countries. In several parts of North America, the term may encompass children from birth to age 6, ages 3 to 6, birth to age 8, or ages 4 to 8. In Great Britain, the age span we address is usually referred to as the *early years*. Furthermore, the term *infant education*, as used in Britain (for 5- to 7-year-olds), has a completely different meaning in most of North America, where infancy refers to babies.

The term *preschool* covers different age groups within some countries as well as among them. In Britain, children in preschools are often referred to as the under 5s, or even rising 5s. At the present time in Britain, more 4-year-olds are being included in regular infant or primary schools in so-called *reception* classes. Some English-speaking countries imply different ages by the term *kindergarten*: in some, kindergarten is a translation for day care centers serving children from 3 to 6 years of age; in others, it is a small school for children from 4 to 6 years. The category *school years* also encompasses different age groups around the world, depending on the age at which school attendance becomes compulsory.

In the hope of minimizing some of the confusion of terms characteristic of the field of early childhood education, we have chosen to refer to programs serving children 4 and 5 years of age as *preschool education*, and those for 5 to 8 years as the *school years*, even though the two groups overlap in age.

English-speaking countries also use different terms for other aspects of education. In general, North Americans share terms, and others employ British terms. We have attempted to present our ideas and examples "bilingually," so to speak. Where we were unable to find a term common to all readers, we have noted a distinctly British usage by inserting a (Br.) notation. We appreciate the patience and understanding in cases where we have failed to address all readers. Although there are differences among early childhood educators in various regions and countries, we assume that all share common concerns and challenges.

USES OF THE BOOK

This book is intended to be used in a number of ways, depending on the reader's background and experience. Readers who are new to the project approach may find it helpful to begin with Chapter 3. There they will find illustrations of project work and gain an impression of what some of the activities look like. Readers who have had some experience with project work may be especially interested in the specific suggestions offered in Chapters 4 through 9. Readers with extensive experience using the project approach may find the research and principles discussed in Chapter 2 especially helpful for explaining the value and appropriateness of project work to colleagues, administrators, and parents.

We do not intend the book to be used as a curriculum plan. Our purpose is to provide an introduction to the principles and practices of the project approach. We suggest ways that it can be applied, and present examples that readers can use as a point of departure in light of their own teaching preferences and contexts.

We hope to hear from readers about their own experiences with the project approach in working with young children.

We are deeply indebted to Sheila Ryan not only for her painstaking and careful editing, but for encouraging us to keep working to complete the manuscript. Without her support, completion of this book would have surely been long delayed. Thanks are due also to Jane Harbor for her help with typing and correcting the manuscript.

Preface to the Second Edition

Much has happened in the field of early childhood education during the 10 years since the publication of the first edition of this book that prompted us to offer this second one.

First, we have had extensive experience of helping teachers implement the project approach all over North America and many other parts of the world. These experiences have suggested some points to emphasize and others in need of clarification that are incorporated throughout this second edition. Two new chapters have been added to the book. Chapter 5 is a discussion of issues in the selection of project topics. Chapter 10 addresses children's drawing and its role in project work.

Second, during this 10-year period considerable research and development in the field of early education curriculum and teaching methods strengthens our conviction that good project work is educationally, culturally, as well as developmentally appropriate. For example, practices associated with the theory of multiple intelligences (Hatch, 1997), integrated curriculum, situated learning, and research on brain/neurological development (Brandt, 1997); social constructivism (Berk & Winsler, 1995; Bodrova & Leong, 1996); and increasing interest in mixed-age grouping (Katz, Evangelou, & Hartman, 1990) all support the potential value of good project work as part of the curriculum.

Just as the manuscript of the first edition of this book was going to press in 1987, the first edition of the National Association for the Education of Young Children's (NAEYC) position statement on developmentally appropriate practice was published. A second edition of that position statement has since been produced (Bredekamp & Copple, 1997) and has provided further support for the project approach and similar practices, particularly its clear call for a *both/and* approach to what should be included in the curriculum for young children.

Third, when we completed our work on the first edition we had not yet heard of the impressive approach to early education in the small northern Italian city of Reggio Emilia. Our first visit to Reggio Emilia came one year after the publication of the first edition. Since our first visit in 1990, we have made many more visits to their preprimary classes, and continue to be inspired and instructed by what we have seen and learned from their approach to the education of young children (Edwards, Gandini, & Forman, 1998). In particular, we have gained much from the practice of children using the "graphic languages" to represent their ideas and observations. In addition, their use of documentation as a central feature of their approach has added much to our appreciation of the roles of both of these features in project work.

A NOTE ABOUT TERMS AND CONTEXTS

Since the preparation of the first edition, Sylvia Chard has moved from Great Britain and made her home in Canada, where she teaches at the University of Alberta in Edmonton. Thus, this new edition forgoes the earlier attempt to use both American and British terms and we trust that this shift will not be distracting to the many overseas readers who are more accustomed to using the latter.

In recent years, we have also become more aware of the extent to which the project approach can be used in after-school program provisions as well as in the varieties of childcare settings available to children from age 3 up through the early childhood and primary years. Even though we have retained the use of the term "teacher," we intend to suggest ways that caregivers and after-school program personnel also can apply the practices we describe.

We wish to encourage readers to take note of the points made in the preface to the first edition concerning terms, contexts, and uses of the book.

PROJECT APPROACH NETWORKING

At the close of the preface to the first edition, we invited readers to let us know of their own experiences with the project approach. During the intervening decade, many readers have contacted us directly and indirectly, at conferences and seminars and through the listserv and e-mail to share their experiences, triumphs, and reverses, to make suggestions and to ask questions. Today, we can exchange information with teachers on the PROJECTS-L listserv, hosted by ERIC/ECE (on the Internet at http://ericeece.org) and through the PROJECTS web pages at http://www.project-approach.com. The web pages offer teachers a location on the Internet where accounts of projects written by teachers can be studied. These accounts are illustrated with pictures of children engaged in projects and samples of their project work. Online courses are also available through this website. In addition, ERIC/EECE now publishes the online peer-reviewed journal *Early Childhood Research and Practice*, which regularly features reports of projects and is accessible at http://ecrp.uiuc.edu.

1

Introduction to the Project Approach

The purpose of this chapter is to outline the aims and benefits of including project work in the curriculum during the early years. The central aspects of the project approach are highlighted as we begin with a brief look at project work in progress in an early childhood classroom:

> Several children in a kindergarten are collaborating on a painting depicting what they have learned about the driving mechanism of the school bus. Their teacher is helping them label the steering wheel, horn, gearshift, ignition, accelerator, hand brake, brake pedal, turn indicators, windshield wipers, and inside and outside rearview mirrors.
>
> A second small group is drawing with felt markers representing parts of the motor, indicating where they believe the oil is added. The children make a diagram representing their understanding of how fuel flows from the gas tank to the motor and how the exhaust makes its way through the tailpipe. As they work, they correct each other and make suggestions about what goes where and what details to include.
>
> A third small group is finishing preparations for a display of their paintings showing the different kinds of lights inside and outside the bus. The display notes which lights are for signals and warnings and which serve to light the way ahead as well as the inside. Some lights are red, some amber, and some white; some flash on and off and some are just reflectors. Their work is accompanied by a lively exchange of information and opinions about what they have seen and how to picture it so that other children can see what they mean.

A fourth group of children has prepared a chart of the gauges and dials on the dashboard, giving a basic idea of the information each one yields. As they work they refer to the field drawings they made of the dashboard while inspecting their school bus.

Two of the children used a rope to establish the width and length of the bus. They have displayed their rope on a counter in front of a sign the teacher helped them to write:

OUR BUS IS:
2 ROPES WIDE & 6 ROPES LONG
IT HAS 6 WHEELS & 42 SEATS

Three children are explaining to a classmate how they measured the bus. Earlier that day they had described the data-gathering processes to the principal of their school.

Two children are completing a large illustration of the safety features on the bus: fire extinguisher, emergency doors and windows, an emergency exit sign, and a first-aid kit.

Six children are playing in and around a large model of the school bus constructed in the classroom. The heavy cardboard container painted in traditional school bus colors by the children includes the name of the school district, license plates, and other words copied down from the real bus during their field studies. A few rows of seats made of large blocks and small chairs, a steering wheel, and a rearview mirror stimulate the spontaneous, animated roleplay that includes a bus driver, traffic officers, and noisy passengers.

Although this project involved the children in a detailed study of their school bus, the knowledge and skills gained are not likely to be assessed on a standardized achievement test. However, the example illustrates the main thesis of this book: including project work in the curriculum promotes *children's intellectual development by engaging their minds in observation and investigation of selected aspects of their experience and environment,* ideally, those aspects worthy of their attention and energy. The special knowledge gained by the children about the school bus was not the only value of the project; it also provided contexts for other kinds of worthwhile learning discussed in detail in Chapter 2.

THE NATURE OF A PROJECT

We use the term *project* to refer to an indepth study of a particular topic, usually undertaken by a whole class working on subtopics in small groups, sometimes by a small group of children within a class, and occasionally by an individual child. The key feature of a project is that it is an investigation—a piece of research that involves children in seeking answers to questions they have formulated by themselves or in cooperation with their teacher and that arise as the investigation proceeds.

The project consists of exploring and investigating a topic such as "going to the hospital," "building a house," or, as in the example above, studying the bus that brings them to school. Work on a project usually extends over a period of days or weeks, depending on the children's ages and the nature of the topic. Preschoolers might spend two or three weeks on a hospital project; older children, on the other hand, might spend two or three times as long on the same topic. Some of the projects undertaken by preprimary children in the Reggio Emilia municipal preprimary schools extend over several months (Edwards, Gandini, & Forman, 1998).

A project involving an indepth study of the neighborhood or of the changes in local weather might be extended over several weeks; however, others might be completed within a week. Unlike spontaneous play, projects usually involve children in advanced planning and in various activities that require several days or weeks of sustained effort. However, shorter, impromptu, or smaller projects might be stimulated by an unexpected event, a visitor, or an unanticipated event that comes up in the course of a well-planned project.

Preschoolers are more likely to work on projects in small groups rather than as individuals or as a whole class. Older children might have leaders who take some responsibility for different aspects of the work to be done by the whole class. At any age, a few children with particular interests may work on individual projects, and the teacher helps their peers to ensure meaningful and satisfying participation in the projects.

THE PROJECT APPROACH TO TEACHING AND LEARNING

We use the term *project approach* for several reasons. First, it reflects our view that projects can be incorporated into the early childhood curriculum in a variety of ways, depending upon the preferences, commitments, and constraints of teachers and schools. In some cases, project work takes up a large proportion of the curriculum. In other cases, project work is offered just two afternoons a week. Some teachers integrate project work into learning centers; still others, especially at the preschool level, devote most of their curriculum to it. In other words, there is no single way to incorporate project work into a curriculum or teaching style; the significant feature is that some time is allocated to experiences in which children make careful observations and inquiries into worthwhile topics over a sustained period of time.

Second, project work as an *approach* to early childhood education refers broadly to a way of teaching and learning, rather than to a particular set of teaching techniques, or invariable sequences of activities, routines, or strategies. This approach emphasizes the teacher's responsiveness to the individual children as well as the whole group in her class. On the basis of her special knowledge of the children, she can encourage them to interact with people, objects, and the environment in ways that have personal meaning for them. As a way of learning, the project approach emphasizes children's active participation in the planning, development, and assessment of their own work; children are encouraged to take initiative and responsibility for the work that is undertaken.

The topic of a project for young children is usually drawn from the world that is familiar to them. Thus, one might expect projects in a rural school to focus on animals and crops cultivated on nearby land. Children in a fishing village might be engaged in projects about boats, fishing, and fisheries. In an urban area, children can undertake projects about types of buildings, construction sites, local industries, traffic patterns, vehicles, and the workers involved. When these children are older it will be highly appropriate for them to study the people, objects, and environments that are not in their own firsthand experiences, but that are more distant in both time and space. In principle, the younger the children, the more important it is that the topics investigated have *horizontal* rather than *vertical* relevance. Vertical relevance refers to learning that is intended to prepare children for the next class or the next school; horizontal relevance refers to learning activities that are meaningful at the time they are experienced. In other words, as children increase in age and have the experience and competencies that accrue with age, it is the responsibility of schools to help them understand and know about phenomena distant from their own firsthand experiences. A major aim of education in the early years, however, is to strengthen children's confidence in their understanding of their own environment and experience.

DISTINCTIONS BETWEEN PROJECTS, THEMES, AND UNITS

Many teachers and curriculum specialists in early and elementary education use the terms *projects, themes,* and *units* interchangeably. Clearly there are many similarities among the activities included in all three, especially in that they are clearly distinct from formal, didactic whole class instruction. However, we find it helpful to keep in mind some distinctions between these three terms.

Themes

The term *theme* usually refers to a set of activities around a broad topic or large concept, such as "spring" or "fall." In connection with the theme, and depending on their ages, children engage in some activities that involve counting, some measuring, some reading, writing, spelling, and so forth, in such a way that the theme serves as a pretext for applying a wide variety of basic skills. The goal seems to be to find a topic around which to apply some basic skills and enjoy some arts and crafts activities. In this way, the organization of work around a main theme is often a case of looking for something related to it. In contrast, as the investigation of a project progresses and the children collect data in answer to their research questions, they look for ways to represent their findings in charts, graphs, diagrams, murals, individual and class books, reports, and so forth, as described in the chapters that follow.

A theme, however, could provide good topics for projects. Around a theme such as "spring," for example, children could develop a set of questions about the kind of changes in flowers, shrubs, bushes, and trees in the immediate neighborhood or grounds of their school, testing predictions and discussing the hypotheses underlying them. As data are collected from systematic observations, field notes, surveys, and interviews, the children use a variety of graphic organizers as well as a whole range of basic skills. In contrast, a theme usually has no sense of direction, though it may consist of completing a list of suitable activities related to it.

Units

A *unit* is usually a set of preplanned lessons on a particular topic, one usually deemed of sufficient importance to ensure that the content covered is not left to chance or to the interests, ideas, or questions that a given group of children might generate. The teacher, the school district, or the textbook authors determine the information to be acquired; the children usually do not participate in the plans for the unit, or formulate questions to be answered. The desired outcomes are predetermined independently of the particular children in the class. Often the set of activities in the unit is repeated every year. Such units have an important place in the primary school curriculum, and can make significant contributions to children's knowledge.

Projects

Unlike themes and units, a *project* is a piece of research about a topic—one that may be related to a larger theme—in which children's ideas, questions, theories, predictions, and interests are major determinants of the experiences provided and the work accomplished. Close examination of the documentation of a project makes frequent references to the children *deciding* something, *arguing* a particular point, *explaining* their ideas to their classmates, *predicting* findings and *hypothesizing* the bases for predictions, *checking* facts and details, *interviewing* persons who might be sources of needed information, *initiating* new directions in the line of inquiry, *drawing* from observation as well as from memory and imagination, and *recording* observations, *reporting* findings, *giving* each other suggestions, *encouraging* one another, trying things again, and in countless other ways, *accepting* and *carrying* responsibility for what is accomplished.

AIMS OF THE PROJECT APPROACH

Our advocacy of the project approach is rooted in our own values and ideas concerning the aims of education in the early years. An overall aim of this approach is to cultivate the life of the young child's mind. In its fullest sense, the term *mind* includes not only knowledge and skills, but also social, emotional, moral, aesthetic, and spiritual sensibilities.

An appropriate education for young children should address the full scope of their growing minds as they strive to make better and fuller sense of their experiences. It encourages them to pose questions, pursue and solve puzzles, and increase their awareness of significant phenomena around them. From 3 to 8 years of age, most children still respond eagerly to adults' suggestions, contribute readily to group efforts, and try out new skills with enthusiasm. We have worked with many teachers—especially in the primary years—whose experience had been mainly whole group activity or formal instruction. These teachers have reported their amazement and delight at how eagerly most children make choices, show initiative and leadership, contribute to group efforts, and respond to adult suggestions when working on a project. Project work provides opportunities for children to do all of these things.

We recommend that the project approach be incorporated into the early childhood and elementary curriculum in the service of the major aims outlined below.

Intellectual Goals and the Life of the Mind

In North America and in many other parts of the world, the education of young children emphasizes academic goals, in particular the acquisition of so-called "basic skills." The academic curriculum is typically organized in lock-step fashion so that all children pass through the same instructional sequences at the same age. The traditional three R's that dominate an academic curriculum are also typically broken into discrete "skill and drill" sequences. The children are formally instructed in small or in large groups and practice the skills by means of separate subtasks in workbooks and on worksheets. The content of these exercises is often unrelated to the world in which they live and learn. Largely mindless, these activities usually mean little to the children, though at the outset most are quite willing to do them.

A curriculum oriented toward academic goals puts a high priority on the needs, demands, and constraints of the academy itself and on acquiring the narrow range of skills and dispositions required to function within it. In such a curriculum, the activities and content have more vertical (that is, future relevance) than horizontal or current relevance.

Many parents and school officials believe that the only alternative to an academically oriented curriculum is one that is focused mainly on socialization and spontaneous play. Sometimes labeled the *traditional* nursery or kindergarten approach, this approach to curriculum offers children the opportunity and materials for spontaneous play and a variety of good instructional games and for a range of arts and crafts, music, literature, and physical activities. While there are several variations on this so-called traditional approach, they share a strong emphasis on spontaneous play as the significant medium for learning.

Our position on the matter of curriculum emphasis is that neither the academic nor the traditional socialization/play approach is adequate for the education of young children because both fail to engage the child's mind sufficiently. The opportunity for spontaneous play and the cognitive growth and socialization that it provides can benefit all children during the early years and certainly many children as young as 5 years of age can profit from some kinds of academic work. But in our view, an appropriate curriculum for young children is one that puts a high priority on *intellectual* goals. By this we mean that children's minds are engaged in ways that deepen their understanding of their own experiences and environment and thereby strengthen their confidence in their own intellectual powers, that is, their dispositions to observe and investigate, for example, discussed more fully in Chapter 2.

Many adults tend to overestimate young children academically but underestimate them intellectually. The extent to which young children's intellectual powers have traditionally been underestimated has been made even more clear in recent years by the impressive work of the children in the preprimary schools in the northern Italian city of Reggio Emilia (Edwards, Forman, & Gandini, 1998; Katz & Cesarone, 1994). The careful and detailed documentation of the children's experiences, conversations, arguments, discussions, theories, and hypotheses provide compelling evidence of the intellectual powers of very young children, and how they can be supported and strengthened in the course of good project work.

It has long been a central tenet in early childhood philosophy and theory that play is a child's natural way of learning. Observations of young children worldwide strongly supports such a view. Indeed, virtually all young mammals spontaneously engage in some play in which they rehearse behavior they will use when they are mature. However, play is not the only natural way that children learn: it is just as natural for them to learn from observation and investigation. Indeed, young children's powerful inborn disposition to investigate, to poke and pry all around them, often challenges the energy and patience of their caregivers, especially during the very early years when their environments are full of potential dangers.

The minds of the children described at the beginning of this chapter were engaged in finding out about the parts of the bus, their functions, safety provisions, and many of its other parts and how they work. The children had the chance to learn that everyday things can be full of interesting features to be studied in detail. Knowledge of the parts of the bus is not "core knowledge" essential to the educational future of the children; rather, the knowledge gained can deepen children's sense of confidence in their grasp of phenomena around them. Even more important, their work provided a context for strengthening important intellectual dispositions. The high priority we give to the goal of intellectual involvement in the early years is related to our understanding of the nature of development and is discussed in more detail in the next chapter.

A Balance of Activities

We are not suggesting that project work should replace all current early childhood or primary school practices. Rather, as a significant portion of the curriculum, project work stimulates emerging skills and helps children to master them because it provide contexts in which they are applied purposefully.

Project work should complement and enhance what young children learn from spontaneous play as well as from systematic instruction. Project work plays a somewhat different role in the preschool and primary grades curricula. For preschool children, project work lends coherence and continuity to their work together. It is that part of the curriculum that the teacher intentionally guides. In this sense, for preschoolers, a project, comparative to other parts of the curriculum, is the relatively *more* teacher-directed part. However, because a project is emergent and negotiated rather than totally preplanned by the teacher in the primary school years, it constitutes the *less* teacher-directed, more informal part of the curriculum.

We realize that many teachers are under strong pressure from school authorities, teachers of older children, and many parents to emphasize academic instruction at the expense of the more spontaneous, emergent, and creative aspects of the curriculum. Nevertheless, for most 4-year-olds, regular whole-class formal instruction in academic skills cannot be justified on the basis of available evidence (see Chapter 2).

As children grow, their capacity to benefit from formal academic instruction increases. From the age of about 5 years, many children can be profitably engaged in some formal small-group instruction in basic academic skills. In our view of children's learning and development, the knowledge and skills acquired by formal instruction are likely to be strengthened by being applied, and by serving purposes that are clear to the children applying them. It is a good idea to keep in mind that skillfulness improves with *use* and not just with instruction and repetition of isolated exercises. This implies that in the early years, a curriculum is best when systematic instruction is balanced with the kind of project work described in the chapters that follow.

School *Is* Life

One overarching aim of the project approach is for adults and children to experience their lives together in school as real life rather than as an anticipation, postponement, or a withdrawal from life, to be resumed only outside the school. From the child's point of view, school experiences are not contrived or pretend. As elsewhere, life in school should make varying demands on concentration, effort, and involvement. Some of the time should be free from external pressures, some time assigned to challenging work, and some allocated to routine work. The inclusion of project work in the daily schedule can provide this variation in the kinds of demands and pressures children encounter.

Older children are likely to see school as a place where certain feelings and concerns have no place. Young children, however, have not yet acquired such a perspective. On the contrary, it is developmentally characteristic of young children to respond in a relatively undifferentiated way to all of their experiences. During the early years, the stream of daily life occurrences does not occur in categories such as science and history. The content of experience is more like events and topics than like separate disciplines. Project work does not require children's minds to be constrained by subject boundaries. In principle, the younger the children, the more appropriate an integrated curriculum becomes.

Community Ethos in the Class

Our fourth aim in advocating the project approach is for the children to experience the class as a community. Community ethos is created when all of the children are expected and encouraged to contribute to the life of the whole group, even though they may do so in different ways. Stevahn, Johnson, Johnson, and Real (1996) point out that competitive environments are those in which individuals have a vested interest in others' failures, each working against the other "to achieve a goal that only one or a few can attain" (p. 803). In a similar way, individualistic environments are those in which individuals work independently of each other to achieve their own personal goals. In both competitive and individualistic contexts, participants tend to be dominated by short-term self-interests. In cooperative settings, on the other hand, individuals work together to achieve mutual goals; their efforts are stimulated by relatively long-term, mutual interests so that they strive to maximize joint outcomes. Project work provides ample opportunity for a cooperative ethos to flourish.

The children who studied their school bus, for example, shared a set of experiences they all had in common. Studying different aspects of the topic of a bus in small groups and sharing their findings strengthened their sense of belonging to a community of young investigators and scholars. Each child could appreciate the contribution of his or her own work to the resulting collective understanding developed by the whole class, encompassing a range of abilities, experiences, developmental levels, and backgrounds. This commitment to a community ethos in the classroom also urges us to provide contexts in which children work together, resolve differences, accept different individual responsibilities, and contribute to the whole in differentiated ways.

Teachers play a major role in supporting children's developing sense of belonging to a group and in helping them to develop the many skills and insights involved in participating in and contributing to group life. A wide range of skills, dispositions, and feelings is experienced and learned when the class works as a lively community doing together what they could not accomplish nearly so well individually or alone—these are life skills, dispositions, and feelings not included on standardized tests.

Education and Democracy

A major aim that we believe is served by the inclusion of project work in the curriculum is to help children to become able to participate competently in and contribute to a democratic society. This fundamental commitment to democracy means that opportunities are provided throughout the early years for children to investigate events and phenomena around them so that (a) they deepen their appreciation of the knowledge, skills, and expertise, as well as the wide variety of ways that the efforts of others contribute to our well-being; (b) learn in detail of the ways in which members of a community are interdependent; and (c) learn to prize differences within their communities and perceive those differences as enriching.

Furthermore, democratic societies are most likely to flourish when their citizens seek an indepth understanding of the complex issues they must address and about which they must make choices and decisions. It is our view that project work provides the contexts in which young children's dispositions to seek an indepth understanding can be strengthened. Project work provides early and regular opportunities to make choices and decisions about topics, responsibilities, and all other aspects of the work undertaken. Furthermore, we suggest that, in principle, unless children have experience of what it feels like to understand some things in depth, they cannot develop the disposition to seek indepth understanding.

Similarly, project work can strengthen children's dispositions to be empirical, that is, to seek and to examine available evidence and facts, to check their predictions and hypotheses, and to learn to be open to alternative ways of interpreting facts and findings. In addition, project work provides opportunities to strengthen their disposition to work hard, presents occasions of having to do some things over again to meet the participants' developing standards, and to find satisfaction in overcoming obstacles and difficulties. All of these are ways that the project approach contributes to children's early experience of aspects of democratic living. Many of the teachers we have worked with have indicated how much they had underestimated children's capacities to gain satisfaction from hard work and from overcoming the obstacles their work entailed (see Beneke, 1998; Helm, Beneke, & Steinheimer, 1998).

The Challenge of Teaching

Another aim of the project approach is for teachers themselves to experience their work as engaging and challenging. We have worked with teachers in many countries in a wide variety of situations and under diverse conditions. Some teachers must cope with poor physical facilities and limited supplies of learning materials. Still other teachers have very large classes and poor staff–child ratios. Many teachers of young children work with two different groups of children per day, some have one group on Mondays, Wednesdays, and Fridays, and another on the other two weekdays, and thus both groups must share the space and equipment in the classroom. Although these realities frequently present severe problems, we have tried to emphasize that they can often be seen as challenges. The two examples below may be helpful.

The teacher of a morning group of 4-year-olds was reluctant to undertake project work because she feared that the morning and the afternoon groups using the same room would spoil each other's work. Once she saw this difficulty as a challenge, however, she used it as an opportunity to help children learn to communicate with others. The morning group dictated a message to her for the afternoon group, saying, "We are building a police station in our class. Have you got some ideas?" The afternoon teacher read the message to her group, solicited their replies, and wrote them down. In the morning, the teacher read the afternoon group's message to the children, and they discussed its contents, offered comments and suggestions for the teacher to relay to the morning builders. The children in the morning group were able to carry on their project, which the afternoon children regularly inspected and commented on without interfering in its progress. Both groups learned something about transmitting information to people who are not present, and thereby gained some fresh understanding of the function and value of written communication.

The second example is that of a teacher of 5- to 7-year-olds who arrived at school one morning to find that a group of workers had started to repair the roof of her temporary classroom building. Neither she nor the principal had been fore-warned, and no alternative classroom was available at the time. After a brief discussion with the principal about possible courses of action, she decided to stay in the classroom and organize a day-long study of the whole event—a mini-project. Some of the children, working in pairs, accepted the responsibility of observing the workers' progress throughout the day. Other children accepted the assignment to interview the men about their tools, the materials, and the processes involved. Some of the children made a scale model of the classroom, roof and all, based on their measurements. Others drew the tools, learned their names, and painted pictures of various aspects of the work. One of the workers was invited to talk to the class about roof repairs. The children studied the tools, the different layers of roofing, and the tar, which had to be heated to specific temperatures before application. By the end of the day and on into the next, the children created a wall display describing the event in rich detail.

In this example, a creative and constructive solution was found in response to a problematic situation. On reflection, the teacher saw the situation in a positive light, accepting it as a challenge, rather than as just an interruption of her earlier plans. Creative solutions to the predicaments of teaching are not always possible. However, the disposition to respond to problems and constraints as challenges is worth cultivating in ourselves as well as in the children. The response of the teacher in our example was successful in part because she had confidence in the children's abilities to take on the challenges with her. A curriculum that limits the teacher primarily to daily instructional lessons or to setting out the same toys, the same learning centers, and the same equipment day after day may eventually make teaching young children dreary and devoid of intellectual challenge.

PROJECT WORK AND OTHER PARTS OF THE CURRICULUM

As already suggested, we do not suggest that teachers discard all of their current practices and replace them with project work. We do recommend, however, that teachers experiment with project work in their present curriculum context and adapt it to their own aims and philosophies. Project work can thus complement and enhance what children learn through other parts of their curriculum.

In preschool and kindergarten settings, projects are among many other available activities. Appropriate materials and opportunities for spontaneous indoor and outdoor play, story reading, music, and other features of a good preschool curriculum continue alongside project work. The work of a project differs from the other parts of the preschool curriculum in that it is based on the plans and intentions of individuals or groups, typically in consultation with the teacher. Preschool activities such as block-building, water play, and spontaneous dramatic play are usually activities that do not focus on a topic or involve detailed planning in advance, or sustained effort over a period of days or weeks.

At the primary school-age level, however, project work is undertaken alongside systematic instruction. Bear in mind one of the underlying principles of the project approach: skills applied purposefully to meaningful activities are more likely to be mastered (Department of Education and Science, 1978). As we have already suggested, for many young children, workbooks and drill sheets are not sufficiently purposeful to them for effective application of skills. Not only do such learning materials usually fail to engage children's minds, but they may also prevent children from understanding the purpose and use of a skill. However, once children have reached about first grade—roughly about age 6—project work complements systematic instruction. Furthermore, as children grow older, they become better able to address routine and repetitive academic tasks because they can more easily comprehend the contribution of drill and practice to the attainment of proficiency and competence.

Formal systematic instruction in basic academic skills is not typically undertaken during the preschool years. Therefore, project work does not differ as much from other aspects of the curriculum as it does during the primary school years. Both spontaneous play and project work are informal in organization. In the primary school years, however, systematic instruction is clearly more formal than project work.

The values of project work in the early years can be seen by contrasting it to systematic instruction, and noting the complementary relationship between the two, especially during the primary years. At least five fundamental contrasts between the two approaches can be distinguished. As discussed below and summarized in Table 1.1, these contrasts indicate how the long and sometimes difficult processes of acquiring proficiency in basic skills through systematic instruction, and, at the same time children's dispositions to use the skills thus acquired, can be supported during project work.

TABLE 1.1.
Five Distinctions Between the Contribution of Systematic Instruction and Project Work

Systematic Instruction	Project Work
The teacher focuses on helping children **acquire** skills	The teacher provides opportunities for the children to **apply** skills
Extrinsic motivation: The children are motivated by their desire to please the teacher and obtain rewards	**Intrinsic** motivation: Children's interest and involvement promote effort and motivation
The **teacher chooses** learning activities and provides materials at the appropriate instructional level	The **children choose** from a variety of activities provided by the teacher; they determine their own level of challenge at which to work
The **teacher is the expert**; the teacher addresses children's deficiencies	The **children are the experts**; the teacher capitalizes on the children's proficiencies
The **teacher is accountable** for the children's learning, progress, and achievement	The **children and teacher share accountability** for learning and achievement

Acquisition and Application of Skills

Systematic instruction is an approach to teaching individual children a progression of interrelated sub-skills, each of which contributes to greater overall proficiency in skills such as those involved in reading, writing, and arithmetic. Systematic instruction refers to processes by which those skills that require specific and sequential sub-skills to attain proficiency are learned. While some children can acquire these skills without systematic assistance, most profit from it. Once acquired, strengthening the disposition to apply the skills requires the provision of contexts in which their application is functional and purposeful. Projects provide such contexts.

Extrinsic and Intrinsic Motivation

Let us look first at the nature of children's motivation. Teachers frequently overcome children's reluctance to work on tasks designed to aid the acquisition of basic skills by offering extrinsic rewards (see Kohn, 1993, 1994). This is especially true when children's attention and persistence are difficult to secure by other means. By contrast, project work relies on intrinsic motivation. It capitalizes on the children's own interest in the work and on the appeal of the activities themselves. The learning is more diffuse than in formal instruction and involves children in applying skills and knowledge in a variety of ways for a variety of purposes. Because project work provides many options, children are rarely required to undertake one particular task rather than another. The tasks involved also vary in levels of difficulty and the demands made on children.

When children are intrinsically motivated, they respond in ways that strengthen their disposition to work independently of the teacher, for example, by helping one another. They can choose for themselves what they want to find out from books, reference materials, adults at home, and other children. The sense of purpose with which children engage in a project activity is just as important as the completion of a particular piece of work. The dispositions to exert effort, to strive for mastery, to overcome difficulties, and to seek challenge can be strengthened when project work is regularly available to children.

Both extrinsic and intrinsic motivational processes are probably required for optimal participation in schooling, as well as in the larger world. In the elementary school years, including both systematic instruction and project work means that the curriculum attends to the development of both types of motivation in a complementary fashion.

Selection of Activities

In systematic instruction, the teacher selects the work and specifies the level at which it is to be carried out. However, in project work, the child can make these choices. Some children will be more adept at making the choices than others; but learning how to do so is a life skill—one that deserves the teacher's help and encouragement. Rarely can the acquisition of complex skills such as reading wait until children spontaneously choose tasks for which learning to read is necessary. In systematic instruction for skill acquisition, an optimum match (Harrison, 1980) is required between task difficulty and the level at which a child needs instruction. Three levels of text readability were proposed. The first, termed the "frustration level," indicates that the reading material is too difficult for the child to benefit from instruction. The second, the "independent level," refers to material that can be read independently but is not helping the child to learn new skills. The third is the "instructional level," when the readability of the material optimizes the effects of instruction for a child. Such material is at an optimum level for acquiring the subskills needed to take the next steps toward full proficiency (Brown & Campione, 1984). This conceptualization of instructional level is increasingly referred to as the "Zone of Proximal Development," as suggested by Russian psychologist L.S. Vygotsky (see Berk & Winsler, 1995) Normally, the teacher is considered responsible for continuously assessing and diagnosing the level at which the child is reading so that effective instruction can be given. Thus, the teaching of complex academic skills usually requires teacher selection of tasks.

When applying skills during project work, however, the children are not required to progress through any recognizable sequence of stages. The children can safely choose their work from a range of options provided by the teacher. At times they may choose to tackle challenging problems, and at other times easy ones. The difference between selecting one level or the other may be accounted for by differences in background knowledge and interest in the topic rather than by differences in ability level. Thus, the two approaches are complementary: the teacher selects the level of work that aids the child in acquiring skills, and the children select work that involves applying those skills.

Furthermore, the wide variety of project tasks and activities typically provides contexts in which children can manifest their dispositions to seek appropriate levels of challenge. Note, however, that children should not feel compelled to work at the upper limits of their ability all of the time. A sufficient variety of activities and tasks should be available so that some can be done routinely, some in a free-wheeling fashion, and others with just enough difficulty to stimulate new learning. In the absence of an optimum mix of these levels of task difficulty, some children will experience excessive stress and discouragement and others may become bored by school experiences of insufficient challenge.

The Expertise of the Teacher and the Child

The location of expertise is another distinction between systematic instruction and project work and relates to the selection of learning activities discussed above. As we have suggested, in the formal teaching of reading, for example, the teacher is the expert responsible for instruction according to her diagnosis of the child's level of proficiency. The teacher directs and monitors skill practice, often through a sequence of graded workbooks, assignment cards, or worksheets. The teacher is the expert on the skills being taught and on how they are best learned.

In project work, children are encouraged to assess their own proficiency in applying skills, to monitor their own activity, and to select manageable tasks for themselves. The children, with experience, become experts on their own learning. The teacher makes suggestions, but the children may be allowed to turn them down and judge for themselves. Poor judgment can be an occasion for teaching. For example, teacher and child can discuss ways of minimizing errors in the future. But if some errors pass unnoticed, they are not critical to the next stage of proficiency, as might be the case in progressing through a finely graded sequence of academic tasks.

A related distinction between systematic instruction and project work is based on alternative views of the learner. In planning formal academic work, teachers have to focus their attention on what the children cannot yet do or do not yet know; their goal is to address any deficiencies in the children. In contrast, when planning project work, the teacher focuses on the children's proficiencies and capabilities, considering ways in which children can apply skills and knowledge in meaningful contexts. Tasks used in systematic instruction often have little personal meaning to the children. In contrast, project work is undertaken in a context that makes sense to the children. The support afforded by the project context encourages the children to actively apply to skills already developed, including observing, exploring, playing, investigating, reading, recording, discussing, and evaluating their progress and assessing the results of their own efforts.

By way of example, a teacher was helping a 7-year-old child who had difficulty with mathematics. In talking with the child, she discovered that he had a great interest in playing marbles. The playground culture of the school at that time included versions of the marbles game with a considerable range of quantitative information built into it. Pursuing this interest, the teacher asked the boy to show her his marbles and tell her about their different values in the game. She took two or three marbles in each hand and asked him which handful he would rather have. He immediately pointed out which one. She changed the combination and showed it to him for a split second. Again, he immediately indicated which of the two was more valuable. She increased the number of marbles and varied them to include more complex value combinations. By this means, she discovered that the child's behavioral knowledge of number values was far ahead of any ability he had shown in the pencil-and-paper tasks of the mathematics curriculum. She then helped the child represent in written form his behavioral understanding of the number values of the marbles. The exercise greatly facilitated his subsequent understanding of the pencil-and-paper tasks. Thus the teacher used the child's proficiency with numbers in a restricted context to teach him how to apply it more flexibly in other contexts. This incident clearly illustrates a point that French (1985) made:

> Perhaps cognitive development can be best characterized as a process of "gradual decontextualization." This position holds that cognitive skills first emerge and are practiced in specific contexts that demand their use, and that over time they may be generalized and extended beyond the initial context to be applied more flexibly. (p. 188)

Thus, when activities in a class include both systematic instruction and project work, teachers can use their expertise as required, and children can select the level of difficulty with which they are comfortable. These two kinds of learning can occur in complementary fashion. Children's own knowledge and experience also contribute to the development of a project. The teacher ensures an appropriate balance between systematic instruction and project work because the expertise of both teacher and children contributes to learning in complementary ways.

The Accountability of the Teacher and the Children

Now let us consider who is accountable for a child's accomplishments. In the case of teaching basic academic skills, teachers are maximally accountable. Teacher accountability is important precisely because it is she who has the expertise and specialized resources available for helping children with the difficulties they are likely to encounter. The teacher must make every effort to help any child experiencing difficulties in acquiring academic skills.

In project work, however, the children and the teacher are accountable together. The cultivation of children's dispositions to reflect on and evaluate their own contributions to a project and to be accountable for them is an important feature of the project approach. If a child does not become proficient at drawing, for example, but does show a vivid imagination in creative writing, the parents and teacher are not likely to be greatly concerned. It is generally accepted that children vary in their strengths and limitations and have uneven patterns of achievement across all curriculum areas. When the curriculum includes both systematic instruction and project work, the accountability for a wide range of potential learning is shared by both teacher and the children.

We wish to emphasize the point that the fact that accountability is shared does not mean there is an absence of standards. Teachers can encourage children to evaluate their own efforts, not so much in terms of whether or not they like what has been accomplished, or whether they judge it to be good or bad; rather, teachers can help children to adopt criteria or develop rubrics for evaluating their efforts by encouraging them to think about whether the work is as *clear, detailed, accurate,* or as *complete* as it could be, or as interesting to their classmates as it can be, and so forth. Teachers can also encourage children to prepare second or third drafts of pieces of writing, charts, and other elements in a display of their findings. The teacher can also indicate her own criteria and standards against which to assess the children, but can also profitably involve the children in developing these. In her research on assessment practices in a third-grade classroom, Williams (1998) states that "by giving children the tools and opportunities to self-assess and self-evaluate their work, we are teaching children to become responsible for their learning and to be responsible for what is expected of them" (p. 182).

In sum, the two aspects of a curriculum, systematic instruction and project work, particularly at the kindergarten and primary levels, constitute aspects of the role of the teacher that provide different experiences for the children, each of which contributes to their growth, development, and learning, albeit in different ways.

THE AGES OF THE CHILDREN

While interesting and worthwhile projects conducted with children under age 3 have been reported (see Edwards & Springate, 1993; Sanderson, 1999), some researchers use the term *project* in a more general sense than we do. As we use the term, we imply a level of initiative and responsibility on the part of the children that would be difficult with most groups of children under 3 years old.

In this book, we address the project approach for a relatively wide age range—3 to 8 years, and beyond. Those who study and work with children in this range usually see it as a period in which intellectual development progresses at a rapid rate. Although continuous, development is also uneven; it progresses in spurts and lingers occasionally on plateaus. Furthermore, development is typically idiosyncratic, varying with the individual characteristics, circumstances, and experiences of the child. The project approach takes into account the unevenness of development by enabling children to undertake open-ended tasks alongside one another at varying levels of complexity and with equally acceptable alternative outcomes. Consider, for example, a project in which 5-year-olds investigate the distance that different balls will roll along the floor after rolling down an inclined plane they created placing a plank against a pile of blocks. One child is just able to release the balls, while another has just enough of the necessary knowledge and skills to note down the measure of the distance rolled. Both children participate and contribute to the completion of the task, but at quite different levels. Age itself is at best a rough predictor of children's capabilities.

Second, the project approach lends itself particularly well to teaching children of different ages within a class or group. In many early childhood settings around the world, teachers work with groups mixed in age as well as in ability. The project approach is particularly suited to capitalizing on the differences among children in mixed age groups. Among the many advantages of project work in mixed age groups (Katz, Evangelou, & Hartman, 1990) is that the younger members are more likely to be included in and challenged by the work initiated by the older children among them than they could be if they were in an age-segregated group.

Third, we especially want to emphasize how the same topics can be fruitfully studied by children from 4 to 8 years of age in accord with their developing intellectual, academic, and social competencies. As children's knowledge and skills accumulate and develop, the work grows in depth, complexity, and sophistication. Thus, for example, kindergarten teachers need not be concerned if their pupils had already studied the weather in their preschool classes. Throughout early childhood, projects on most topics can be undertaken in such a way that knowledge and understanding continue to deepen and become more differentiated and complex.

In the project work described in the chapters that follow, children of varying ages and abilities work together, contributing to the group effort, studying the same topic continuously, extending and deepening their knowledge of it, and increasing the skillfulness with which they work.

THE PROJECT APPROACH IN HISTORICAL AND INTERNATIONAL PERSPECTIVE

The practices included under the term *project approach* are not new to early childhood or elementary education (Prawat, 1995; Van Ausdal, 1988). Stewart (1986) asserts that the idea of learning through projects originally gained popularity in the United States, where it was advocated by both Dewey and Kilpatrick. It can also be seen in Isaacs's (1966) descriptions of children's work in England in the 1920s. The project approach also closely resembles the Bank Street curriculum model developed over many years at the Bank Street College of Education in New York City (Zimilies, 1987).

Project work was a central feature of the practices identified, described, and advocated in Great Britain in the document that came to be known as the "Plowden Report" (Plowden Committee Report, 1967; see also Department of Education and Science, 1978). British educators labeled them variously as the "integrated day," "integrated curriculum," and "informal education." During those years, hundreds of North American educators visited infant schools all over Britain to observe high quality project work. During the late 1960s and early 1970s, many Americans incorporated these methods under the title "open education." The complex reasons for the decline of progressive education at the end of the 1930s, the open-education movement in the United States in the mid-1970s, and the "integrated day" in Britain in the 1980s cannot be taken up in any detail here. However, it is often noted that educational philosophies and ideologies swing back and forth in pendulum fashion (see, for example, Alexander, Murphy, & Woods, 1996; Kliebard, 1985).

From time to time, a particular approach to early childhood education is enthusiastically embraced and implemented. Within a few years a counter-movement emerges, resulting in overcorrections in the opposite direction, only to be followed some years later by overcorrections that again lead to reverting to earlier methods. It seems to be in the nature of education in general, and the field of early childhood education in particular, that opinions and ideologies concerning appropriate curricula and methods are argued with great conviction by each generation of parents, educators, and politicians (Dearden, 1984; Katz, 1995).

Perhaps one reason the open-education movement declined was that many teachers believed themselves to be in an either–or situation: they felt obliged to adopt *either* progressive-open *or* formal traditional methods. Many believed they had to abandon all of their previous practices, but were not given sufficient support for embracing the new ones (Gross, Giancquinta, & Bernstein, 1975). Furthermore, pressures from parents to ensure their children's academic success, whether merely perceived or actual, intimidated many administrators and teachers into abandoning plans for more informal open methods.

The issue of "recurring innovations" has been examined closely by Alexander, Murphy, and Woods (1996). They ask also why educators "cast education as *either* individual *or* social, good instruction as *either* direct *or* discovery, and so forth?" (p. 32). They suggest instead that the more important questions are when, where, and for whom a particular approach might be most appropriate. They also suggest that

> expertise in any domain is built around central principles or concepts that give that domain its identity or form ... fostering a principled understanding may serve as a powerful grounding or ballast for teachers and learners, even through fierce storms of controversy or concern. (p. 36)

Several factors may account for current renewed and increasing interest in the project approach. First, as we argue in Chapter 2, an accumulating body of research on children's development and learning supports the proposition that good project work is an appropriate way to stimulate, strengthen, and enhance children's intellectual and social development as well as competence in basic skills.

Second, no evidence suggests that the project approach puts children's intellectual or academic development at risk. However, like any other innovation, curriculum, or teaching method, the effectiveness of the project approach depends on the quality of its implementation, which in turn depends on many factors addressed in the chapters to follow.

Third, as indicated in the earlier discussion of the complementary roles of systematic instruction and project work, we advocate the approach as *part of* a balanced curriculum throughout the preschool and primary school years. During the preschool period, a large part—but not all—of the curriculum is allocated to spontaneous play. As children get older, increasing proportions of the curriculum are given to systematic instruction. It is our view that project work is an appropriate part of the curriculum throughout the preschool and elementary school years.

Finally, like numerous other educators of young children, we continue to be inspired, informed, and instructed by the variety of projects conducted by young children in the Reggio Emilia preprimary schools. In particular, their detailed documentation of the children's experiences and ideas has provoked many educators of young children to turn to projects as a significant part of the curriculum.

SUMMARY

During the preschool years, spontaneous play and project work are closely intertwined and can occur side by side. Preschool children are encouraged to engage in spontaneous play related to the events and constructions they have worked on. For older children, each aspect of the curriculum—systematic instruction and project work—makes essential and complementary contributions to their education.

At all age levels, project work provides contexts for careful observation, indepth investigation, exchange of ideas, mutual support, resolution of conflicts, cooperation, collaboration, and other important experiences while in the process of learning about significant aspects of the local world of people, objects, and events.

2

Principles of Practice in the Early Years

As we indicated in the previous chapter, the involvement of children in extended projects is not new. At the time of this writing, it seems to be in its third revival. Unlike previous movements toward project work, we now have a substantial body of research about the development and learning of young children to support its advocacy. This chapter presents a summary of the relevant research and offers principles of practice derived from it in support of the proposition that good project work can engage young children's minds in ways that strengthen their intellectual dispositions as well as support their growing competence in basic skills. We begin with a discussion of the concept of development, follow by discussing four types of learning goals, and then take up research on curriculum and teaching methods.

In this way, we present a rationale for including project work in early childhood and primary education based largely on insights from recent research findings and enriched by more than a decade of experience of working with teachers who have been using it. Throughout this chapter, we offer principles of development and of practice that serve as a basis for making many of the complex decisions involved in teaching young children.

THE CONCEPT OF DEVELOPMENT

Following a brief discussion of the concept of development, we present research and principles of practice relevant to four main kinds of learning goals. This section is followed by a brief discussion of the implications of research on various aspects of the project approach.

Early childhood education has traditionally drawn heavily upon studies of human development. As academic specialties, child study and child development have contributed greatly to the field (Greenberg, 1987). The study of child development in particular is commonly a major component of early childhood teacher preparation, though in recent times the cultural bias of developmental theories and research has been a subject of animated discussion and debate (Katz, 1996).

We find it helpful to think of the concept of development as having two major dimensions: the *normative* and the *dynamic* (Maccoby, 1984; Radke-Yarrow, 1987). Each of these dimensions has implications for curriculum and teaching methods.

The Normative Dimension of Development

As most commonly used, the concept of development draws on the normative dimension. This dimension addresses matters such as what most children can and cannot do at a given age, that is, age norms. Patterns of behavior, abilities, and understandings that are typical and most frequently observed in children at a particular age are thus treated as age norms. For example, we are applying the normative dimension when we say something about how many words most children know at a particular age, or about the average age at which they can be expected to take their first step, understand time, conserve volume, and so forth. When we say that an activity is developmentally appropriate, or speak of grade-level achievement, we are employing the normative dimension of the concept of development.

Knowledge of the age norms of abilities provides a basis for planning environments and activities likely to be suitable and interesting to children of a given age group. Such knowledge can alert teachers to patterns of behavior or abilities in a child that are sufficiently above or below age norms that they warrant closer observation, examination, and special provisions.

The Dynamic Dimension of Development

The other major dimension of development is the dynamic one. This has three interrelated aspects. One deals with the ways that human beings *change* over time and with the physiological development and the experience that accumulates with it. It addresses the sequence of learning, the transformations that accrue in capabilities from one age to another, and the order in which the stages of development and learning occur. Thus, some specialists study the sequential transitions in infants as they progress from babbling in babyhood to becoming competent speakers of a language by age 4 or 5.

A second aspect of the dynamic dimension is that of *delayed impact* (Radke-Yarrow, 1987). This concerns the way that the effects of early experience, not evident at the time, may affect later functioning, particularly with respect to affective and personality development. It attends to determinants of behavior that may be unconscious and because they occurred early, are no longer easily accessible to conscious attention. For example, the assumption that early separation from mother or caregiver may have a delayed impact on later mental health continues to be debated in the field of human development.

A third aspect of the dynamic dimension are the potential long-term *cumulative effects* of repeated or frequent experiences. An experience might, for example, have no effect on a child's development if it occurs only once in a while, but have a harmful effect if it occurs frequently over a long period of time. For example, a teacher might not worry if a child is occasionally confused when approaching school tasks; but frequent or repeated confusion may have strong cumulative effects on the child's self-confidence. Occasional exposure to horror movies might not affect a child in any noticeable way; but frequent exposure might have deleterious effects in the long term.

These three aspects of the dynamic dimension—change, delayed impact, and cumulative effects—remind us to consider children's early experiences in light of their potential long-term consequences.

When both the normative and dynamic dimensions of development are taken into account, it seems reasonable to suggest that, in principle, *just because children* can *do something when they are young does not mean that they* should *do it.* The distinction between what young children can do and what they should do is especially serious because most children appear willing, if not eager, to do most of what is asked of them; they rarely appear to be suffering, and most often enjoy the activities offered. Most young children are eager to please their teachers. But children's willingness and enjoyment are potentially misleading criteria for judging the value of an activity. After all, young children enjoy junk food, questionable video games, and television programs of doubtful value. Enjoyable experiences that people generally agree are not in a child's best interests can be tolerated on a few occasions. However, their potentially damaging *cumulative effects* are of concern to many adults.

Within and across cultures, it is well established that young children's activities and behavior vary widely. In some parts of the world, many young children, especially girls, assume heavy responsibility for the care of their younger siblings. While they *can* do so, it does not follow that they should, or that these responsibilities are in the best interests of their long-term development. In some communities, toddlers are taught to "read" flash cards. In others, preschool children can and do perform rote counting up to the hundreds. In some preschool classes, young children fill out worksheets daily and frequently work assiduously to receive tangible rewards, such as gold stars and colorful stickers on their papers or even tokens and candies. Such teaching methods seem to "work" quite well in the short term; however, the potentially damaging long-term effects warrant serious concern about their appropriateness (Kohn, 1994).

In some preschool classes, children are engaged daily in the "calendar ritual" well in advance of the capacities of most of them to understand the complex concepts involved in it. The following is an observation of a small group of 4-year-olds seated on the floor facing a large calendar showing the month of February. The teacher asked them what day it was. They called out days of the week in apparently random fashion; none offers the correct answer, which was Thursday. The teacher then asked, "What day was it yesterday?" The same array of guesses is offered, which fortunately includes Wednesday. She responds "That's right! So if it was Wednesday yesterday, what day is it today?" Eventually she coaxed them into agreeing on the correct answer. When she asked next for the date (the 19th), no one replied. She then asks one of the children to come forward and write the correct numbers in the appropriate empty box on the calendar. When he hesitated, she suggested that he look at the number (versus date) for the day. Unfortunately, he looked in the box above rather than to the left of the empty one; because it contained the number 12, the child hesitantly suggested 13. Pointing out that he has looked "the wrong way," the teacher asks, "What comes after 18?" She thereby persuaded him to agree on the date, which he manages to write barely legibly in the correct box. The teacher continued the exercise, soliciting the name of the month and the year.

This ritual consumed at least 15 minutes. Apparently it had taken up about the same amount of time daily since the beginning of the school year in late August. According to *normative* data on children's understanding of time (Blyth, J., 1984), the group observed in the calendar ritual probably understood little of the concepts involved in the calendar. If they had been asked what day or date it would be after dinner, very likely they would have been unsure of the correct answer. Daily discussions of the calendar seem appropriate for children a few years older than those observed. But 4-year-olds lack the readiness to grasp the basic concepts of the calendar. Nevertheless, because the children were eager to please the teacher, they behaved as if they understood the concepts, when in fact they understood them very poorly, if at all. The fact that children at age 4 can and do willingly engage in such an exercise does not justify including it in the curriculum.

We are not implying that such activities are inevitably damaging to the children. Experience of the calendar ritual at age 4 is unlikely to be harmful if it occurs perhaps once a month. However, the potential long-term or cumulative effects of daily participation warrant the concern of educators. Specifically, behaving occasionally as if one understands something when one really does not may not matter in the long run. Perhaps some come to see themselves as slow, or believe that they are not expected to be able to understand what occurs during whole group activities, but must simply comply with expected behavior. Perhaps some deal with their confusion by creating distractions from the proceedings for themselves and perhaps for their peers. We suggest that, in principle, *the cumulative effect on children of being asked to behave as though they understand the matter at hand when they either do not, or understand it very poorly, can—in the long term—undermine their confidence in their own intellectual competence.* Such a cumulative effect is antithetical to the purpose of education. Furthermore, based on our understanding of development, especially in the long term, school time could be allocated to experiences other than the calendar ritual of potentially greater value to their intellectual development, such as, for example, the absorbing and stimulating experiences provided by indepth investigations of phenomena around them.

When considering this principle, it is useful to keep in mind that children are always learning, and that the term *learning* is a neutral one: children learn undesirable as well as desirable things, for example, to mistrust as well as to trust, to hurt as well as to help. The developmental question is not so much what children *can do*; the critical developmental question for educators is what young children *should do and should learn* that best serves their development in the long term. Thus, professional judgment about what young children should be doing and learning takes into account not only what they can and cannot do at given ages—that is, the normative dimension of development—but also the best available knowledge of the long-term dynamic sequences, delayed and cumulative effects of the choices at hand. The long-term developmental considerations can be applied to all of the important types of learning that continue throughout the early years of life.

THE FOUR CATEGORIES OF LEARNING GOALS

When the question of what children should learn is addressed in general terms, it is fairly easy to reach agreement. We readily agree that children should learn the knowledge and skills that will enable them to become productive, contributing, and competent members of society, that they should learn to be honest, responsible, cooperative, and so on, and in other ways, realize as much as possible of their potential. However, when it comes to planning specific experiences for a given group of 4- to 7-year-olds, the question typically becomes problematic. From extensive experience of working with schools and preschool programs across North America, the question of what should children be learning is typically answered by: the alphabet, the calendar, colors and shapes, holidays, dinosaurs, and traditional stories. In some countries, even 4-year-olds are also expected to begin learning basic phonics and arithmetic as well. While these topics and their related activities are unlikely to be harmful, they are hardly mind-engaging for young children.

We suggest that curricula and teaching methods are appropriate when they take into account four broad categories of learning goals: (a) knowledge, (b) skills, (c) dispositions, and (d) feelings, all of which overlap in several ways. These are briefly defined as follows:

Knowledge refers to "contents of mind" such as facts, information, concepts, ideas, constructs, stories, myths, and the like.

Skills are discrete units of action that can be fairly easily observed or inferred from observable behavior and that are executed within a relatively short time. Examples of skills are recognizing the sounds of initial letters of words, drawing, and cutting with scissors.

Dispositions can be roughly defined as habits of mind or tendencies to respond to situations in characteristic ways. Examples are inquisitiveness or persistence at a task in the face of difficulty.

Feelings are subjective emotional or affective states, such as feeling accepted, confident, or anxious (see Katz, 1995).

Research and principles relevant to each of these four categories of learning goals are discussed below.

Acquisition and Construction of Knowledge

The precise nature of knowledge has occupied epistemologists for hundreds of years and remains difficult to define (Sfard, 1998). It seems clear that with increasing age and experience, the knowledge children acquire and construct becomes more highly differentiated and increasingly hierarchically organized and is stored in memory in complex ways. Our understanding of how children's knowledge develops, what they can understand and how they understand their experience as development proceeds is another basis for curriculum planning.

Deciding what knowledge is worth having at a given age or stage of development is difficult and complex. One basis upon which to make decisions is what the adults in children's culture believe is important for them to know (Spodek, 1987), though *when* they should know it is a separate issue. Another basis is our understanding of how children's knowledge develops and what they can understand as development proceeds.

A Constructivist Perspective

Current literature in early education and development asserts that children "construct their own knowledge" (compare Kamii & Ewing, 1996). While it is reasonable to assume that children "make up their own minds" about how to understand their experiences, when they must master such arbitrary knowledge or facts as the alphabet or the calendar, it does not seem helpful to claim that they have constructed it themselves. Indeed, one of the reasons why the skillfulness of the teacher is so important is because young children frequently misconstruct their knowledge!

When young children first learn that the red light is the one that means "stop," they have adopted or internalized information they have heard or been told by others—the redness of the light has no inherently or internally logical relationship to stopping; it is a sign or symbol agreed upon by a particular community. The names of colors are learned, acquired, or internalized from exposure to others' use of the words to label them rather than by children's autonomous constructions. Some children will "construct" for themselves the knowledge that mixing black and white paint will create gray; others will acquire that knowledge when it is told to them by a peer or adult, perhaps accompanied by a demonstration. Whether the quality or meaning of the knowledge is related to the extent to which it was "constructed" or "instructed" is not clear.

One of the central concepts of constructivism is the zone of proximal development (ZPD) defined by Berk and Winsler (1995) as:

> [t]he distance between what a child can accomplish during independent problem-solving and what he or she can accomplish with the help of an adult or more competent member of the culture. (p. 5)

However, in this definition, reference is made to what children "accomplish" rather than their construction of knowledge per se. Similarly, Bodrova and Leong (1996), taking a Vygotskian approach to constructivism, cite Wood, Bruner, and Ross's original conception of scaffolding to the effect that

> [t]he expert provides *scaffolding* within the ZPD to enable the novice to perform at a higher level. With scaffolding the task itself is not changed, but what the learner initially does is made easier with assistance. (p. 42)

Here, the constructivists are concerned with helping children to *perform tasks* and do not make clear that these tasks involve constructing knowledge. It is not clear why this description of "scaffolding" is different from the concept of teaching. Similarly, Julyan and Duckworth (1996) state that

> Jean Piaget in his numerous studies detailed examples of the construction of knowledge by children as they acted on objects.... In fact, the way a child constructs understanding of how things work is not significantly different from the way that adults build their understanding. Our beliefs about how the world works are formed around the meanings we construe from the data of our experiences. (pp. 56–57)

Within these few sentences, the words used include "knowledge," "understandings," "meanings," and "beliefs," leaving the meaning of the assertion that "children construct their own knowledge" somewhat unclear. As Smagorinsky (1995) points out:

> The ZPD ... has been interpreted in three completely different ways; it has been invoked to account for the success of theoretically incompatible pedagogical approaches such as the whole-language approach that minimizes teacher direction and reciprocal teaching in which membership in the group is not democratic: the adult teacher is definitely a first among equals. (p. 193)

Nevertheless, it seems useful for teachers to accept the idea that children construct their own understandings and misunderstandings of their experiences, and that a major role of adults is to ascertain what these understandings and misunderstandings are, and to help the children refine, improve, and deepen their understandings and clarify or minimize their misunderstandings.

We take the view that children acquire much knowledge, information, concepts, and facts from those around them, who share what they know in effective ways. We take a constructivist view of the way children construct and misconstruct their understandings of the world around them.

We suggest that there are some things children can find out easily for themselves, some that they struggle to understand, and some that they adopt as true or simply memorize when adults tell them what they know. Some children are willing to accept the fact that they will understand some important things more fully as time passes and experience accumulates. From our perspective, the role of the teacher is one of inviting children to bring what they already know and what they already understand—however deeply or accurately—into a productive relationship with what she wants them to understand more fully, deeply, and accurately. We advocate incorporating the project approach into the curriculum as a way of increasing children's opportunities to actively construct and deepen their understandings of significant phenomena around them.

Contemporary insights into the nature of development and learning in the early years reaffirm the idea that young children are intensely engaged in the quest for understanding their experiences (see Donaldson, 1983). Although investigators use various terms for the processes involved, they generally agree that the disposition to make sense of experience is a powerful disposition in all young children (Blyth, W. A. L., 1984).

The strength of this disposition was evident when Hughes and Grieve (1983) asked young children bizarre questions such as "Is milk bigger than water?" and "Is red heavier than yellow?" Five-year-olds attempted to treat these questions sensibly and to produce plausible answers: "Milk is bigger because it's got a color" and "Red is heavier than yellow because there's water in it" (pp. 108–109). Older, more knowledgeable, and experienced children were much more likely to respond by pointing out that these were silly questions.

Most teachers of young children have a store of anecdotes about the interesting and often charming ways that children have made their own sense of experiences beyond their interpretive capacities. Children's sense-making activities can be seen as efforts to achieve the best understanding they can with the intellectual capacities they possess and the experiences they have had at a given stage of development. This suggests that a major responsibility of parents and teachers is to help children make fuller, deeper, and more accurate sense of their experiences. While parents contribute informally and spontaneously to children's understanding, teachers are the adults in children's lives who undertake this role deliberately and intentionally (see Katz, 1995).

Behavioral and Representational Knowledge

In mature learners, knowledge is often classified into two main types. One type, *behavioral knowledge*, is primarily practical or procedural in nature (Pinard, 1986; Shuell, 1986). Behavioral knowledge consists of how to enact various procedures and roles and to perform skills. Knowing how to ride a tricycle or push oneself on a swing are examples of behavioral knowledge in young children.

In contrast, *representational knowledge* consists of mental representations of the concepts, ideas, facts, propositions, and schemata that are abstracted from direct and indirect experience. While behavioral knowledge is also represented in memory, it is represented primarily as the behaviors associated with events or related actions rather than as concepts or abstract symbols. Although abstract representational knowledge consists of schemata that may include behaviors, it consists mostly of higher order conceptual schemata abstracted and constructed from experience. A young child may have the behavioral knowledge of riding a bicycle or pushing a swing, but is unlikely to have abstract representational knowledge of how either of the phenomena work.

Young children's knowledge is mainly behavioral and is strongly embedded in the context in which it has been learned. A 3-year-old may possess the behavioral knowledge to navigate throughout the rooms of her own home and perhaps her immediate neighborhood, but she probably cannot represent this knowledge abstractly in the form of a sketch or map. Even her ability to instruct someone else on how to get from one room to another may not fully match the extent of her behavioral knowledge. Similarly, 5-year-olds typically have the behavioral knowledge to speak their mother tongue fluently. They do not need abstract representational knowledge in the form of the rules of syntax and grammar in order to express themselves clearly and to use the language correctly for their own purposes.

Even though the two types of knowledge, behavioral and representational, surely interact with each other in the course of daily life, the typology is useful for thinking about young children's intellectual development. A rich store of experiences for building behavioral knowledge can provide a firm basis for subsequent development of abstract representational knowledge. Thus, a child can represent the behavior involved in navigating her house if she first has full behavioral knowledge of it. The developmental sequence seems to be *from behavioral to representational knowledge*, although the two forms of knowledge increasingly interact with each other as a child grows.

Formal academic instruction emphasizes the transmission of abstract representational knowledge. In traditional educational institutions, the behavioral knowledge of the learners and how it might be related to what is taught is not usually taken into account. Much contemporary conventional schooling, characterized by Heath (1987) as the "transmission model" of education, assumes that learners can acquire representational knowledge and transform it into appropriate and desired behaviors—the reverse of the direction suggested above. While the reverse direction may be applicable to children in the later school years, a relevant principle for the early years is that *an appropriate curriculum first strengthens and extends children's behavioral knowledge and then helps them to employ a variety of abstract representations directly related to it.* Many documented projects undertaken by the preprimary children in Reggio Emilia show the rich interactions between children's behavioral knowledge of their own direct experiences and the learning generated by a variety of ways of representing them (compare Reggio Children, 1998). Similarly, one of the major features of the project approach is the work of representing the findings of the investigations in a variety of ways, thereby strengthening both the knowledge gained and the skillfulness with which children use a variety of representational methods and media.

Event and Script Knowledge

Along similar lines, Schank and Abelson (1977) assert that much knowledge, especially in preschool children, is represented in a form that resemble scripts. A script specifies the actors, actions, and props used to implement the goals of the scripted event. The extensive research of Nelson and her colleagues (Nelson, 1986; Nelson & Seidman, 1984; see also French, 1985) on how young children's representations of knowledge develop from scripts provides useful insights for early childhood curriculum planning.

Nelson (1986) points out that "the young child's cognitive processing is contextualized in terms of everyday experience" (p. 4) and that "real world knowledge comes to the child almost exclusively from direct experience primarily from the analysis of [her] own experience rather than from mediated sources" (p. 5). Nelson suggests that children are constantly engaged in reorganizing the data they collect from experience, first into events and then into scripts.

An *event* representation is a memory of an event and all of the associations the child has with it. For example, the "bedtime" event would be represented in memory with the objects, persons, and other salient matters related to it.

A *script* representation is a memory of an event and its associations, which includes temporal sequences of what the participants do and say to each other as the event unfolds. Scripts "involve people in purposeful activities, and acting on objects and interacting with each other to achieve some result" (Nelson, 1986, p. 11). Thus, a young child can represent the sequence of events contained in her bedtime routines. At times young children can in fact become quite indignant if the sequence is changed by leaving out even a minor detail.

In the preschool years, scripts are organized around familiar sequences and the behavior and props involved in them. Observation of children during spontaneous play gives us a sample of the script knowledge they are building. Thus, spontaneous play is frequently about life at home, school, and other scenes and settings to which they have been exposed. With age and experience, children develop scripts that become longer, more detailed and complex, and less bound by direct firsthand experience.

Therefore, young children constantly assimilate information to the scripts they already know and accommodate their script representations to make sense of new experiences. As children share scripts with others in the course of spontaneous interaction and more formal discussion, scripts assume a public form: they include the same features as the scripts of other members of their culture. Children gradually recognize what is idiosyncratic within their own experience and what is held in common with others' experience. For example, the breakfast event has public, culturally shared elements. Within any culture, however, individuals may have breakfasts that take very different forms. As children work on projects, the teacher can capitalize on the pool of event knowledge in a class of children from diverse backgrounds.

Nelson (1986) suggests that, while older children and adults learn from indirect or secondary sources of knowledge such as textbooks and formal instruction, young children are unable to do so. Indirect sources of knowledge are not easily available to them because they are "unable to make use of language to construct world knowledge independently of their own prior experience for several years after first learning to talk" (p. 5). Children can learn much from stories and books, especially when they can relate the knowledge in them to their own direct experience.

The variety of backgrounds that children bring to the group enriches the sources of information about how different people enact familiar events and what they do often, only occasionally, or rarely in relation to common scripts. Projects involving familiar events can be used to introduce new variations and information related to them. Project work on topics familiar to the children can provide contexts in which they can refine and add to their growing repertoire of scripts.

In sum, the question of what knowledge young children should be acquiring and constructing, and the many processes by which they do so raise complex issues for curriculum planning and teaching methods. We suggest that good project work helps children to acquire and construct understandings of their own experience and environments, which will then strengthen their confidence in their capacities to make sense of their world and their desire to master skills that will assist them in doing so.

Acquisition of Skills

As previously suggested, skills can be defined as small units of action that can be fairly easily observed or inferred from observable behavior. The accumulation of a repertoire of skills continues to be a common basis for designing curricula for young children. The list of skills that young children learn spontaneously and with the help of adults in a variety of contexts is very long. It includes many kinds of physical, social, communicative, and cognitive skills of varied specificity. Unlike parents, teachers typically use systematic procedures to help children acquire basic skills, especially those related to reading, writing, and mathematics. While many children are able to acquire such skills spontaneously, most need a teacher's help to achieve mastery.

Virtually all learners require some amount of practice to achieve proficiency in using skills. Practice typically takes the form of drills and exercises. But activities to which the skills are applied are also a form of practice. As suggested in Chapter 1, in principle, skillfulness improves with *use*, and not only with formal drill and practice. Furthermore, actual use of skills often strengthens children's motivation to increase their proficiency in them. Including project work in the early childhood curriculum provides opportunities for the acquisition and practice and application of many basic skills. Almost all projects of interest to young children can provide contexts for acquiring and applying emerging skills in literacy and numeracy. As we noted in Chapter 1, project work is best seen as complementary to the more formal aspects of early childhood curriculum.

Skills Required for Social Competence

Although definitions of social competence vary, they generally include the capacity to initiate, develop, and maintain satisfying reciprocal relationships with others, especially peers. Components of social competence include social knowledge and cognition (French, 1985) and emotion regulation, as well as prosocial interactive skills.

Accumulating evidence indicates that young children who fail to develop at least a minimal level of social competence during the first five or six years are at significant risk in adulthood (Katz & McClellan, 1997). The risks include increased probability of dropping out of school, involvement in juvenile or adult delinquency, and of experiencing problems related to mental health (Parker & Asher, 1987).

Achieving social competence involves many complex processes that begin at birth. The development of social competence involves addressing all four types of learning goals discussed earlier in this chapter: knowledge, skills, dispositions, and feelings. Teachers of young children are in an ideal position to foster the development of all these components by providing contexts in which they can be expressed in meaningful ways. It should be noted that both appropriate and inappropriate social responses are learned through interaction with caregivers and peers. Maladaptive patterns of social responses may be intensified and strengthened during interaction unless the child is helped to alter them. Simply providing group interaction does not guarantee that all young children will acquire desirable peer interactive skills. Many children need adult help to master them.

Early social competence is unlikely to be learned or improved by instruction or exhortation. Rather, it is fostered with the assistance of a knowledgeable teacher who provides insight, guidance, and suggestions in the course of a child's interaction with peers. Fortunately, teachers now have a range of techniques available for fostering the development of social competence (see Katz & McClellan, 1997).

In the course of project work, children have ample genuine opportunity to listen to each other's ideas and questions, to anticipate each other's wishes and questions, to resolve arguments, to offer assistance to each other, to communicate their own suggestions and thoughts to their coworkers, and to coordinate their efforts with others. Furthermore, they often will have the opportunity to learn to work with peers they do not especially like or prefer. Thus, all of these experiences offer occasions to acquire and practice social competencies that are life skills—skills not included on tests or report cards.

Communicative Competence

All who are concerned with young children's development and learning recognize that early childhood is a critical period in the development of all aspects of communicative competence. Communicative competence includes complex knowledge as well as skills. Contemporary research indicates that all three basic functions of language, namely, communication, expression, and reasoning, are enhanced when children engage in conversation (Nelson, 1985; Wells, 1983, 1986). Passive exposure to language by itself is not sufficient for the development and strengthening of communicative competence.

Most children in the preschool years are still in the process of developing their conversational skills. Most teachers recognize the difficulty of encouraging real conversation and discussion during group sessions. Much effort is given to reminding children to wait for their turn to speak. A kindergarten teacher was observed attempting to engage a class of 5-year-old children in a group discussion by asking each in turn, "What is your news today?" Each child struggled to find something headline-worthy to report to his or her indifferent, squirming classmates. Perhaps some of these children were learning to "listen" as the teacher intended; but many appeared to be learning to "tune out" their stammering, hesitant classmates.

Conversations are a special type of interaction in which the content of each participant's contribution is contingent upon the other's in a sequential string of responses. If the contributions are not sequentially contingent, the event consists of parallel monologues. The work of Bruner (1980) and others suggests that conversations are most likely to occur when children are in small groups of three or four, with or without an adult present. Furthermore, it is reasonably clear that children are most likely to converse when something of sufficient importance or interest to them occurs in context (Clark & Wade, 1983). The findings of the Oxford Research Project (Bruner, 1980) indicate that the content of interactions in preschool programs is typically managerial and fails to engage the kind of concern and interest that would support genuine conversations among children.

Blank (1985) also suggests that conversations are more likely to be prolonged when adults make comments to children rather than simply ask questions. This suggest that in principle *children's conversational interactions are facilitated when adults offer comments and solicit their opinions and ideas*. Many teachers attempt to engage children in conversation by asking them questions. There are, however, several types of questions, not all of them equally likely to result in sustained conversation (Wood & Wood, 1983). The most common type of questioning that teachers use is formal interrogation, resembling a cross-examination aimed at specific answers expected by the questioner. Questions like "What color is your shirt?" or "What did I say?" are examples of formal interrogations, that is, questions to which it is clear that the adult knows the right answers and is seeking and will only accept specific responses. Interrogation-type questions have a distinctly unauthentic aspect to them. A nursery school teacher was observed questioning her pupils about a visit they had made to an aquarium on the preceding day. When she asked the children "How did the fish get into the tank?," one of them responded earnestly by asking her, "Have you forgotten already?"

One effect of the excessive use of such interrogations is to create interactive patterns that are phony and unlike discourse outside of school. Another is to make respondents feel intimidated or even threatened by the possibility that they will fail to give the desired answer. When such questions dominate interaction in the class, pupils often become reluctant to reveal their confusion and to ask for help.

An alternative to the interrogation approach is for the teacher to ask children soliciting questions, which encourage them to give her information she does not already have. If a teacher is required to discuss the names of colors, she can ask, for example, "Is that color shirt one of your favorites?" "Do you especially like the color blue?" The child's answer can then be responded to with appropriate comments and conversation. However, an interrogation is occasionally appropriate. If so, the teacher could say something like "I want to know if you know your address. Would you please tell me what it is?" In this way, the teacher's question is genuine, and her relationship to the child remains authentic and respectful.

A principle suggested by much recent research is that *young children's communicative competence can be enhanced by work in small groups on projects that provide rich content for conversation.* In other words, if children are to have frequent and satisfying experiences of conversation, they must have content about which to converse—content that is of concern, importance, or of interest to them. Our experience of the project approach is that during all three phases, children have rich content for conversations.

Development of Dispositions

As previously indicated, dispositions are broadly defined as relatively enduring habits of mind and action, or tendencies to respond to categories of experience across classes of situations (Katz, 1995). Buss and Craik (1983) define dispositions technically as summaries of act frequencies. They assert that when an individual enacts certain behaviors with sufficient frequency, one can infer that he or she has a given disposition. In this sense, the term *disposition* denotes many of the same qualities as the term *personality trait* (Katz & Raths, 1985), and these qualities are manifested in a variety of behaviors that occur with relative observable frequency.

A disposition is not an "end state" similar to the mastery of a piece of knowledge or the command of a particular skill. Dispositions are habits of action and reaction to classes of events and situations. Desirable dispositions include many of an intellectual nature as well as curiosity, humor, generosity, and helpfulness. Undesirable dispositions include avarice, quarrelsomeness, and callousness.

Intellectual Dispositions

As suggested earlier, academic goals are those concerned with the mastery of basic literacy and numeracy skills, many of which cannot be learned spontaneously or by discovery, or in other ways cannot be "picked up" by most children. They are relatively small units of behavior or skills that require some careful individual or small group instruction from an adult. They are also the items of knowledge that have to be memorized and rehearsed, as in the case of the alphabet; knowledge of the alphabet and its correspondence to the phonemes of the language may be "constructed" by children, as in invented spelling, but in such cases they are misconstructed. These kinds of skills also require practice. However, they are likely to get better with frequent use rather than just practice and instruction.

Intellectual goals, however, are those concerned with a broader definition of the life of the mind, and include a wide range of human experience, such as aesthetics, moral sensibilities, identifying and understanding emotions, and many other cognitive processes involved in understanding experience.

The intellectual goals of education address the development and strengthening of dispositions, that is, habits of mind. The intellectual dispositions that can be expressed and strengthened during project work include the dispositions to analyze, hypothesize, and synthesize, to predict and check predictions, to theorize about cause–effect relationships, the consequences of actions, to be empirical, to strive for accuracy, and many others.

Basic academic skills serve the school's or the society's purposes. They are part of the processes of socializing the young and preparing them to participate in the adult world to which they are ultimately expected to contribute. Intellectual goals are also part of socialization. However, many intellectual dispostions are likely to be inborn and fairly robust in most children upon entry to school. For example, the disposition to make sense of experience can be assumed to be inborn in all humans. However, unless the curriculum provides contexts in which intellectual dispositions can be strengthened by being used and applied, they may be seriously weakened or even lost. It seems reasonable to assume that once they are lost they are likely to be very difficult to put back in again.

Intellectual Dispositions and Academic Skills

Curriculum approaches employed in early childhood programs vary in the extent to which they emphasize formal instruction in basic academic skills (Maccoby & Zellner, 1970; Schweinhart & Weikart, 1997). Some approaches achieve a more even balance than others, between the proportion of time allocated to basic academic skills instruction and spontaneous play or work in learning centers. In general, including instruction and exercises in basic skills for 4- and 5-year-olds has increased significantly in the last decade. This matter has been the subject of vigorous discussion and debate among educators and parents over several decades (Bereiter, 1986; Bredekamp & Copple, 1997; Gersten, 1986; Marcon, 1995; Schweinhart, 1997; Schweinhart, Weikart, & Larner, 1986a, 1986b, 1997).

Many preschool children show a spontaneous interest in various aspects of literacy (Schickedanz, 1999). Certainly these interests should be encouraged and supported, albeit in an informal way. As indicated in Chapters 4 and 5, project work provides many opportunities for children to apply the rudiments of the basic literacy and numeracy skills they are developing.

Observation of children in a wide variety of academically oriented programs supports the claim that young children *can* engage in formal exercises designed to instruct them in basic skills, such as phonics, phonemics, counting, and handwriting. But the extent to which they *should* do so must be evaluated in light of the potential cumulative effects that these exercises may have on the development of desirable dispositions.

Dispositions deserve the attention of teachers during the early years for several reasons. The first and more obvious reason is that educators and parents readily nominate many dispositions when asked to indicate their hopes for the outcome of education. They generally agree on the desirability of encouraging children's curiosity, creativity, resourcefulness, independence, initiative, perseverance, responsibility, and other positive dispositions.

Second, the development of dispositions also deserves attention because some approaches to teaching and instruction may possibly undermine the disposition to use them. Of particular concern is the risk that introducing formal direct academic instruction in the early years may jeopardize the development of desirable dispositions. Furthermore, there is no compelling evidence that early introduction to academic work guarantees success in school in the long term. But there is reason to believe that, due to cumulative effects, early introduction of academic exercises could work against developing desirable dispositions related to learning and achievement.

The main issue is that early achievements, for example, in phonics or arithmetic, may threaten development of the dispositions to be readers and to be willing users of mathematical skills, given the amount of drill and practice usually required for success in mastering these skills at an early age. This issue can be referred to as the *damaged disposition hypothesis* (Katz, 1995).

The risk of undermining desirable dispositions related to education may go unnoticed for two reasons. First, young children who are given formal direct instruction in basic skills appear to do well—in the short term—on the kinds of standardized tests used by school authorities. When a curriculum is designed as a strongly remedial program and allocates large proportions of time to practicing basic academic skills, the initial test results are generally encouraging, and the program can report positive results. But these positive outcomes are mainly of short duration. On the other hand, curriculum approaches that provide for strengthening dispositions such as interest, initiative, and curiosity by allowing for play and project activities show relatively unimpressive test results in the short term, but considerable benefits in the long term. Second, dispositions (for example, curiosity, interest, persistence, and so on) are rarely effects considered worthy of being evaluated in early childhood programs.

The damaged disposition hypothesis seems to be a reasonable interpretation of the results of several longitudinal studies (Karnes, Schwedel, & Williams, 1983;

Miller & Bizzell, 1983; Schweinhart, Weikart, & Larner, 1986a; see also Consortium for Longitudinal Studies, 1983; Marcon, 1995; Walberg, 1984). As we look at the results of these studies, the early pressure on young children to perform academic tasks (for example, practice in phonics, workbook exercises) appears quite harmless or even beneficial at first. Many children *can* perform the tasks involved. But professional educators are obliged to take into account the potential cumulative effects of early experiences, no matter how benign those experiences appear to be at the time they occur.

The most recent reports of longitudinal studies of children considered "at risk" for academic difficulties have confirmed our concern about the differences between the short-term and long-term benefits of various curriculum approaches. On the whole these studies confirm earlier research results. They suggest again that while early formal instructional methods appear to be beneficial in the short term, they fail to produce positive effects on academic, intellectual, and social development in the long term as the more child-sensitive approaches (Marcon, 1992, 1995; Schweinhart, 1997; Schweinhart & Weikart, 1997). In particular, the long-term follow-up studies of children in High/Scope's Perry Preschool Program (see Schweinhart, 1997) and the follow-up studies of Marcon (1995) indicate that *in the long term* children benefit greatly academically, intellectually, and socially from early childhood programs that provide opportunities for them to take initiative, and to be actively engaged in their own learning experiences. Marcon (1995) refers to the long-term negative effects of early formal direct instructional programs as the "fourth-grade slump." Marcon summarizes her findings as follows:

> the negative impact of overly academic early childhood programs on achievement and social development was clearly apparent by the fourth grade. Children who had attended [academically directed] prekindergarten programs were scoring noticeably lower in fourth grade despite their adequate performance on third-grade standardized achievement tests. The [academically directed] children were also developmentally behind their peers and displayed notably higher levels of maladaptive behavior (i.e., defiant behavior, anxiety, and distractibility). (p. 19)

Results from these longitudinal studies suggest that curriculum design for young children should be approached in a way that optimizes the *simultaneous* acquisition of knowledge, skills, *and* desirable dispositions. It is clearly not very useful to have skills if the disposition to use them is undermined in the process of acquiring them. On the other hand, having the disposition without the skills is also inconsistent with the goals of education. The challenge, then, is to help the learner with both the acquisition of skills and with desirable dispositions that invoke the application of those skills.

Teachers can help minimize damaging emerging dispositions to use new skills by being alert to situations in which it is advisable not to require further practice or more workbook exercises, lest a disposition to be a writer, for example, be weakened by the excessive drill. This view of the relationship between skills and dispositions reflects the principle *that emphasis must be balanced so that both the skills and dispositions to use them are simultaneously enhanced.* Identifying and observing children's dispositional development should thus be taken into account in teacher decision making.

As we have already suggested, a third reason for emphasizing dispositional development in the early years is that it is reasonable to assume that many of the important intellectual dispositions are inborn and robust in all children, though there are likely to be individual differences in their strength. As already indicated, these intellectual dispositions include the disposition to make sense of experience, to theorize and hypothesize about cause–effect relationships and how things work, and to analyze, predict, synthesize, and in other ways give meaning to experience. An appropriate curriculum thus includes ample opportunity for strengthening and using these dispositions, as in project work.

A fourth reason for emphasis on dispositional development in the early years is our assumption that once these powerful intellectual dispositions are either damaged by excessive emphasis on academic drills, neglected by mindless activities, or lost due to insufficient opportunity to express them, they are likely to be very difficult to reinstate.

In sum, project work is the part of early childhood curriculum that provides contexts for children to strengthen their intellectual dispositions as well as to *apply* their developing academic skills and to strengthen the dispositions to use them.

The Development of the Capacity for Interest

One of the important dispositions of concern to educators of young children is *interest,* tentatively defined here as the capacity to "lose oneself" in an activity or concern outside of oneself. Although frequently used by educators, psychologists, and others, the term *interest* is difficult to define with precision. We use it to refer to the disposition to pursue an activity or goal in the absence of coercion or expected rewards. We include the tendency to become deeply absorbed enough in an activity to pursue it over an extended period of time, with sufficient commitment to accept its routine as well as novel aspects. Sometimes called "intrinsic motivation" (Deci & Ryan, 1985; Morgan, 1984), "continuing motivation" (Maehr, 1982), or "self-directed learning" (Benware & Deci, 1984), this disposition in rudimentary form appears to be present in the normal human at birth and is affected by a variety of social-psychological processes throughout childhood.

Research indicates that children's interest and intrinsic motivation are affected by the kind of feedback they receive (Ryan, Connell, & Deci, 1985). Studies of the overjustification effect (Lepper, 1981) suggest that when children are rewarded for tasks in which they had initially shown spontaneous interest, the reward is followed by diminished interest. In other words, rewards may reduce children's desire to engage in an activity spontaneously. The term *overjustification effect* reflects the idea that the satisfaction children derive from activities undertaken spontaneously provides its own justification. Therefore, offering a reward therefore *overjustifies* the activity. The researchers suggest that children respond to such rewards by saying to themselves, as it were, "It must be wrong to like doing X if I am given a reward for doing it" (Deci & Ryan, 1982).

Hunter and Barker (1987) have analyzed the effects that rewards have on children's self-attributions about their own efforts. They point out that when extrinsic rewards are made salient, children have no choice but to attribute their effort to a factor or force *outside* themselves. If, on the other hand, rewards are not obvious, children can attribute their effort to their own initiative and to forces *inside* themselves. Hunter's and Barker's analysis suggests that children are less able to perceive the responsibility for what happens to them as their own if extrinsic rewards are overemphasized in the classroom.

Similarly, in an experiment with preschoolers on ideational fluency, one index of creativity, by Groves, Sawyers, and Moran (1987), showed that children in the rewarded group scored lower than nonrewarded groups on creativity tasks, thus "supporting the growing body of evidence that rewards are detrimental to creative functioning" (p. 339). Boggiano and Main (1986) showed that the *bonus effect* of a reward can change the interest value of the activity for which the reward is given. Experiments on the bonus effect indicate that, when participation in one activity is contingent on having completed another, the latter's value is automatically depressed. Thus, if we were to insist that carrots can be eaten only if dessert has been finished (the reverse of the usual order), the desirability of carrots would increase substantially. The appeal of the dessert also becomes depressed. Needless to say, the bonus effect is bound to be restricted: increases in the liking for some foods are likely to be limited.

The deleterious effects of rewards and bonuses apply especially to activities that children find appealing at first. Special care must therefore be taken not to offer rewards for those activities. Since most young children are easily attracted to almost any novel activity, the practice of introducing tangible rewards is generally unwarranted. Teachers all over the world using the project approach tell us regularly of their amazement at the level of the children's interest, absorption, and commitment to their work. Their children's efforts are sustained in spite of periods of frustration and various setbacks. A powerful motivator of their efforts seems to be the purposefulness with which they approach the tasks involved in the investigation and reporting of findings.

The growing body of research on the effects of rewards and bonuses also implies that the tendency of teachers to tell children they may do artwork only after completing their reading assignments is likely to depress the value and liking that children have for reading. They may perceive such contingencies to mean that little satisfaction can be expected from reading. Furthermore, making art activities contingent on completing other work may also give children mixed messages about the teacher's view of the value of art. It is unrealistic to expect children to be equally enthusiastic about all of the activities offered. Teaching strategies that unwittingly reinforce negative attitudes toward any of them should be avoided. Children do not have to like every activity or task required of them; but it is a good idea that they be able to grasp their value and importance at some level.

A parallel line of research on the development of interest suggests that when positive feedback is general in nature, productivity increases but interest declines (deCharms, 1983). Children are likely to respond to general positive feedback by increasing the amount of work they produce, but are likely to show less willingness to work on the tasks when the feedback is withdrawn. General positive feedback includes global comments such as "Very good!" "Well done!" "Great!," and the drawing of smiling faces or placement of decorative stickers or gold stars on the children's products. When positive feedback is specific, however, particularly if it includes information about the competence of the work, children's willingness to continue without external pressure increases, although the amount of work produced does not necessarily increase. Specific, informative feedback is called a *tribute*, and general, nonspecific feedback is called an *inducement*. A tribute is associated with increasing interest in the task, whereas an inducement is associated with loss of interest but increased productivity, except when rewards are withdrawn.

Along similar lines, Grolnick and Ryan (1987) compared the effects that different amounts of control, direction, and spontaneity have on children's motivation in experimental learning conditions. The researchers reported evidence of greater deterioration in rote recall several days following the experimental lesson that had greater control and direction. The finding "suggests that material learned under strong external pressures may be less likely to be maintained" (p. 897). The data also showed that under conditions in which the learners became apprehensive about grades, rote learning was promoted, but it "undermined interest and active integration of the material" (p. 897).

It is not yet clear how rewards and general positive feedback exert their negative effects on interest. But it seems reasonable to assume that they distract children from involvement in the tasks at hand. McCullers, Fabes, and Moran (1987) examined the link between the detrimental effects of rewards on interest and subsequent immediate task performance. Their view is that "the adverse effects of material rewards are due to a temporary, reward-induced regression in psychological organization and function" (p. 1027). They assert that rewards shift subjects to a more "primitive" level of psychological functioning, and have the effect of "changing the level of challenge from an optimal (intrinsically motivating) to a nonoptimal one" (p. 1032). Thus, "tasks that are interesting and challenging under nonrewarded conditions become frustratingly difficult under reward [conditions]" (p. 1032). McCullers and colleagues suggest that when a reward is anticipated, it is reasonable to choose simpler, less challenging tasks by which to improve one's chances of obtaining the reward. Occasional striving for rewards and honors may be appropriate and beneficial. However, the cumulative effects of frequent and constant expectation of rewards from early childhood onward may damage interest and challenge-seeking in the long run.

Academically oriented programs typically emphasize general positive feedback, ostensibly to give children feelings of success and to spur productivity. This strategy appears to work well to induce young children to keep working at discrete, disembedded, decontextualized, and often very trivial tasks. Few of the kinds of tasks offered in such programs seem to engage children's inquisitive minds. Most young children approach these tasks quite willingly early in their school experience. However, research on the effects of rewards strongly suggests that children may suffer academic "burnout," or what Marcon (1995) has labeled the "fourth-grade slump," after several years of general, positive, extrinsic rewards.

Curricula and teaching methods that attempt to provide children with constant amusement, fun, or excitement also risk undermining the development of children's dispositions to be interested and absorbed in worthwhile activities (Katz, 1995). For example, telling stories of the romanticized and exciting but unlawful activity of pirates is not really necessary to make the topic of the sea interesting—especially if the children are close enough to it to observe it. The size, force, and sound of the waves; the movement of the tides; the expanse of sandy beach, seaweed, pebbles, and shells; soaring cliffs; teeming tide pools; and much more of the real world around the sea are sufficiently intriguing and engaging to children without extraneous inducement.

The teacher's role in strengthening children's dispositions to be interested in relevant and worthwhile phenomena is a complex and critical one. If dispositions are to be strengthened, opportunities to manifest them must be available. In the case of interest, the topics and activities themselves can be the source of satisfaction. Interest can also be strengthened when other people, particularly adults, acknowledge and appreciate its expression. For example, if a child asks a question while interacting with others, the teacher might return a day or two later with a pertinent artifact, indicating that she has recognized the child's expression of interest. She might say, "Yesterday you were wondering what hermit crabs look like. Well, I found a book with some pictures of them and thought it might interest you." Such a response to the child's behavior is positive without taking her mind off the subject.

Interest and the capacity for absorption can be strengthened when children are encouraged to engage in projects that call for sustained effort and involvement over a period of several days or weeks. Such projects provide contexts for extending, elaborating, and continued work and play (Rosenfield, Folger, & Adelman, 1980). Academic exercises and drills are usually presented to children as one-shot tasks to be completed within brief periods and rarely include extended or continuing involvement in a topic. Workbook exercises seldom evoke the disposition to make a second or third attempt at mastery. Typically, each worksheet is handed in for correction and returned on a later day. The disposition to lose oneself in an activity may be threatened by frequent interruptions. A classroom schedule that segments the day into many activities lasting only 15 or 20 minutes may undermine the disposition to become deeply involved in worthwhile effort. The daily program for young children should be flexible rather than fragmented in allocating time to various activities. The principle behind project work is that *activities lasting an extended period of time strengthen the disposition to become continuously involved and absorbed in mind-engaging work.*

Effort, Mastery, and Challenge Seeking

Extensive research by Dweck (1986, 1987; Smiley & Dweck, 1994) suggests that the goals teachers set have significant cumulative effects on children's dispositions to seek mastery, reach for learning, engage in effort persistence, and challenge seeking. Dweck asserts that school tasks can be set in terms of *performance goals* or *learning goals*. When a teacher introduces an activity by saying something like, "Today I want to see how good you are at X" or "How many problems you can get right" or "How well you can do," she sets performance goals. If on the other hand, the teacher says something like "Today I want to see how far you can get on X" or "How much you can find out about Y" or, "I would like you to try and find out how far and how fast these cars roll on different surfaces," she sets learning goals.

These two conditions arouse different kinds of responses that affect children's dispositions toward effort and mastery. Under conditions of strong performance pressure, children focus on gaining favorable judgments of their ability or avoiding negative ones. Under conditions of learning goals, children seek to increase their understanding or mastery of something new. Dweck (1986) defines the mastery disposition as adaptive, accompanied by "challenge seeking and high, effective persistence in the face of obstacles" (p. 1040). She defines the maladaptive disposition as helplessness, manifested by "challenge avoidance, low persistence in the face of difficulty" (1986, p. 1042), accompanied by negative affect, anxiety, and negative self-attribution with respect to ability. The evidence also indicates that adaptive and maladaptive dispositions are independent of actual intellectual ability (Dweck & Leggett, 1988).

According to many studies, these two types of goals produce different effects on children's concerns as they address the tasks assigned. Under performance goals, children show concern about their ability. The confident ones may accept the task eagerly, though a few will worry lest they fail to measure up to their reputations as highly able on a particular occasion. Other children tend to engage in defensive withdrawal from the task to avoid expected negative judgments of their ability. Performance goals "promote defensive strategies that can interfere with challenge seeking" (Dweck, 1986, p. 1043). As Dweck's experiments revealed, children faced with learning goals chose challenging tasks regardless of whether they believed themselves to have high or low ability; they were also not unwilling to display their ignorance. Tending to think more about the required skills and the interest of the topic, they were less oriented internally toward their own ability and how they might look to others.

In tasks and assignments oriented toward performance goals, children who do not succeed tend to attribute their failure to their lack of ability. This kind of self-attribution usually leads to anxiety, which may interfere with their performance, and ultimately to withholding effort. A few children even become overwhelmed by worry about goal attainment. However, during learning goal assignments, children perceive obstacles and difficulties as cues to increase their effort, to analyze and vary their strategies, and thus to improve their work. As Dweck (1986) points out,

"The more children focus on learning or progress, the greater the likelihood of maintaining effective strategies (or improving their strategies) under difficulty or failure" (p. 1044).

The two different types of task goals also give rise to different sources of satisfaction. Children perceive the performance goals condition as an opportunity to display their abilities and take pride in them if indeed they are able, or they experience embarrassment and shame when they fail. Children may come to the conclusion that effort indicates low ability. They may then attempt to disguise or deny that they have to apply real effort, fearing it will reveal that they actually have little ability. Children with a strong performance orientation derive satisfaction from outshining others; they often respond to the failure of others with a sense of relief; those who perceive themselves as able tend to welcome a competitive reward structure.

In the case of learning goals, children enjoy the effort involved in the tasks and gain satisfaction from the mastery achieved. Learning-oriented children have also been found to be more magnanimous toward their peers in noncompetitive situations (Dweck, 1986, 1991). Research also indicates a greater retention and transfer of learning and more active attempts to apply what has been learned to novel problems.

According to one hypothesis about the possible outcome of extensive experience with performance goals, children who see themselves as having moderate or low ability come to disavow grades, test scores, and other indices of performance. This hypothesis is related to Dweck's (1991) assertion that in some cultures people acquire in the early years a strong belief that ability is a fixed entity: one either has ability or not. Repeated pressures to perform would be accompanied by repeated exposures to one's own inadequacies. One way of coping with these exposures might be to distance oneself from the institution that passes judgment and from its workers, methods, and symbols.

The potentially negative effects of overemphasis on performance goals are similar to the detrimental effects of rewards. In an educational setting where teachers encourage working for rewards, children would be unwise or even foolish to undertake risky or challenging tasks. The most adaptive response in such settings is to do the simplest tasks to increase the chance of obtaining the rewards the adults put so much stock in. Although working for a reward might be appropriate or harmless on rare occasions, repeated daily injunctions to strive for rewards could have undesirable, long-term cumulative effects. Contrary to common sense, "[c]ontinued success on personally easy tasks with a performance goal...is ineffective in producing stable confidence, challenge seeking and persistence" (Dweck, 1986, p. 1046).

This research suggests that young children's dispositions to learn can be threatened by excessive emphasis on skilled performance in academically oriented curricula. Dweck (1986) notes that emphasizing performance "may well create the very conditions that have been found to undermine intrinsic interest" (1986, p.1042). One of the many reasons we advocate including project work as part of early childhood curriculum is that it emphasizes learning goals and provides contexts that focus on what individuals and groups can learn while exploring topics and investigating phenomena together.

Social Dispositions

Parents, teachers, and others in our communities are also concerned about strengthening dispositions related to social competence, for example, helpfulness, charitableness, and appreciation of others' efforts. These dispositions must first be elicited and acknowledged if they are to be strengthened. Project work provides natural contexts in which such dispositions and their component behaviors are elicited, refined, strengthened, and appreciated by others.

Ames and Ames (1984) have shown how the goal structure of the classroom affects children's responses in terms of social dispositions. The researchers point out that goal plus reward structure is a pervasive feature of most classroom situations in the United States. Such a structure "defines which goals students are to accomplish, how students are to be evaluated, and how students are to relate to each other and to the task" (p. 535). Ames and Ames identified three basic types of goal structures: competitive, cooperative, and individualistic, as well as hybrids of the three. In a *competitive* goal structure, "[s]tudents work against each other such that the probability of one student achieving a goal or reward is reduced by the presence of capable others" (p. 536). In a *cooperative* goal structure, on the other hand, "[t]he probability of one student receiving a reward is enhanced by the presence of capable others" (p. 536). In an *individualistic* goal structure, the probability of receiving a reward is unrelated to the capabilities of others. On the contrary, it involves a "fusing of the person with the demands of the task such that the task itself becomes the goal" (p. 536).

As extensive research indicates, the individualistic and cooperative types of class structure are more likely to foster dispositions toward effort, mastery, and cooperativeness. These findings support the proposition that young children's dispositions to mastery, effort, and interest may be at risk in a program that fails to provide sufficient activities in which noncompetitive, individual, and cooperative achievements are valued. As children work on projects together, both individual and group efforts are stimulated, encouraged, and valued.

Teachers can strengthen desirable dispositions in several ways. One is to provide ample opportunity for their manifestation, followed by acknowledgment and appreciation. Another is to minimize extrinsic rewards and competitive goals and to give specific informative feedback rather than general feedback (Kohn, 1994). The dispositions to be cooperative and charitable are unlikely to be well learned from instruction or from posters in which a smiling animal declares that happiness results "when everyone gets along." Such dispositions are more likely to be strengthened when children cooperate during carefully planned group project work. Since emulating models may also be important, teachers themselves can help when they show that they, too, are intrigued by phenomena worth learning about and take appropriate opportunities to benefit from others' knowledge and skills.

Development of Feelings

Feelings are difficult to define precisely. For our purposes, however, we define them as subjective emotional or affective states. Educators and parents are concerned about the feelings children develop toward school and their many experiences within it. We generally want children to feel accepted, comfortable, and competent, to feel that they belong to the class group and that their contributions to shared experiences are generally welcomed. Such feelings can be learned while interacting with significant others in the group.

We are especially concerned about the feelings many young children may acquire when academic skills are not sufficiently balanced with opportunities for spontaneous play and other informal activities. When an early childhood curriculum excessively focuses on academic tasks, many children are likely to be at risk in important ways. For example, because academically oriented curricula tend to use a restricted range of teaching methods and materials, it is unlikely that all children in the group can feel and be equally successful. As yet, no clear evidence indicates the optimal proportions of the groups capable of doing the required tasks. Nevertheless, it is reasonable to assume that teachers aim the tasks they set to what they perceived to be the average ability level of the group. We hypothesize that the knowledge and skills included will be at about the right level of difficulty for one third or one half of the children in a given group. For another one fourth or one third, the knowledge and skills are likely to be in their repertoires already. The remaining children are unlikely to be unable to respond to the tasks effectively.

In a study of the learning experiences of 6- and 7-year-olds in Britain, investigators (Bennett, Desforges, Cockburn, & Wilkinson, 1984) reported that 40 percent of the high-achieving children studied were assigned tasks below their ability, and 44 percent of the low-achieving children were expected to undertake tasks too difficult for them. In the classes studied, the tasks seemed unmatched to the abilities or outside of the Zone of Proximal Development (ZPD) of most of the children. Such high percentages of mismatches between children's abilities and the work assigned to them are likely to engender stress, despair, or boredom in a majority of the children.

From time to time and from place to place, the percentages of mismatches may vary. We suggest that to the extent that a standard teaching method or a single set of learning tasks is assigned to a whole class at the same time, significant proportions of children are condemned to fail. Failure has dynamic consequences, the full impact of which may not show during the early years. In principle, *when a young child's confusion, misunderstanding, misconceptions, and other difficulties do not cause the teacher to modify the instruction, vary the materials, or otherwise change her approach, the child may learn to feel helpless, hopeless, inadequate, and generally incompetent.* Indeed, in such situations the child *is* incompetent (see Skinner, Zimmer-Cembeck, & Connell, 1998).

Occasional feelings of incompetence may be benign. But when children have such feelings frequently and regularly over extended periods of time, the cumulative effect is likely to be that they learn to feel stupid and ultimately to give up. We refer to this self-attribution as *learned stupidity*. There is reason to believe that children tend to bring their behavior into line with their self-attributions (Grusec & Arnason, 1982). When college students are confused by the content of a lecture, they can and frequently do attribute their difficulty to the lecturer's incompetence. But young children cannot as yet decenter in the same way. They have to attribute their difficulties to their own lack of abilities (Dweck, 1986).

Some children may cope with feelings of incompetence by being disruptive; others may respond by redoubling their efforts. But the large majority of young children subjected to tasks too far beyond their competence and outside their own experiences eventually give up and become psychological dropouts. No doubt some give up sooner than others. Giving up is probably one of the less objectionable ways of coping. Such children are the victims of a kind of "academic burnout" already mentioned. As Donaldson (1978) points out:

> In the first few years at school all appears to go very well. The children seem eager, lively, happy.... However, when we consider what has happened by the time the children reach adolescence, we are forced to recognize that the promise of the early years frequently remains unfulfilled. Large numbers leave school with the bitter taste of defeat in them.... The problem then is to understand how something that begins so well can often end so badly. (pp. 13–14)

It is useful to keep in mind that the processes leading to a self-attribution of low ability or stupidity are not usually or easily discernible to teachers. For some time young children remain remarkably willing to undertake any number of decontextualized, abstract, or even frivolous and superficial tasks. Their eagerness to please the teacher, their general good will toward her, and their desire to participate in the ongoing life of the class typically last through the first few years of school. As frequently observed, children in academically oriented early childhood education programs are so eager to answer a teacher's question that they frequently raise their hands whether they know the answer or not, and often before she has even finished asking the question! A few years later, however, teachers of the same children regularly ask for help and suggestions about how to motivate them. As Bennett, Desforges, Cockburn, and Wilkinson (1984) point out on the basis of their study of mismatches between tasks and ability,

> [i]n the short term, inappropriate work appeared to have little direct emotional or motivational consequences for children of this age [6 and 7]. Although cognitive problems, which manifested themselves in unproductive or confusing learning experiences, were all too clearly apparent in the post task interviews, this cognitive confusion was masked from the teachers by the children's cheerfulness and industry. The teachers avoided the immediate consequences of such confusion by rewarding individual endeavor, and by restricting their considerations of children's work to the product, not the process of such work. (p. 215)

When opportunities to work on projects are properly balanced with appropriate academic exercises, all children can be encouraged to participate in classroom life in accord with their individual preparedness for particular tasks. In a given preschool class, for example, some of the children will work exclusively on projects; others can profitably spend some part of their time on formal academic exercises individually or in small groups. Periodically, the teacher can assess the project group's readiness to join the group learning and practicing basic skills. Including projects in the daily work of the whole group alleviates the pressure on all children to succeed at the same tasks at the same time. All children can thus learn to feel competent and that they belong to the class and can contribute effectively to its activities. Furthermore, project work provides opportunities for children to grasp the purposes of the academic skills they are expected to master during the more formal part of the curriculum, thus helping them to feel more positive about the tasks involved in mastery of them. Furthermore, in our experience of working with many teachers as they involve their young pupils in projects, we are persuaded that it is common among educators and parents to overestimate children's readiness to master academic skills, and underestimate their readiness and ability to apply their many intellectual dispositions.

CURRICULUM AND TEACHING METHODS

The previous discussion focused on the effects that various teaching and curriculum strategies have on children's dispositions and feelings. In this section, we discuss more general aspects of children's development and learning and how they are affected by various curriculum approaches (Beneke, 1998; Helm, 1996, 1998).

The Role of Interaction in Learning

It is easy to see that social competence develops in the course of interaction with others. However, intellectual development is also facilitated by interaction (Azmitia, 1988; Brown & Campione, 1982; Bruner, 1985; Glaser, 1984; Karmiloff-Smith, 1984; Nelson, 1985; Rogoff, 1982; Slavin, 1987a, 1987b, 1987c). Rogoff (1982) points out that "cognitive development depends on children's adapting and adopting the intellectual tools and skills of the larger sociocultural context, aided by other people" (p. 154). Young children's intellectual development is probably best served by opportunities to interact with adults, each other, the environment, and with a variety of materials.

In principle, *the younger the children, the more likely it is that interaction facilitates a wide variety of learning.* This principle implies that young children should be engaged in more active and expressive processes than in passive and receptive ones. For this reason, many children benefit from being introduced to writing before reading, because writing involves more action and expression than reading does. Selected interactive computer programs can also be appropriate in the early years, even before children's writing and reading skills are fully developed.

Interaction cannot occur in a vacuum, however. Something of interest and concern to the interactors is required to sustain interaction. The relevant principle of practice is that *sustained interaction requires content that is relevant, vivid, engaging, significant, and meaningful to the participants.*

In classrooms dominated by formal academic instruction, much of the interaction is taken up with following directions and instructions. The content of interaction is likely to be procedural rather than substantive, addressing matters of routines and directions (see Willes, 1983). Pupils' attention is drawn more to how to behave and perform than to the content of what is to be learned. As already suggested, the work of Dweck (1986, 1987) suggests that emphasis on performance outcomes orients children internally toward their own abilities and how they are judged by others, whereas activities with learning outcomes orient them to the topic and work at hand. Similarly, as reported above, Ames and Ames (1984) showed that, when the goals of tasks are set for cooperative or noncompetitive individual rewards and achievement, children approach the tasks in terms of the knowledge and effort necessary to proceed. Under competitive conditions, children become distracted by concerns about where they stand with respect to classmates. This body of research confirms the following view: when a curriculum is organized primarily around formal instruction for the whole group, the content of interaction among pupils and between pupils and their teachers revolves around matters other than ideas, information, concepts, and other mind-engaging phenomena.

Another principle of practice in early childhood education is that *the younger the children, the more the content of interaction should relate to their own firsthand experiences and real environment.* With increasing age and experience, children can and should be encouraged to develop their understanding of indirect experiences. In the later years, the content of interaction can be broadened to include the experiences and environments of others, those at a distance both in time and place. During the early years, however, the content of interaction and activity is likely to engage children's minds when it is related to what is salient and familiar to them. As Carey (1986) points out, children gain understanding by relating what they are learning to what they already know. This is the cognitive rather than motivational reason for studying topics that are relevant to children's experiences.

The Benefits of Optimal Informality

By its very nature, group life in school requires some classroom procedures. The practical issue, especially in the early years, is to ensure that procedures and routines serve the knowledge and skills to be learned. As a principle of practice, then, *programs for young children are likely to be beneficial when they adopt only those procedures necessary to ensure that the really mind-engaging activities can occur.* There is an optimal number of rules and routines: having too many may result in the content of interaction being dominated by nonintellectual concerns; having too few may result in confusion or chaos. An optimal amount of routine and order is liberating.

Helping children acquire a fuller understanding of their experiences means that informal contexts should be provided in which children can reveal their understanding. These revelations help the teacher to know which understandings should be further developed, refined, corrected, or otherwise improved. The underlying principle is that *the more informal the learning environment, the greater the teacher's access to the learners' representations, understandings, and misunderstandings.* A related principle is that *the better informed teachers are about these aspects of children's thinking, the better able they are to make appropriate curriculum decisions.* However, as in the case of avoiding chaos, an *optimal* rather than maximum or minimum amount of informality is recommended. Too much informality may slow down children's progress through the intended learnings, and insufficient informality cuts off teachers' sources of information about where the children are, which could be used in planning.

The principle of optimal informality suggests a related principle of practice: *Children's learning is enhanced when they are taught strategies by which to let their teachers know of their confusions and questions, and in general how to request the help they think they need with intellectual and academic tasks.* Thus, children can be encouraged to say, when appropriate, things like, "Would you explain it again, please?" "I'm lost!" "Can you help me with this?" "Could you go over this again slowly with me please?" "Is this what you mean?" "May I do another one? I understand it better now."

Children can also be helped to evaluate their own work, and in the process, take on greater responsibility for their progress. In American schools, children commonly take the products of their work home everyday. This practice places undue emphasis on one-shot tasks and individual products. Instead, children could collect their work in a portfolio and at the end of a week or so select one piece they especially want to share with the family. Their disposition to evaluate their own efforts could then be strengthened. On the basis of such self-evaluations, they might wish to repeat a task, do it differently, or elaborate upon it. If the curriculum is flexible and optimally informal, the teacher will have enough time and opportunity to participate in the evaluation process and to respond appropriately. One of the important features of project work is the debriefing and evaluation the children can engage in the final phase of the work.

In addition, if sufficient time is available, teachers can take periodic opportunities to discuss with each individual pupil their responses to questions like the following: What do you think you are making good progress on? What do you think you need to work harder on? What would you like someone to help you with? Although a few children may claim to be excellent at all skills and subjects, and a few may assert the opposite, most children are likely to be quite realistic in responses to these questions; these self-appraisals can serve as a basis for children developing a sense of responsibility for their own progress.

In the process of project work, there are many opportunities for children to become thoughtful evaluators of their work. As suggested in Chapter 1, in the course of daily debriefings, the teacher can encourage exchange among children concerning the progress of their work. The teacher can provoke consideration of a variety of criteria for evaluation. She might ask, for example, whether the group working on particular parts of the project are satisfied with the amount of information they have, whether they consider their reports sufficiently detailed, complete, interesting, clear, and so forth. In this way, the teacher encourages the children to adopt criteria against which to evaluate their work, and standards at which the criteria should be met.

With optimal informality, teachers also have access to children's knowledge and understanding by observing and listening to them at play. Montessori long ago alerted teachers to the importance of observation as a way to learn about children's growing and "absorbent minds." But observation is not an end in itself. Its function is to obtain the kind of information that can serve as a basis for a wide variety of teaching and curriculum decisions.

The informal part of a curriculum can include two types of activity: spontaneous play and project work. Spontaneous play is stimulated and encouraged by the array of materials and equipment typically available in nursery and kindergarten classes. Blocks, dress-up clothes, easels, sandboxes, and many other items can be counted on to elicit and facilitate the young child's disposition to play. The body of research supporting the contribution of play to all major aspects of children's development continues to grow (see Bretherton, 1984; Fein & Rivkin, 1986; Garvey, 1983). Although informal, project work differs from spontaneous play in that the project activities are more purposeful, deliberate, and intentional than play, and the teacher has an important role in guiding and facilitating the work undertaken.

VARIETY OF TEACHING METHODS

Early childhood programs that emphasize basic academic skills tend to use a single teaching method and a narrow curriculum. A single teaching method can be thought of as a *homogeneous* treatment; that is, every pupil is subjected to the same treatment. For a group of children of diverse backgrounds and developmental patterns, a homogeneous treatment is bound to produce *heterogeneous* outcomes.

Our goal is not that children become alike in all respects; differences in abilities and talents are valued in most communities. There are some important outcomes of education that we trust will lead to heterogeneous outcomes. But many outcomes with respect to knowledge, skills, dispositions, and feelings should be achieved homogeneously, in that we want some outcomes for all children. For all children to develop a robust disposition to be readers, for example, requires heterogeneous treatments. In other words, in principle, *to achieve the same objectives with diverse children, different teaching strategies and curriculum elements are required.* This principle is based on two assumptions. First, the younger the pupils, the less likely they are to have been socialized into a standard way of responding to their environment. Second, the younger the pupils, the more likely it is that their background experiences are unique and idiosyncratic rather than common and shared. If homogeneous outcomes are best achieved by heterogeneous treatments, it follows that when a single teaching method is used for a diverse group, a significant proportion will fail to benefit from it.

A related principle is that *the younger the children, the greater should be the variety of teaching methods* (Durkin, 1980; see also Nelson & Seidman, 1984). For stability and practicality, however, the variety of teaching methods that can be used in particular contexts is likely to have some limits.

Heterogeneous Ability and Age Grouping

Teachers who use a single teaching method or a restricted curriculum usually attempt to deal with heterogeneity by assigning children to ability groups. In the early years, this practice may create more problems than it solves. In the first place, obtaining accurate and reliable measures of young children's true abilities is difficult at best. They have had little or no experience in testlike situations. Obtaining a representative or large enough sample of their behavior across a wide enough range of their typical functioning takes both time and patience. Such being the case, the younger the children, the greater the chance that many will be falsely classified either as "low" or "slow" or even as "high" or "fast" learners. In addition, since the rate of development and children's experiential backgrounds vary, some children may be labeled "low" or "slow," when perhaps within a short time the assessed behavior will change. As long as a standard measure is applied to a group, some scores will be lower than others; but the earlier children are tested, the greater the risk of mistaking poor performance (pseudoslowness) for a true learning disability.

Furthermore, grouping by ability presents other hazards (Slavin, 1987a, 1987b). There is a strong tendency for the "slow" children to slow each other down (Wisconsin Center for Educational Research, 1984). Many teachers report that, when slow children are grouped together, they tend to drift, daydream, or interact unproductively. There is cause to be concerned about the top ability groups as well. Able children tend to speed each other up, and many among them experience considerable stress and anxiety about the danger of "falling out" of the group. Furthermore, even young children are aware of which group they are in and assess their own competence accordingly. Once a child has been labeled as "slow" and has internalized slowness as a self-attribution, the label may have a cumulative effect and the chances of discarding the label are small.

The practice of segregating children by ability in early childhood programs seems to come and go regularly. However, evidence continues to accumulate on the rich educative potential of mixed-ability and mixed-age grouping (Katz, Evangelou, & Hartman, 1990; McClellan & Kinsey, 1999; Mounts & Roopnarine, 1987; Slavin, 1987a, 1987b). In a review of research on mixed-age groups, Lougee and Graziano (n.d.) point out that mixed-age grouping also has many advantages for the development of social competence. Lougee and Graziano cite a report to the effect that, when some disruptive children were casually asked to remind younger children about the rules, they too became observant of them, presumably identifying with the teacher's role. Mounts and Roopnarine (1987) and Howes & Farver (1987) have shown that younger children engage in more complex play when grouped with older children. Apparently, small children can participate even though they are unable to initiate more complex activities themselves.

In a related experiment, Tudge (1986) reported on the experience of children assigned tasks in pairs. If one in the pair grasps the relevant concept and the other does not, the latter is likely to learn from the former. However, learning occurs only if the child who understands the concept has a firm and confident enough understanding of it to be able to explain it to the other in various ways and to resist regressing to the level of the other. The data also show that learning occurred only in those pairs who exchanged differences of opinion and argued about how to solve the problems in the task. An experiment in which pairs of preschool children worked on a complex block-building task demonstrated that when the "novice" builders were paired with the "expert" builders, significant improvements in their performance carried over to subsequent tasks (Azmitia, 1988).

Projects can include a sufficient variety of tasks to accommodate the diverse contributions from mixed groups—mixed in ability as well as in age. Furthermore, project work gives younger children the chance to observe and learn the more sophisticated skills and knowledge of the older children. Similarly, older children can strengthen their own understanding by teaching younger ones (Benware & Deci, 1984).

Curriculum Models Research

As suggested in the review of research above, the long-term effects of different kinds of early childhood curricula support the view put forward here: the curriculum should provide interactive and active rather than passive experiences, and ample opportunity to initiate and be engaged in interesting work. According to Walberg (1984), a synthesis of 153 studies of open education, including 90 dissertations, indicates that, while children in so-called open education were no different from others in achievement, locus of control, self-concept, and anxiety, they were at an advantage in their attitudes toward schools and teachers, curiosity, and general mental ability. They also had an advantage in cooperativeness, creativity, and independence. Walberg adds, "Thus students in open classes do no worse in standardized achievement and slightly to moderately better on several outcomes that educators, parents and students hold to be of great value" (p. 25).

Fry and Addington (1984) followed children for two years after they had been in open informal and in traditional kindergarten programs. Compared with children from the traditional classes, those from the more open curriculum classes performed better on social problem-solving skills two years following their kindergarten experiences.

Koester and Farley (1982) examined the effects of open and traditional classes on children diagnosed as either high or low on a physiological measure of "internal arousal." Children who are low on measures of internal arousal are commonly classified as hyperactive, currently classified as suffering from attention deficit and hyperactive disorders (ADHD). It is assumed that they are hyperactive because their low levels of internal arousal cause them to provoke the external environment into being a source of stimulation that can raise their own arousal levels. But contrary to common sense, as Koester and Farley found, hyperactive children placed in an open curriculum fared much better than in a traditional one. According to the interpretation offered by the experimenters, the informal curriculum provided hyperactive children with sufficient external sources of arousal that they were not compelled to disrupt the environment to create arousal for themselves. In the traditional formal curriculum, the level of external stimulation was so low that the children created stimulation by their hyperactive behavior.

A rich body of research on curriculum approaches designed for *cooperative learning* (Johnson & Johnson, 1985; Johnson, Johnson, Holubec, & Roy, 1984; Krathwohl, 1985; Slavin, 1983) provides compelling evidence that long-term academic and dispositional outcomes are achieved when children are taught in groups that are mixed in ability, age, and ethnic and socioeconomic background and that are oriented toward cooperative goals (see also Katz, Evangelou, & Hartman, 1990). Consistent with research outlined earlier, Johnson and Johnson (1985) point out that cooperative learning experiences "tend to promote higher motivation to learn, especially intrinsic motivation ... more positive attitudes toward the instructional experiences and the instructors" (p. 23), and higher academic achievement than competitive or individualistically oriented classes. In addition, "cooperative learning is associated with higher levels of self-esteem and healthier processes for deriving conclusions about one's self-worth ... and result in stronger perceptions that other students care about how much one learns, and that other students want to provide assistance" (p. 23).

SUMMARY

The inclusion of project work in early childhood curriculum is neither new nor revolutionary. Several variations of it have been used by many teachers in many countries for a long time (Zimilies, 1987). Although some schools always maintain it as part of their curriculum, its wider use appears to come and go as ideologies and national priorities fluctuate. Our reassertion of its potential value to education in the early years is based on our understanding of contemporary research on the complex processes of development in young children. It is reasonably clear to us that formal instruction in the early years may serve the normative ends at the expense of the dynamic long-term aims of education. Given what is being learned about the nature and acquisition of knowledge, we suggest the principle *that the younger the children, the more informal and integrated the curriculum should be.*

Project work takes into account all four kinds of learning goals: the acquisition and construction of knowledge, the mastery of social and basic skills, and the strengthening of important intellectual and social dispositions, as well as the development of desirable feelings. It can provide learning situations in which context and content-enriched interactions and conversations can occur about matters familiar to the children. Project work can provide activities in which children of many different ability levels can contribute to the ongoing life and work of the group. Working together on projects also provides situations and events in which social skills are functional and can be strengthened. Because project topics are drawn from children's familiar environments and interests, the knowledge and understandings gained can have real cultural relevance for them. Last but not least, we advocate the project approach because it provides continuous challenges for teachers and thus can contribute to making the teacher's work interesting and professionally satisfying.

3

Project Work in Action

For readers unfamiliar with the project approach, this chapter presents illustrations of how projects usually proceed. Some of the illustrations are from our direct experiences with teachers and children; others are based on reports teachers have shared with us (see also Beneke, 1998; Helm, 1996, 1998). The range of potentially valuable topics for projects is very wide and the many issues involved in selecting them are discussed in the next chapter. However, our purpose here is to outline a few examples of the kind of work children undertake in projects.

PROJECTS ON GOING SHOPPING

Most preschool children have experience of going shopping. By the time they reach primary school age, they probably have visited many different kinds of stores, supermarkets, and shopping malls, and have even made their own purchases. Although shops around the world vary considerably, it is likely that at least one child in a class of children with diverse backgrounds is familiar with the most common kind of local store.

At the beginning of a project with preschoolers on shopping, dramatic play and discussion reveals children's widely varied experiences with stores. In early discussions, children are encouraged to tell what they know about the event of going shopping, the stores they visit, and where food and other goods are usually purchased. Most children are able to tell their classmates about going shopping with parents or friends. Preschool children can represent recollections of their experiences and imaginary ideas by drawing or painting or dictating them to an older child or teacher. Older children's written accounts of shopping trips can be put into a class book and illustrated with drawings and paintings. The teacher can write captions for the drawings dictated by the younger children. Many of the older ones can write their own captions or stories and may even label drawings for those not yet able to write.

From the beginning of the project, the children can discuss and implement a plan to set up a store in the play area of the classroom. At first the props will be simple—shelves, a few items to buy or sell, a counter, cash register, shopping carts, baskets, and money. As the work progresses, more props will be added. Children can make signs denoting departments for various goods. Their understanding of money can be developed and enriched throughout the project. Those who already understand pricing may want to announce sales. Depending on ability, each child will use numbers at different levels of complexity.

The children can also visit a local supermarket, bicycle repair shop, fish market, open-air market, plant nursery, or garden center. The choice will depend on the opportunities afforded by the community where the school is located. In some parts of the world, for example, the children can visit a vegetable stall in a neighborhood market. During preliminary group discussions, the teacher can help them plan questions to ask the salespersons. All children in this age range can interview salespersons and store managers. The teacher helps the youngest children to each take responsibility for one question and encourages them to listen closely to the answer so as to be able to report it during discussion upon their return to the classroom.

Depending on the ages of the children, they can ask salespeople how they got the vegetables, which ones are weighed when sold, which are sold singly or by the dozen, which sell best, which perish fastest, and which last longest. The children can discuss which vegetables and fruits have to be peeled, cleaned, chopped, or cooked; which are eaten raw; which items become soft when cooked, and which items cost most and least. Many teachers find it helpful to tape-record these interviews and transcribe them on return from the field trip. These transcriptions are included in the documentation panels displayed in the classroom or hallways so that parents can become familiar with their children's experiences and understandings.

The children can bring some items back to their classroom, and begin to classify them (leafy, juicy, hard or soft, sweet or sour, with or without seeds, smelly). They can appreciate the idea of pricing and selling by weight and note the different kinds of weighing scales used for lighter and heavier and smaller and larger goods. The older the children, the more able they are to take field notes, to record answers to their questions on special forms or checklists prepared in advance of the field trip. At all ages, the children can draw the scenes observed. These drawings often serve as a basis for animated discussion upon the children's return to the classroom.

The field trip experience brings new life to the classroom store. The children may decide to set up a market of stalls with facsimiles of items for sale, a weighing scale, and money that they make for use in the transactions. The field work also stimulates a variety of drawings, paintings, models, graphs, diagrams, written reports and stories, and calculations. Individuals can work alone, or pairs, and groups may want to collaborate on their work. The teacher of younger children can help each group prepare paintings and drawings so that they can report what they learned to other groups who visited different market stalls, such as clothing or kitchen wares. The work thus produced can be displayed as documentation of all aspects of their experiences.

As the project unfolds, dramatic play is enhanced by the terms learned on a visit to a real store and from real shop workers. Additional props reflecting the newly acquired information greatly enrich dramatic play. The children "use" stock books, order books, sales slips, receipts for deliveries from the wholesaler, and they record customers' purchases. The complexity of the dramatic play will depend to a great extent on the level of understanding and background experience of the children involved. In a group of mixed ability and experience, the participants can take simple or more complex roles. Thus, children whose understanding or experience is more limited can learn by observing, playing, and working alongside more knowledgeable classmates.

Along similar lines, a small group of preschoolers in India visited a bicycle repair shop set up on a nearby sidewalk. Although many of the children had passed by the shop daily on their way to and from the school, their attention had never before been drawn to it. They asked the repairman about his tools, the materials used for repairs, and what kinds of repairs were common. He gave them some old pedals, tools, and bits of bicycle chain to take back to their class, where they set up a repair shop. Roleplaying continued for about a week, with some children riding tricycles and getting them repaired. During the dramatic play, some of the children became interested in license plates and made some to attach to tricycles and wagons. The project could have been extended to other forms of transportation, visiting a gas station in the neighborhood, collecting used tools and materials, and constructing a gas station in the school yard.

If supermarkets are plentiful in the community, a visit to one in the neighborhood can be planned in detail. The planning includes telling the workers beforehand about the goals of the project and the characteristics of the children. The teacher and children discuss which aspects of the supermarket to look at closely. Children can join small groups that can volunteer to examine particular departments closely. The children can investigate many features that will help them understand how the supermarket operates and what the workers do there and what the workers have to know and plan in advance.

In a study of what store assistants do, the older children can learn about sales, stocking the shelves, pricing, storing fresh deliveries, and moving goods from one part of the shop to another. Most supermarkets have large docks where goods are delivered. The children can inspect the dollies, trolleys, or other special equipment used for unloading and moving large piles of cartons. The children can make a list of the equipment used for lifting and transporting goods within the shop and examine how the equipment works.

The children can also learn about the store and the stockrooms. They can note the contrasting temperatures of the shopping aisles, refrigerators, and freezers and they can find out which items must be stored cold, and which must be kept frozen. In studying a department store, the children can sort the wide variety of goods into different categories and discuss the relative merits of their ideas. Activities such as pricing, comparing temperatures, and sorting merchandise can deepen children's understanding of the uses of mathematical operations and strengthen their skills in applying their own developing numerical recording.

The children's vocabularies grow as they become familiar with terms such as *taking stock* and *stocking up* and what it means when something is "out of stock" or "running out." Children can be encouraged to ponder the distinctions among the terms *shop, store, supermarket, department store, market, shopping mall, shopping arcade, trading post, kiosk, bazaar,* and *boutique,* as appropriate to their experience and environment.

If the class is large enough that small groups need to be formed, each group can be responsible for preparing a shopping list, identifying particular kinds of items to look at (for example, house-cleaning items, produce, breads, canned goods, dairy products, beverages). The children can ask clerks which items are sold most often, what they cost, who marks the prices, why some are refrigerated, and anything else they would like to know.

The children can transform their simple classroom store into a supermarket by adding more sale items, cash registers, bags, and so forth. "Zooming" in on particular aspects of packaging goods, some children can take responsibility for stocking the classroom supermarket with items sold in sacks, boxes, waxed cartons, plastic and glass bottles, squeeze bottles, tins and cans, and plastic and paper bags. The collections can include goods wrapped in paper, foil, transparent plastic, styrofoam, corrugated cardboard (for light bulbs), crates, net bags, and tubes (for ointment and toothpaste). The stock can also include a magazine and newspaper rack.

While some children will act out roles of workers within the supermarket, others will deliver goods from big trucks, and still others will gladly be shoppers. During dramatic play, if someone's car or bicycle breaks down, a gas station and garage mechanic may need to be added. As a project on shopping progresses, children may change the type of store or add another part to it. More specialized props can be added to stimulate more complex play.

The classroom studies for the older children may diverge somewhat at this stage as children extend their understanding and branch out to related topics. Alternative perspectives may be taken to help children reach a fuller understanding of the process of shopping, and the interdependence of customer, retailer, truck driver, farmer, and so on. For instance, the customer's point of view in the shopping event might be more fully explored. Customers in the class shop might be interviewed for their views of the facilities and services offered: getting to the store, vehicle parking, opening hours, bags for carrying purchases, the right to return damaged or unsatisfactory items, and attractive window displays.

In one school, a class of 5-year-olds collected plastic shopping bags. They experimented with them by carrying heavy items across the school playground to determine which kinds of handles were best designed for comfort. Group members were then surveyed to find out and record their preferences. One kind of handle was clearly favored by most of the children. Following such an experiment, children may decide to compose a report and send it to the appropriate store and manufacturer. They could also systematically test the sturdiness of bags of different materials and similarly report their findings.

One kindergarten teacher reported that when two sales clerks in the classroom supermarket ran out of money, they discussed the crisis together with great animation. They agreed that a bank was required, but, lacking construction materials, they quite spontaneously built an imaginary bank with imaginary nails and hammers. They informed bank customers in no uncertain terms of the precise location of the entrance, counters, and tellers as they distributed imaginary money.

Throughout the life of such a project, stories and picture books on related topics can be introduced and consulted. The children can also collect their own paintings, and with the teacher's help they can make a book entitled "Going to the Market" or "A Visit to the Bicycle Repair Shop."

Older children can also look at a sequence of events in which the store is only one part of the process of getting products to the customer. In a study of where products come from, they may look at the transformation of raw materials, for example, sheep's wool as it is transformed into fabric for clothes. From sheep to clothing store, the wool takes an interesting journey while being processed along the way. Perhaps the children's town has a clothing factory that loads bales onto barges for transporting the wool to another stage in the production chain. Even though somewhat remote from "going shopping," a visit to watch the loading process might be an effective way to elaborate the understanding of a few children whose interest needs additional stimulus. Digression from the main theme, undertaken in the last phase of a project, may serve to point the teacher and children toward the next project, for example, a study of different modes of transportation.

PROJECTS ON THE WEATHER

Preschool and primary school classes often include a time during the morning when children take note of the day's weather. At the preschool stage, the weather provides relatively few events to act out or few roles for dramatic play. Nevertheless, climate and weather are sufficiently complex topics that can be studied for a lifetime.

Depending on the local climate and weather patterns, the weather can affect children's lives more or less directly in many ways. A project on the weather is likely to be most engaging in environments where the weather changes fairly rapidly and varies visibly, at least from week to week. On the whole, this topic involves more investigation than dramatic play. Depending on the ages of the children in the group, the project can "zoom in" on specific subtopics such as heat, light, and clothing.

An initial discussion reveals the children's levels of awareness and understanding of the weather and how it affects daily life. Most preschoolers can talk about how the sun, rain, snow, and wind feel on the skin and about the sounds of storms, high winds, and heavy rain. Some will recall dark clouds and rainbows and their feelings upon seeing them. In many localities children talk about snowballs and snowmen, slipping on the ice, shivering in the cold, winter sports, and their experience with travel in the snow.

The project work can begin with paintings and drawings of their own impressions, recollections, and ideas about the weather. Children can be encouraged to illustrate hot sunny days, a clear starry sky, storm clouds, and rain. Older children will also write about events or adventures featuring weather conditions. Stories, poems, songs, and books about familiar experiences will further stimulate discussion. Books with pertinent new information can be introduced throughout the project.

Weather Forecasters

School-age children can play the roles of people in the meteorological office responsible for forecasting and recording the weather. They can play the weather person on television, using a large cardboard box with a television screen "window" cut out of the front. For the background, the children can make a satellite picture, a radar map, and charts of statistics about maximum and minimum temperatures and the times of sunrise and sunset, each of which can be flipped out of the way as discussion of them ends.

Activities related to the weather can include daily observations of the brightness of sunshine, precipitation, wind, and temperature. Each of these can be depicted on cards reflecting gross categories of variation. Younger children can make small drawings with colors added exemplifying sunshine or rainfall; these pictures can then be placed on a chart recording each day or each morning and afternoon. Older children can consider recording finer variations in the relative amounts of clouds, sun, precipitation, and so forth. They can plot the readings for a week or two or longer.

Weather variables can be plotted in broad terms such as "very sunny," "mostly cloudy," "sun and clouds," "thick fog," "damp," "frost," or "dew." Similarly, the rain can be described as "heavy," "light," "sprinkles," and "drizzle." Written descriptive reports can also accompany the chart record. Duration can be described as "all day," "early morning," or "afternoon." Rate and amount of snowfall and size of snowflakes can be included where appropriate.

Temperature Studies

A group of preschool children might investigate temperatures, using a large thermometer next to which different shades of red parallel the degree markings (pale pink = 0 degrees Celsius to 3 degrees; deep red = 45 degrees to 48 degrees). The group can chart their "readings" at different locations indoors and outdoors and compare morning and afternoon temperatures. Older children can write about things that affect the temperature in different places, such as prevailing wind, time of day, sun, fog, and rainfall.

Temperature investigations can include studies of ice. Children can observe the rate at which icicles melt and the investigation can include experiments to test predictions. For example, using icicles of different sizes brought into the classroom, the children can predict how much water each icicle will produce when it melts. Predictions and outcomes can then be recorded on a chart and discussed with classmates. Preschoolers can make ice cubes from water tinted with different colors and then predict which colored ice cube will melt first and last. The ice cubes can be wrapped in different kinds and thicknesses of fabric to see which ones will take longest to melt. The children's attention can also be drawn to how their classroom and their homes are heated, aired, or kept cool.

Older children can discuss the variables in the experiments with greater understanding of cause and effect than younger children can. They can also generally predict with greater precision and record their observations more fully.

Wind Studies

Detailed work can be carried out in groups that take responsibility for specific subtopics. The teacher can help a "wind study" group to make a windsock and place various sizes of windmills or pinwheels around the school grounds. The group can also look for weathervanes around their neighborhood and places visited. They can be encouraged to make their own weathervane. Older children will be able to infer something about the force and direction of the wind by observing the smoke from a chimney or smokestack.

The "wind study" group can take responsibility for recording the force of wind at several locations. After making a few observations, younger children can make drawings on separate cards depicting how the windsock, pinwheels, and windmills look when the wind is strong, mild, and light and then place these cards on the chart. Older children will be able to make more precise recordings on a chart. This group might also look for books and stories about wind damage, tornadoes, cyclones, and hurricanes.

The weather investigation could branch out to the subject of kite flying, varieties of kites, and the construction of kites and paper planes. The youngest children can participate in these activities with various kinds of balloons. They can attach paper of different shapes to string to see how the paper flaps in the wind. Older children can more precisely analyze the variables relevant to the flying potential of different shapes. They can describe their trials and discoveries and write instructions telling someone else how to replicate their most successful flyer.

Shade and Shadow Studies

One group of children can investigate shade and shadows. The project can include charting the darkness–lightness and sharpness of shadows each day. Special objects and sticks can be placed around the school for observing the length and angle of shadows. Some of the older children in the group can experiment with translucent materials such as plastic wrapping of various colors. Or they can collect different-colored sunglasses and predict and observe the effects of the differences on the sharpness, glare, and color of shadows. Older children with a good understanding of clock time can try to design a simple sundial. Some children might take responsibility for observing the kinds of awnings and shop window shades in the neighborhood or town and report their observations to the class.

In a location where there is a reasonable amount of sunshine, children can identify a window in a wall that faces the sun during the day and develop a procedure for recording the angle of the shade it creates at a certain hour every Monday, Wednesday, and Friday morning. When such a record is kept from August to December, or January to June, the recorded marks should clearly indicate to them how the angle of the sun changes as the season progresses. By the time children are in the primary grades, such a record can form a good basis for a preliminary understanding of the solar system.

Rain Studies

A group responsible for rain studies can experiment with different materials to see how waterproof they are. Children can be encouraged to predict which material will be the most or the least waterproof. The teacher can help them develop a simple graph for recording their predictions and results. This work can be followed by examining their raincoats, boots, shoes, and umbrellas. Another group can keep track of rainfall when it occurs. This might include checking puddles for size and depth. They might also make chalk marks around the edge of the puddles to observe how quickly they dry in shade versus sunshine.

The internationally acclaimed exhibition of the work of young children in toddler centers and preprimary schools in the city of Reggio Emilia, in northern Italy, entitled "The Hundred Languages of Children," includes documentation of young children's investigations of the rain in their city. The work included direct experience of the rainfall, puddles, reflections in puddles, and included children's representations of their theories of what causes lightning and thunder, and many other features of the environment as affected by rain. The exhibit also includes the children's explorations of the nature of light and shadows.

Animals

In many parts of the world, autumn is a time when hibernating animals can be watched from a classroom window as they eat and store food for the winter. In the spring, the children can make the first sightings of animals and birds that have been hidden for some months. In the winter in many parts of the world birds that have struggled to survive respond eagerly when the children offer them food and water daily outside a classroom window. The habits and food preferences of birds can be recorded. If the local museum has stuffed birds, perhaps they can be taken out on loan so that the children can study them closely and draw them from observation. Such observational drawings typically give rise to questions about the details of the birds, their wings and colors and other features, all of which can be followed up with books, Internet information resources, and perhaps a visit from a member of the local bird-watching society.

Climate

Climate is another subtopic of the weather. By primary school age, many children may well have heard something about the polar regions, deserts, and rain forests. The prevailing weather in different climates highlights interesting phenomena of adaptation, ecology, camouflage, and migration. The importance of sanctuaries for protecting threatened wildlife can be discussed. Some children may want to know more about the satellites that provide the meteorological office with photographic data. Other children may want to focus on tornadoes, hurricanes, typhoons, sand-storms, avalanches, and tidal waves that occasionally take place around the world.

Sayings and Myths

Most likely all cultures have a great deal of folklore about the weather. The English language provides many good examples of sayings, proverbs, aphorisms, and metaphors based on the weather of its place of origin. Some of the children can collect sayings about it: "Make hay while the sun shines"; "Red sky in the morning, shepherd's warning; red sky at night, shepherd's delight"; "Save for a rainy day"; "When it rains, it pours"; "An ill wind blows no good"; "Every cloud has a silver lin-ing"; and so on. Some metaphorical expressions are of interest: "pouring rain," "driving rain," "sheets of rain," "it's raining cats and dogs," and so forth. Children can also invent new figurative expressions for different kinds of weather conditions. By definition, the weather is a difficult topic for project activities; undertaking and completing work on it literally depends on the weather! However, as the weather and seasons permit, groups can be invited to report their findings to others. The reporting process should allow for questions and suggestions from children partici-pating in other parts of the weather project. The older children can discuss the weather that prevails in different seasons and study the habits of animals that have to accommodate to these changes. This learning will draw heavily on books and films or slides because only one season can be studied at a time. However, the season, whether spring or autumn, should be studied firsthand.

PROJECTS ABOUT A CONSTRUCTION SITE

Most young children will be interested in a project on building, especially if there are construction sites in their neighborhood or on their route to school. Indeed, Sanderson (1999) describes a rich variety of interesting experiences of a small group of toddlers as they engaged in a project involving close study of a playground construction site behind their building. While building methods and materials vary around the world, children can learn much about what builders do and the tools, equipment, and materials they use. In the process of finding out about builders and construction, children can learn about their own homes and neighborhoods. A project on this topic can include a variety of investigations, constructions, and dramatic play.

Initial discussion reveals the children's current knowledge and understanding of how buildings are constructed and the extent of their exposure to the topic. The discussion can include children's ideas of the sequences in putting up a building. When the roof is put on, when stairs are built, when pipes are laid, and how these things are accomplished can be discussed. The children can reflect their present understanding in pictures and block building in the classroom. If some children live close to an active construction site, they can be asked to bring back reports and descriptions of the equipment and materials observed. Books and pictures of large building equipment and of construction workers are also useful in the early stages of the project.

The children can also make a class book with drawings, paintings, and writing about their own houses and how these are constructed. They can take rubbings of the texture of the walls, showing whether the walls are made of bricks, stone, wood, or stucco. They can count the number of rooms, windows, and doors and note their shapes. They can ask questions of their parents about the construction of the house or apartment building and how old it is.

A visit to a local building site can be an interesting source of questions and information, especially if the visit follows careful planning with the children. Planning a visit includes talking about what to look for and what to ask builders, who will take responsibility for drawing various features likely to be observed. The children can be encouraged to note and draw the tools, equipment, and work clothes of the workers. Materials such as cables, wires, sand, cement, bricks, mortar, lumber, buckets, pipes, blowtorches, pneumatic drills, and scaffolding can be noted. Equipment such as dump trucks, cement trucks, earthmovers, bulldozers, and cranes will also interest the children. If the building is to be very large, visits can be made periodically to note its progress. A large construction site usually includes a workers' hut, which is likely to interest the children. The foreman responsible for the workers and the contractor in charge of the whole effort can be interviewed about various aspects of their work, as well as the architectural and engineering drawings they use.

Parents or grandparents who work in one of the building trades can be invited to talk about their work and tools and to answer questions. It might be possible to borrow some tools for study in the classroom for a week or two. These can be examined closely, drawn, and written about. After visits to construction sites, the children can discuss making a building site of their own in the classroom. Small groups can focus on particular parts of the classroom's construction site.

One group can construct a cement truck from large crates, scrap wood, or packing boxes (for example, from a washing machine or refrigerator). A steering wheel can be included in the driver's cabin. The truck can be painted, and appropriate signs added. Children can also make props representing bags of cement. Other groups can build a bulldozer, dump truck, or crane.

Another group can build walls of bricks made from milk or egg cartons or other boxes of manageable size. The bricks can be pasted or taped together to make sturdy walls. The children can discuss how to make doors and windows. A small stepladder, wheelbarrow, shovel, trowel, plumb line, crash helmets, and heavy work clothes are useful props to include. A workers' hut can be constructed on the classroom site as well. One or two children may build a road and a parking lot for the new building.

Most children are interested in handling real materials. Real bricks—old and new, rough and smooth, large and small, differently colored—can be collected and studied for their properties. Many children will find it fascinating to realize how heavy each brick is and how large they look close up when they seem so small in the context of a high wall. The children can make rubbings and drawings of the bricks. Differences in the age, texture, size, and color of bricks offer interesting topics of discussion about how those differences affect the process of building. A brick factory, if the neighborhood has one, is also a very interesting place for children to visit. Books can be consulted on the development of brick-making. Different kinds of roofing materials can be investigated: tiles of various kinds, slate, wood, and glass. A local museum or other historical site might provide older children with examples of early construction, such as log cabins and sod houses.

Experiments can be designed by some of the older children to find out the insulation properties of different materials designed to protect houses from the cold of winter and the heat of summer. Insulation experiments can be carried out quite simply by timing the melting of ice cubes enclosed in containers made of different materials. The findings of these experiments can be displayed on the walls above labeled exhibits of the different materials tested.

Buildings can be looked at in any amount of detail. For example, the space inside the building can be partitioned into rooms in various ways. Children can be alerted to the different kinds of connections between one room and the next. They can discuss how the function of different rooms might dictate building requirements.

Children can note that doors and windows will have fastenings of various kinds. The mechanisms of locks that have been discarded or replaced can be studied in the classroom. Problem-solving activities might include designing alternative mechanisms for closing and locking. The children might study the very earliest examples of log cabin locks, which had an inside latch with string going out through a hole in the door so that the latch could also be operated from the outside. At night, when the string was pulled in through the door, it could be opened only from the inside.

As the children build and make things for the project, their understanding of buildings and the work of the bricklayers, masons, glaziers, roofers, plumbers, electricians, surveyors, carpenters, landscapers, and the foreman and engineers is developed. Children will become familiar with the types of workers and what each contributes to the building. Specific knowledge about construction materials will be enhanced. This developing knowledge can be applied to their own homes and their school building. Construction activities in the classroom also involve the use of fine motor skills. In the process of making bricks and building walls, the children can be alerted to their shapes and how to match brick sizes to make corners. Many problem-solving skills are likely to be called on during the processes required for constructing the site and its various elements.

The dramatic play stimulated by the topic provides a context for children to consolidate their new knowledge and to enact the various roles involved. The vehicles that children construct should be large enough for them to load and unload bricks and bags of cement. The vehicles should have cabins large enough for the drivers to get into and out of easily. Similarly, the workers' hut should be roomy enough so that the workers can take their coffee breaks in comfort. Large-sized constructions enable the dramatic play to be sustained and productive for several weeks.

Two kindergarten teachers in a midwestern U.S. city engaged their pupils in a project they titled "Houses: How Are They Built?" The children visited five houses in different stages of construction adjacent to their school grounds. Excerpts from the teachers' journal noting the children's comments and questions are included in Appendix A. The children's comments and questions reflect their interest in what they observed. Follow-up activities in the classroom may involve discussing what they saw, as well as building with a variety of materials that include foundations, window wells, posts, joists, and beams that they began to learn about from their talks with the builders.

SUMMARY

These descriptions of projects are intended to give some idea of what good project work looks like in action. The main events in project work are described: class discussion, dramatic play, investigations, field trips, visiting and interviewing experts, and real objects in the classroom documentation and display of work and findings. Well-planned project work provides a range of activities from which children can choose. As children become engaged in various aspects of project work, their teachers can identify opportunities to enhance their knowledge, improve their skills, strengthen worthwhile dispositions, and ensure healthy feelings about their lives in the community of learners.

In the next chapter, we analyze in more detail what occurs in the classroom during project work, and we describe more fully the role of the teacher in organizing class projects.

More information about projects conducted by teachers in a variety of settings can be seen on a website about projects at: http://www.ualberta.ca/~schard/projects.htm. Readers are also encouraged to join a special listserv devoted to the project approach at PROJECTS-L@postoffice.cso.uiuc.edu.

Reports of successful projects are also available in a catalog of project displays titled *Project Approach Catalog 2*, 1998, edited by J. Helm and available from the ERIC Clearinghouse on Elementary and Early Childhood Education at the University of Illinois, Urbana-Champaign.

4

Phases and Features of the Project Approach

In the previous chapter, we presented a picture of what project work looks like in the classroom. In this chapter, we outline principal features of the project approach that underlie the projects illustrated in Chapter 3.

The principal features discussed in this chapter concern detailed procedures for implementing the project approach. We begin with a time-scale perspective on projects and the characterization of the early, middle, and later phases in the life of a project. We then describe five features that function across all three phases to facilitate the planning and evaluation of the project as it progresses. These five features are:

1. discussion;
2. field work;
3. investigation;
4. representation; and
5. display.

This chapter concludes with a discussion of the benefits to the learner of exercising genuine choice in many aspects of project work, followed by an overview of the teacher's role in creating the classroom. The structure underlying the implementation of the project approach is one that enables the teacher to be flexible and responsive to children's interests and learning needs while continuing to exercise leadership in facilitating work of high quality for all children.

PHASES OF PROJECT WORK

Projects resemble the structure of a good story in that they have a beginning, a middle, and an ending. These structural elements are defined as three general phases that typically merge into each other. This temporal framework is designed to help teachers focus children's attention and effort on a topic of study over an extended period of time. Within this framework, we suggest ways that certain structural features (discussion, fieldwork, investigation, representation, and display) can help a teacher ensure that projects are optimally productive and memorable. Outlined briefly below, each phase is explicated more fully in later chapters.

Phase I: Planning and Getting Started

A project can begin in several ways. Some begin when one or more of the children in a group express an interest in something that attracts their attention. Some projects begin when the teacher introduces a topic or when a topic is selected by agreement between the teacher and the children. A more detailed discussion on topic selection is presented in Chapter 5.

The main thrust of the first phase of project work is to establish common ground among the participating children by pooling the information, ideas, and experiences they already have about the topic. During Phase 1, the teacher helps the children to build a shared perspective on the topic and to formulate a set of questions that will guide their investigation. For instance, in the school bus project, the children discussed their experiences, noting those that were common to all of them: waiting for the bus, climbing aboard, finding a seat, riding through town, and getting off at school. They also shared less common experiences such as being the first or the last to board the bus, just missing the bus and having to get to school some other way, observing the bus driver arguing with a policeman, and being on the bus the morning it broke down.

During these Phase 1 preliminary discussions, the teacher encourages the children to talk about the topic, to engage in dramatic play related to the topic, to draw or write about it, and to depict their current understandings of it in other ways, depending on their ages and levels of competence. The teacher acts as a source of advice and suggestions during this phase. At this time, parents can be informed of the topic of study and invited to participate in any way they can in the project. Children are also invited to bring pertinent objects from home and collect materials for the construction activities of the project.

The exchange of personal experiences gives rise to an appreciation of both common and individual experiences the children have had. It also helps the teacher to learn which children already know a great deal about the topic and which children have only limited experience. Sometimes children with similar experiences have very different ways of understanding those experiences.

Teachers can probe the children's accounts of their experience and invite them to share their understandings. This process helps to distinguish between stories of experiences and explanations of them. A focus on explanation in discussion offers children opportunities to wonder about the cause-and-effect relationships that underlie experiences. For example, there are many reasons why a family might have chosen to own a particular kind of pet. Consideration of such reasons would emerge as the project on pets progressed. Yet there may be many children who would not be able to go beyond describing their pet in the early discussions of stories of experience.

Discussions in the first phase of the project may suggest many aspects of the topic to wonder about: Why do some people decide to keep snakes, cats, or guinea pigs? How much does it cost to keep different kinds of pets? Where do different kinds of pets sleep? What do they eat? Many children are very willing to offer opinions on these matters and the differences among them helps the teacher to formulate questions with the children to which their research in Phase 2 can yield pertinent information and answers.

The children and teacher can develop plans for conducting investigations, make arrangements for visits, nominate visitors, and develop a variety of initial questions to be answered by the investigations. Procedures for obtaining construction materials are also worked out at this time. Some preliminary investigations upon which to build later ones might also be introduced during this phase. For example, a project about clothes might begin by taking a close look at the children's coats and noting colors, types of buttons, belts, zippers, and fabrics.

Phase II: Projects in Progress

During the second phase, the teacher's main emphasis is on enabling the children to learn new information and knowledge. The teacher arranges visits outside the school or invites visitors with relevant expertise to talk to the children or demonstrate special expertise. The teacher also collects related objects, books, photographs, or artifacts for the children to study in the classroom. For example, a group (or a whole class) of children studying stores might visit a wide variety of those nearby. The visit is carefully planned so that the children, even at the preschool level, are clear about what they are to find out during fieldwork and the visits with experts. The visits to the stores may include talking to store managers and cashiers, and buying some items to take back to the classroom. This shared event provides a common background of experience on which to negotiate new understandings. The visit can enhance the realism with which the children play "stores" and "shopping" in the classroom. Visits also increase the likelihood that the children will ask for clarification of their perceptions of what they have experienced together.

In a hospital project, the teacher might arrange to have a nurse or a doctor talk with the children about their work and leave them some spare instruments or X-rays as props for their play. Before these visits, the children discuss together and with the teacher what they want the visitor to talk about and who will be responsible for asking them which questions. The children could explore new sources of information, assimilate new knowledge, and identify and revise misconceptions through interaction with visitors, their classmates, and the teacher.

In the second phase of a project about going to school on a bus, the teacher might arrange for a detailed study of the bus itself and ask that it be brought to school earlier than usual so that the children can talk to the driver and inspect the different parts of the vehicle (see Harkema, 1999). They might build a bus in the classroom. The children could also draw, paint, and write about the bus, its routes to school, traffic regulations, the role of the police, the different modes of transport by which the children come to school, the distances and times that different children travel, the number of stops, and so forth. The second phase, along with the first, gives children common script knowledge about going to school on the bus. They also learn about less common occurrences, dangers, and emergencies, as well as normal experiences and safety precautions.

An important role of the teacher during this phase is to encourage children's independent use of the skills they already have. These skills include observation, communication, drawing, and painting. Older children can apply their developing competence in writing, reading, and calculating. In this phase, the teacher also attends to strengthening the children's dispositions to seek information and to pursue in depth a topic that interests them. The teacher provides materials and offers suggestions and advice about appropriate ways to represent their findings and ideas.

Phase III: Reflections and Conclusions

The main thrust of the third phase of a project is to help bring it to completion with group and individual work and to summarize what has been learned. In the third phase, it is hoped that most of the children will share a thorough, indepth understanding of the topic. Introducing new information at this time may be inadvisable. Instead, what is required is an elaboration of the children's learning so that its meaning is enhanced and made personal. We assume that as children apply their new knowledge, they can make it truly their own.

For older children, the third phase is a time of rehearsal and reflection on the new levels of understanding and knowledge acquired. They express their increased knowledge not only in play, but also in wall displays, music, drama, and dance, making class books, games, and folders of individual work. Sometimes a culminating activity can be organized so that children can present what they have learned to their classmates. They may invite their parents or children from other classes to see their work and to whom they tell the story of their work, explain what they have learned, how they learned it, and the procedures they used to conduct their investigation.

For 3- and 4-year-olds, the third phase is usually a time for them to roleplay in their project constructions. Thus, if they have built a doctor's office or a store, this phase will consist mainly of enacting the various roles they associate with those settings. The social and dramatic play helps them to integrate their modified and fuller understanding of the real world.

In the third phase of the school bus project, the teacher can help children to elaborate their play with the bus they constructed. The class can discuss possible school bus stories for dramatic play: a story or play about the day the school bus had to go a different way because a tree had fallen across the road in a storm; or the day the children helped the driver change a flat tire. They can also dictate or write their stories. They can play or make up games, such as dice and board games in which the progress of the bus is hindered or facilitated along the way to school. They can make up new songs and poems about the bus, if they have not done so already. They can make a pictorial representation of the journey to school.

The Three Phases Illustrated in Dramatic Play

In dramatic play in the context of a project, children negotiate and refine their growing understanding by consulting with other children and the teacher. For example, in the first phase of the hospital project, prior understandings are expressed and shared in play. Early in the project, children might roleplay their experiences of visits to the doctor, being ill at home, or patching up a grazed knee.

In the second phase, new information is tried out. The teacher may have read the children a story about a girl who broke her arm and had to go to the hospital, have it set in a plaster cast, and have the cast removed. The children might try out their newly acquired script information by acting out a visit to the hospital to have an injured arm X-rayed, followed by the succession of events as described in the story.

In the third phase, children consolidate new understandings. During the dramatic play of the third phase of a hospital project, the children may be happy to play various combinations of events: accidents involving broken bones, visits to the doctor's office and to the hospital to see the specialist, being X-rayed, having plaster casts put on and removed. In this more extended and elaborate play, old understandings are clarified and enriched by newly acquired script knowledge.

FIVE STRATEGIC FEATURES OF PROJECT WORK

Good project work is the result of judicious structuring of the project by the teacher. Successful projects have a flexible framework made up of several structural features that apply across the three phases in the life of a project. In this section of the chapter, we describe five features in particular that enable teachers to develop projects that respond to children's interests and learning needs: discussion, fieldwork, representation, investigation, and display. These features can help children become highly motivated, feel actively engaged in their learning, and produce work of high quality.

Discussion

Discussion can take place in a whole class meeting, among a small group of children, or between two children. Discussion can be engaged in by children with the teacher or other adult, teacher's aide, parent volunteer, or visiting expert to the classroom. Many discussions may also be part of children's collaborative activity without the direct involvement of the teacher.

Discussion in the context of a project is different from the kind of whole-group teacher interaction that often takes place, for example, in a direct instructional lesson. Discussion in a project involves children talking to each other and not having to refer back to the teacher between each child's contribution. Children learn to talk to each other, to question each other, to comment on each other's ideas, and to request clarification or additional information from other children, as well as from the teacher. This kind of discussion is well described by Gallas as "what happens to talk when children are encouraged to speak collaboratively and develop ideas from their own life experience" (1994, p. 84). Discussion has several important functions for adults and children in a project. Five of these will be mentioned here.

First, discussion is a way of exchanging information about the topic of study. As the children increase their knowledge about the topic, they can share their discoveries with their peers. In this way, they are able to review what they have learned through explaining it to their classmates for the agreed purpose of making sure that everyone is informed about what is being learned by others. Second, the children can discuss the strategies they are engaged in for investigation and representation in the context of the project. Discussion of these strategies helps all children in their work, reminding them of the range of different ways they can learn. Third, discussion provides children with opportunities to solicit suggestions from peers of how to improve a piece of work or solve a problem. This function of discussion allows children to learn from the work of other children and develop confidence in the different kinds of help available in their classroom. Fourth, discussion provides a context within which children can demonstrate their growing understanding to the teacher. Fifth, the children can be involved with the teacher in planning the development of the project as the study progresses.

Field Work

The study of real world topics where there is local expertise available offers great advantages to the teacher. The children can learn from many sources of information, such as visits to local field sites and interviews with local experts. It is also helpful to see how many of the children's families have access to relevant expertise through training, experience, interest, or travel.

Field work might be seen to be any activity that takes place outside the classroom. In the first phase of a project, children may interview their parents about experiences they have had that are relevant to the topic. In the second phase, the teacher can take children out into the community where there are relevant objects, vehicles, machines, people, events and processes to observe firsthand. Children are ideally suited to learn from complex reality, as is shown by the ease with which they learn a new language when they hear it spoken all around them. The individuals in a class of children deliberately observe different details at a field site. They can become quite efficient at recording these observations in field notes, a genre of representation that may combine drawing, writing, and numbers. A rich pool of information can result from one field visit when the teacher can find ways to collect, sort, and make available all the children's observations to each other.

Representation

Children can represent their experience, prior knowledge, questions, research findings, and explanations in a variety of ways through dramatic play, drawing, construction, writing, and designing graphic organizers. From the beginning of any project, the teacher can help children share experiences, knowledge, and skills with one another through selected representations. Children can also combine representational strategies to clarify and elaborate the information they plan to share. The older children become, the greater the range of representational strategies they have available to them. In the context of a project where different children may at any one time be using a variety of such strategies, children are frequently reminded of the representational strategies open to them in their work.

Investigation

Projects always involve some kind of research. Much research can be firsthand and findings are gained from close observation and interviewing experts. There is also an increasing use of secondary sources of information as children become older: finding out information from books, videos, the Internet, museum exhibits, and other sources where information has been prepared and presented by other researchers.

Firsthand research can be done through field work. In classrooms, it can also take the form of explorations or experiments with material, objects, or substances. Small animals or insects can be studied firsthand in classrooms with the proviso that due care is taken to treat live material in an ethically responsible way.

Display

Teachers can use bulletin boards, classroom walls, shelves, and table surfaces to display information, children's work, collections of objects, lists of words, books to consult, instructions for procedures, and materials and equipment to work with. These displays help children to be more independent of the teacher as they work. Teachers who have experience working this way value the time thus released to observe and interact with children involved in dramatic play or to help with construction techniques. This approach also enables the teacher to move around the classroom for much of the time and to keep in touch with what all of the children are doing. The teacher can use the time to encourage their efforts and, where appropriate, to suggest ideas. In project work, the teacher's role is more that of adviser and guide than an instructor.

Over the course of a project, the teacher can orchestrate the developments by collecting and displaying work products, presenting the progress of groups and individuals to the whole class by means of discussion and display. There can be ongoing evaluation as different items are selected for display on the walls of the classroom. In the first phase, the teacher can display the representations of children's prior experience and knowledge. These representations may include the following: results of surveys; bar charts of the experiences of groups or of the whole class (for example, grocery shopping, pet ownership, grandparents living locally); comparisons of one child's experience with another (for example, traveling on a ferry or going fishing); drawings with captions or written descriptions with picture illustrations (accounts of personal experience); reports of interviews (one child with another in which one child explains his or her experience to another child who has not had the same experience); and so forth.

THE OPPORTUNITY TO MAKE CHOICES

The opportunity to make choices is an important general feature of project work. Many teachers find that increasing the opportunities for children to make genuine choices are accompanied by increases in children's interest and commitment to the work undertaken. Project work offers children the opportunity to make choices at several levels, each with different educational implications. Some choices are procedural, some aesthetic, and some functionally intrinsic to the activity. Choices have implications for learning in cognitive, aesthetic, social, emotional, and moral areas. The choices vary in importance; some may have no far-reaching effects, but others may contribute to the success or failure of a major effort. Some options may be freely available, while others may involve negotiating with the teacher.

Whatever the nature of the choice, the children can consult the teacher for advice, thus giving her an opportunity to talk with them about the work and to share her views and expectations. The practicalities of offering choices to children during project work can be thought of in terms of several options: choices concerning what to do, and when, where, and with whom to do it. Whether to do something and for what reasons are very often matters that the children negotiate with the teacher. Each of these questions is discussed below.

Choice About What Work to Do

There are limits to the extent to which a child may choose not to undertake a given activity. A child cannot, for example, be allowed not to learn to read or write. However, many other, more specific activities might be offered as genuine alternatives; similar tasks can often take very different forms. Writing a letter, a story, or a factual description of an event may serve equally to strengthen writing skills. A sequence of drawings with captions may be presented in the form of an accordion book, or in a book with pages (shown in Figure 4.1), or in a pie-chart presentation of the four seasons (shown in Figure 4.2).

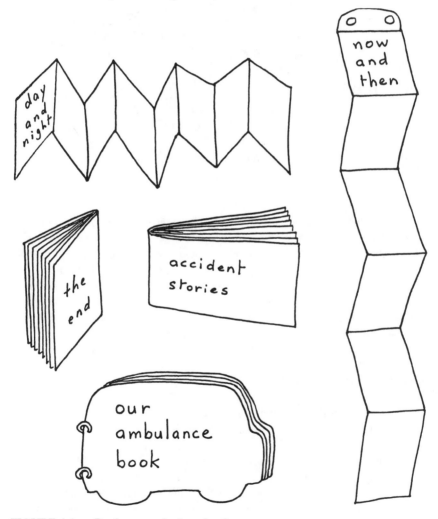

FIGURE 4.1. **Books to make in school**

Winter

Spring

Autumn

Summer

FIGURE 4.2.   Pie-chart representation of the four seasons

The teacher must be alert to the range of activities that children undertake to ensure that they do not miss out on many enriching experiences. Children who regularly refuse to paint or to make models should get help to overcome their reluctance because we have reason to believe that young children benefit from acquiring a broad range of expressive skills. Refusals may present an occasion for the teacher to probe the bases for the child's resistance. In this way, children learn to become accountable for their decisions and for justifying and explaining their choices. Through project work, the teacher may be able to suggest alternative learning activities that can be undertaken in different ways for different purposes.

Choice About When to Work

Children also have the opportunity to choose when to carry out tasks. As long as a particular piece of work is undertaken within a given period, two days for example, a child may choose to do it sooner or later, at the beginning of the time period or toward the end. Each choice has advantages and disadvantages, which can be discussed with the children. Discussion may lead them to favor completing one task early and another one later. Sometimes a child may be among the first to attempt a piece of work; at another time, the same child may prefer to wait and see what other children make of the same task before attempting it themselves.

In one case in which the teacher offered the children a fairly open assignment, some of them sought the challenge of having the first try, while others waited to build on earlier attempts. Those who waited learned alternative ways of approaching the activity from having watched their classmates. Because there were several different responses to the task, learning was much deeper than mere copying. Children who did copy the ideas of their classmates, however, discussed which model to copy. The following detailed description of this example illustrates the kind of learning potential offered by many open-ended tasks.

The activity consisted of painting checkered flags on large pieces of white paper for props in a play. The first child produced an interesting abstract design of randomly placed rectangular black shapes of different sizes. Immediately after, a second child painted rows of black rectangles separated by white spaces. Two days later, a third child painted alternate black and white squares row by row, producing the conventional checkered pattern. This child, a slow-moving and deliberate person, spoke to the teacher conspiratorially as she came to see him painting: "I have been thinking how I would do this," he said. No child spontaneously tried painting vertical and horizontal lines and subsequently filling the alternate squares or boxes, as an adult might approach the task. During the three days during which this activity was undertaken by different children, a considerable amount of mathematical language was used to describe and compare the products. Clearly, there was no single, right way of carrying out the task.

On another occasion, a picture-map drawing activity that a few children had undertaken was discussed at the end of the day. Early the next morning, three of the children whose work had been discussed asked whether they might try it again. Their second attempts showed a marked progression in complexity and cohesion. Had they been required to wait until some later time before being allowed a second try, some of the interesting developments in their work might have been lost. Within the balance of activities, however, it was important to make sure over a week's time that these children did not spend a disproportionate amount of their time drawing, or if they did, that the same thing would not occur repeatedly.

Choice of Where to Work

Within one classroom, different kinds of space can be created for children to work in: lighter or darker; more open or more confined; facing other children or facing the wall or a window; working with a group of others or on one's own; standing, sitting up at a table, or lounging comfortably on cushions on the floor. Sometimes a direct relationship exists between the task and the chosen place, such as painting at an easel. On other occasions, the relationship is not so direct; a piece of writing might be undertaken in an open area or in a small space, with or without other children close by.

Children can learn that alternative settings have different benefits to their work or to their mood at the time. Some children's choice of where to work is best curtailed for a period of time by the teacher. When the beneficial effects of working in different places are discussed with the children, they can understand the reason for the teacher's advice or demand. General recognition of such alternatives helps children make thoughtful choices that support their efforts and facilitate their learning.

Choice of Co-workers

At this early age, friendships are constantly forming, developing, or breaking down under the pressures of classroom life. Important discoveries are being made about what is involved in friendship, communication, cooperation, collaboration, and conflict. Young children vary enormously in the range and quality of interpersonal experiences that they have had outside of school. Social difficulties that persist throughout the early years of schooling are likely to cause distress and pain, and reduce the quality of life for a person during that time and perhaps for several decades beyond it.

Children can be greatly helped by teachers who offer alternative strategies for solving social problems. Through project work, children can develop social competence through opportunities to talk, work, and play together in the classroom. The teacher can encourage cooperation and collaboration by presenting appropriate problems to children. Some children prefer to work privately on making a book of their own. For others, the work is undertaken with much more enthusiasm if it is prepared by a group to be presented as part of a display. The teacher can encourage children to work under both conditions, helping them to see the benefits to be derived from alternative working arrangements. The following account gives examples of activities requiring negotiation and collaboration.

After visiting a large, local garden center or nursery, a class of 6- and 7-year-old children was given a 2-meter square of white cardboard (packing material pasted together with butcher paper). The square was spread out on an area of the floor cleared for this purpose. The activity was preceded by a brief discussion of what the children had seen at the center and what items might be included in a large collaborative painting. Only three procedural instructions were given: (1) three children were to work together for a short but unspecified period of time; (2) each child was to paint one or two items in the total picture; and (3) each child was to give up his or her turn to another child who had not yet made a contribution. The children took their turns, shorter or longer ones, and painted their ideas in the available spaces, which became smaller as the work progressed.

At least two-thirds of the class participated in the activity. The final result showed the care taken to preserve the unity of the picture. The items, of which there were many, were roughly in proportion to each other and observed the general rules of spatial relations, such as above, below, at the side, and in front. Items included a closed-circuit television monitor; a checkout counter; a set of patio furniture; shelves of watering cans, gardening gloves, ornamental dried flowers, feather dusters, bug sprays, packets of seeds, sacks of compost, potted plants, and cut flowers; and many figures representing customers and workers. The overall effect was movingly suggestive of the place the children had visited as a class on the previous day.

The teacher intervened only toward the end, not without some trepidation, to suggest that the children see what the picture would look like if they filled the gaps between the objects with a "wash" of some sort. They tried using a pale yellow ocher. The overall effect was remarkably pleasing, and the whole class was happy with the result. It must be said that this work was achieved later in the school year, after the children had developed the social skills necessary to facilitate collaboration in the classroom.

Examples of choice, such as those described above, are easier to observe in more informal classrooms where the curriculum is integrated. Teachers wishing to introduce this kind of informal work can find many helpful suggestions and a description of classrooms graded according to extent of informality and integration in the book *Organising and Integrating the First School Day* (Taylor, 1983).

The project approach offers children a learning environment that develops their sense of their own competence and worth. It creates a classroom ethos in which children's points of view are taken seriously and their feelings and opinions treated respectfully. It offers the opportunity for children to try out their developing powers of judgment and to learn with confidence from their mistakes. Children's use of judgment can be practiced in situations calling for negotiation and decision making where genuine choices can be made. However, choice is itself a neutral term. If the alternatives to choose from are of little educative value, then motivation is unlikely to be enhanced. The available alternatives must be carefully prepared and monitored by the teacher.

THE ROLE OF THE TEACHER

In Chapter 1, we discussed the differences between project work and systematic instruction. The four distinctions listed in Table 1.1 have implications for the way that children interact with the teacher and with each other in class discussion. It is the teacher's responsibility to set clear expectations and standards of work and conduct and a prevailing tone that facilitates the open exchange of information.

Procedures are very important in the project approach because children work individually and in small groups over periods of several days or weeks. Thus, children must be clear about the teacher's expectations of them. In contrast, systematic instruction generally calls for children to act in the short term, primarily in response to specific instructions. Young children need frequent reminders about the alternatives open to them, about what they should be doing, and about where, when, and with whom they should be doing it. These reminders are not always stated in the form of instructions. Many are expressed as suggestions or options to be considered by specific groups or individuals. Other reminders can take the form of examples referring to individuals who worked in a particularly successful way, who chose carefully, and who can talk about the reasons for their decisions. Children do not usually recount their experiences to show off or to intimidate other children, but to explain how they approached the problems they encountered. Older children's attention can often be drawn to the signs, announcements, and notices around the room, indicating what to do and how to set about doing it. Notices might be entitled: "Things you can do alone or with a friend," "Things to be finished before Thursday," and "How to mount your drawing." An example of how a notice entitled "How to make your own book" might look is given in Appendix D.

Teachers can use many devices to strengthen the children's dispositions to be resourceful and independent as they work on projects. For instance, the teacher can ensure that children have easy access to materials and equipment set out for them, that books and displays are readily available for them to consult for information, and that resources such as word banks are conveniently located around the classroom so that they can find words for their writing. During class discussion, children can be reminded of the procedures for helping themselves and each other when the teacher's attention is taken up elsewhere.

In classrooms where projects are being developed, the free exchange of information contributes to the smooth running of the class. Here, the information emanates not only from the teacher, but also from children's reports of their own understanding and the progress they are making. Children can help one another a great deal by example and as consultants and collaborators. Since much of this work represents information, it can be displayed to serve as a resource for other children while they pursue their investigations. The teacher also has an important role to play in helping children appreciate and value each other's work.

SUMMARY

The principal features of the project approach have been outlined in this chapter along with practical examples. The temporal structure of a project as it develops over three phases was outlined. Five features of project work, which have a role to play in each of the phases, were also discussed in terms of their value for the teacher in guiding the project work. This analysis of features is intended to make more explicit what happens behind scenes such as those described in Chapter 3. In many cases, we have described events in the classrooms of teachers experienced with project work. More recently, many teachers who have introduced the project approach into their classrooms have begun to use this approach in a small way and have extended their project work as they developed techniques that worked particularly effectively for them in their own situation.

5

Issues in Selecting Topics
for Projects

To a large extent, the benefits of project work are related to topics on which they are focused. The ultimate responsibility for topic selection is the teachers', in that they must judge whether those selected are appropriate to the children's development, whether they are worthy of children's time, and whether they meet a variety of other criteria suggested in this chapter. Furthermore, to support good project work, teachers themselves must often undertake extensive preparation, study, and exploration. Therefore, it is a good idea to determine whether the topics are of sufficient substance to warrant both children's and teachers' time and effort. In this chapter, we address the issues involved in the selection of project topics and offer a list of criteria that teachers have found useful for making decisions about project topics.

CHILDREN'S INTERESTS

Extensive experience of working with teachers implementing the project approach all over the world indicates that one of their major considerations in topic selection is usually their children's actual or potential interest in it. Issues raised by this concern are taken up below.

Following Children's Interests

Teachers sometimes select project topics on the basis of the children's expressed interest in them. Even though this strategy can often yield appropriate and enriching topics, basing projects on the interest of an individual, a group of children, or a whole class, it presents several potential pitfalls in topic selection.

The first issue this strategy raises is: What does it mean in to say that an individual child or group of children, or even a whole class, is "interested" in a topic? The word *interest* in this context is not entirely clear. Interests can be of relatively low value (for example, how to pull the legs off of flies [Wilson, 1971]); they might be passing thoughts, fleeting concerns, phobias, fetishes, obsessions, or topics nominated by a child whose motive is to please the teacher.

Second, just because an individual or group expresses interest in a given topic, for example, dinosaurs or pirates, does not mean that the interest deserves to be supported and strengthened through project work. It may be that children become interested in pirates after having seen an entertaining movie about them. In such cases, the children can be given opportunity for spontaneous dramatic play involving pirates; they can be encouraged to discuss their reactions to the movie; listen to the reading of favorite pirate stories and discuss them; and so forth. But such interest does not imply that an indepth *investigation* of the topic of pirates is in their best developmental, educational, or even moral interests. We suggest that there is an important distinction between providing opportunity for child-initiated spontaneous discussion and play around a topic, and a teacher investing a great deal of time and energy in organizing a long range project focused upon it and thereby according the topic greater value than it merits.

Fourth, we suggest that project topic selection should be consistent with the general commitment of educators in taking children and their intellectual powers seriously, treating them matter-of-factly and straightforwardly as young investigators of serious phenomena worthy of their attention. Our experience of working with many teachers suggests that adults frequently underestimate children's capacities to find satisfaction and meaningfulness in the persistent hard work required for close observation and data gathering involved in the study of everyday phenomena around them.

Fifth, adults have the responsibility to educate children's interests. Children's awareness of the teacher's real and deep interest in a topic (for example, changes in the natural environment over a six-week period) very often engenders some level of interest in the topic among the children who respect and look up to them.

Finally, in a class of 25 children, the number of possible "interests" is too large to take up in any single year! How should those to be addressed be determined? Again, the teacher carries the central responsibility for selecting the project topics.

Exciting Children's Interest

Sometimes adults promote exotic and exciting topics for projects in the hope of capturing the attention of children, especially those who often seem reluctant to join in the work of the class. For example, projects revolving around the rain forest undertaken in schools located on the northern plains of the United States may very well entice young children into enthusiastic participation. We have also observed many projects in several countries focused on medieval castles where none exist, typically achieving animated participation by young children. Similarly, we know of several teachers who have responded to young children's lively, spontaneous discussions of the sinking of the Titanic, stimulated by the movie and television documentaries. While their interest in the phenomenon was certainly palpable, the topic does not lend itself to firsthand investigations. However, good discussion and reading, led by a teacher who helps them interpret the new knowledge, would be appropriate in such cases. Furthermore, though such topics do no harm, our experience indicates that young children can be no less absorbed and intrigued by the experience of close observation and study of their own natural environments, whether they are prairies, cornfields, apple orchards, or a nearby bicycle shop.

Children do not have to be fascinated, spellbound, enchanted, or bewitched by a topic. Indeed, as indicated in Chapter 2, one of the potentially valuable contributions of good project work is that it can strengthen children's dispositions to be interested, absorbed, and involved in indepth observation, investigation, and representation of worthwhile phenomena in their own environments.

Furthermore, if the topic of a project is an exotic and therefore remote one, it is difficult for the children to contribute to its direction and design. In principle, the less firsthand experience the children can have in relation to the topic, the more dependent they are on the teacher for the ideas, information, questions, hypotheses, and other elements that constitute the essence of good project work.

Young children are indeed dependent on adults for many important aspects of their lives. However, as indicated in Chapter 2, project work is the part of the curriculum in which children are encouraged to take initiative in setting the questions to be answered, influencing the direction of the work to be undertaken, and in accepting responsibility for what is accomplished.

Along similar lines, topics are sometimes chosen because they are expected to amuse or even entertain the children. Such topics are thought by teachers to stimulate children's imaginations (for example, mermaids, teddy bears, the circus). However, these topics are more fanciful than imaginative, and they are unlikely to provide contexts for direct investigation and observation.

In good project work, children have ample opportunity to use and strengthen their imaginations. This happens when they make predictions before taking a field trip about what they will find and when they predict the answers to their interview questions and when they argue with each other about possible causes and effects related to the phenomena under investigation. Project work stimulates and strengthens young children's imaginations also during the first phase, when they are encouraged to report their own memories and actual experiences related to the topic, and to make up their own stories related to them (for example, stories of actual experiences of riding a tricycle, and imaginary and fictional stories of bike rides).

Optimal Use of School Time

Concern for optimal use of school time includes assessing the appropriateness of a topic in terms of whether the participating children are likely to have opportunities to explore it outside of school. Similarly, assessing the appropriateness of topics includes evaluating whether they will strengthen children's sense of competence in dealing with and understanding their own daily experiences and environments.

Occasionally teachers select topics with the intention of "sneaking" learning into the children through a "hands-on" activity while they are not looking—so to speak. Thus, a teacher might initiate a project on a dentist as a way of getting the children to remember the basics of dental hygiene. If dental hygiene is an important topic, it should be addressed directly, in its own right, and not necessarily as a project. Not everything that is important for children to know and learn is appropriate for project work.

DIVERSITY CONCERNS

Diversity of Experiences

In some classes, the diversity of the incoming pupils' experiences might be so great that it would be beneficial to *begin* the year with a topic the teacher is reasonably certain is familiar to all children. A sense of community in the class is more likely to develop when all the children have sufficient experience related to the topic to be able to participate in a discussion with some confidence, and to be able to recognize and relate their own relevant experiences. As the school year progresses and the children become accustomed to project work and adept at the tasks involved, they can more readily appreciate the fact that individuals and groups have different interests, preferring to work on different topics or subtopics. In this way, they can learn to share with the whole class what each of them has learned. The diversity of work can stimulate and deepen children's appreciation and prizing of differences in experience, interests, and abilities among their peers.

Diversity of Cultures

As defined and recommended throughout this book, the project approach is a highly appropriate way to respond to diversity of cultures within the group of participating children. However, we find it useful to make a distinction between a child's *culture* and a child's *heritage*. The former refers to the current day-to-day experiences and environment of the children; the latter refers to historic and ancestral attributes associated with their families' origins. In the early years, projects are most likely to be enriching if the topics are taken from the children's *culture* rather than *heritage*, though aspects of the latter can and should be introduced to the children in other parts of the curriculum. Again, not all important topics can be taken up in the form of projects.

RELATIONSHIP OF TOPICS TO CURRICULUM REQUIREMENTS

Most official curriculum guides are cast in such broad terms that it is invariably possible to select good project topics from among the lists of knowledge and concepts mandated or recommended. Making explicit the relationship between the topic of the project and the prescribed curriculum requirements for the parents can help reassure them that their children's education conforms to official guidelines.

PREPARATION FOR PARTICIPATION IN A DEMOCRATIC SOCIETY

One important consideration we propose in the selection of project topics is a commitment to helping children to become competent participants in a democratic society. In the interest of this goal, good topics would be those that deepen children's understanding, knowledge, and appreciation of the contribution of others to their well-being and the welfare of the larger community in which they live.

Second, in the interests of the goal of preparing for participation in democracy, topics are appropriate if they strengthen and/or deepen the disposition for close examination of real phenomena and appreciation of their complexities.

Third, one of the many benefits of project work is that it provides many processes and skills useful for participation in a democracy within the classroom itself. Good project work provides contexts for developing agreements on actions to be taken, sharing responsibility for carrying out plans, resolving conflicts about findings, making suggestions to one another, prizing the different ways individuals can contribute to the total work accomplished, and so forth. In the more formal parts of the curriculum, children rarely have early experience of such democratic processes.

RELATIONSHIP OF THE TOPIC TO SUBSEQUENT LEARNING

In many cases, the knowledge gained by children working on a project would be learned or "picked up" later on in other ways. For example, all children eventually learn the main ideas about the behavior of shadows, or the basics of what goes on behind the scenes of a supermarket. Thus, one could ask why these might be worthwhile topics for young children. (Note that the opposite is also true: much that is learned through formal instruction in school that is thought to be essential to later life or to "cultural literacy" is forgotten soon after the learning experiences are over.) We are not claiming that processes (for example, of studying the behavior of shadows) are more important than new knowledge. We suggest that educators at every level are equally responsible for the qualities of the *processes and of the content and of the products* involved in children's work. Though we are not primarily concerned with a particular product or the prespecified knowledge-acquisition outcome in project work, all of the kinds of learning we are concerned about—knowledge, skills, dispositions, and feelings—should be addressed in the course of investigating worthwhile topics. While project work provides pretexts, texts, and contexts for a wide range of important skills and dispositions to be strengthened, ideally these experiences occur in the course of investigating worthwhile topics. In other words, in our view, it is not satisfactory to have good processes used to study worthless content, energy devoted to worthwhile content in the context of inappropriate processes, or inappropriate content and processes in the service of good products; all three aspects of children's work: content or topics, processes, and products deserve careful consideration and selection at all levels of education.

POTENTIAL DELICACY OF THE TOPIC

Some topics are potentially delicate because of their religious or sexual implications, or because they might in some way offend some of the families served by the early childhood program or the school. Some topics might also be delicate in the sense that they touch on matters individual children may not want to share their experience of, for example, some children may not want to talk about their own houses or even their own families. Teachers are in the best position to evaluate the potential delicacy of a topic when they have come to know the children well.

CLINICAL CONSIDERATIONS

Occasionally, a teacher is responsible for an individual child or small group of children whose personal situations are such that a topic ordinarily considered inappropriate would be selected or avoided so as to address or be sensitive to the special case. For example, many teachers of young children have guided them through detailed study of a local hospital. However, it might be the case on occasion that a child has had a very recent traumatic experience—perhaps losing a loved one—or a frightening hospitalization experience of her own, suggesting that the study of that topic might best be postponed until a later time. Similarly, it is possible that a child is extremely difficult to reach or has no interest in topics usually appealing to his or her age group. The teacher decides to respond to his or her sole interest, for example, war planes or glamorous dolls, using these less-than-optimal topics as a means to establishing relationships to build on.

PRESSURES FOR ACCOUNTABILITY

One important consideration in topic selection is whether the knowledge and skills gained by the children can contribute to a teacher's meeting demands for account-ability. Sometimes teachers attribute restrictions concerning topics for projects to district curriculum requirements, even though no such restrictions are actually there. Occasionally, teachers indicate that they are conducting particular lessons because the state or district requires them to do so, even though no such require-ment actually exists. It is thus a good idea to check carefully in advance concerning recommended and mandated subjects and topics.

A TENTATIVE LIST OF CRITERIA

It is a good idea to keep in mind that predicting which topics will work well with any particular group of children is not easy. Many experienced teachers have been sur-prised by those topics about which they had doubts that actually turned out to be beneficial, and vice versa. Based on the issues raised above, we offer a tentative set of criteria for topic selection, which follows.

A topic is appropriate if:

1. sufficient relevant phenomena are directly observable in the children's own environments, in that the topic will provide ample opportunity for firsthand and direct contact with aspects of the topic;
2. it is within some of the children's own experiences;
3. firsthand direct investigation is feasible (and not potentially dangerous);
4. local resources and experts are readily available and field sites accessible;
5. it has good potential for representation in a variety of media (for example, roleplay, construction, graphic, and so on);
6. parental participation and contributions are likely and many parents can eas-ily become involved;
7. it is sensitive to the local culture, as well as culturally appropriate in general;
8. it is potentially interesting to many of the children, or it is an interest that adults consider worthy of developing in children;
9. it is related to the curriculum goals of the school, district, state, and so on;
10. it provides ample opportunity to begin mastery and application of basic lit-eracy and numeracy skills (depending on the ages of the children);

11. it is *optimally* specific—not too narrow and not too broad (for example, a study of the teacher's own dog or "buttons" at one end, and the topic of "music" or "the seasons" at the other); however, narrow topics could provoke good mini-projects, and broad topics can become a source of subtopics of the right size;

12. the teacher's own knowledge of and experience related to the topic will strengthen his or her ability to enrich the children's experiences during the project; and

13. it is rich enough to allow for extended and indepth investigation activities over a period of several weeks.

SUMMARY

The selection of project topics is ideally negotiated in discussions of the teacher with the children, even though the teacher has the ultimate responsibility for it. Furthermore, no matter how interesting a topic might be initially, it could happen that over time interest in it might subside. It is up to the teacher to monitor the children's involvement and to determine when it might be advisable to bring the investigation to a close or whether it might be necessary to introduce a fresh aspect of the topic to restimulate interest.

6

Teacher Planning

Projects can be short-term undertakings or they might enliven a classroom for eight weeks or longer. Short-term, small-group, or spontaneously generated projects, which we refer to as "mini-projects," require little advanced teacher planning. Occasionally, a mini-project arises from an unexpected event, such as the resurfacing of the school yard or bees swarming nearby. In such cases, advanced planning is not possible. However, if a project is to last several weeks and involve the whole class, advanced planning improves the chances of fruitful investigation and accomplishment. This chapter describes some techniques for initial project planning and suggests ways to elaborate plans and adapt topics for particular groups of children.

SELECTING A TOPIC

As indicated in the discussion of issues in topic selection in Chapter 5, the choice of topics for projects may be made in a variety of ways according to the practices and preferences of the school. Individual teachers may independently select topics for their classes, or schools may develop a policy of offering specific major projects in each grade each year. Teachers develop some projects on the basis of a social studies or science curriculum guide required by school authorities. Sometimes a whole school undertakes one project. In such cases, teachers plan as a team, and each class takes responsibility for a particular area or subtopic related to the main topic. Occasionally, the children in a class select a topic and the teacher helps them develop its scope in discussion with them.

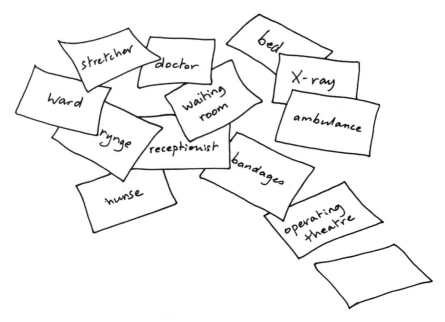

FIGURE 6.1.   Topic web for "going to the hospital."

Once a suitable topic has been selected, the teacher sets out some provisional plans on paper. One technique that many teachers have adapted for this purpose is that of creating what we call a "topic web." This is a diagram in which ideas and information are grouped under sub-topic headings (see Figure 6.1). The major advantage of a topic web is that the ideas can be generated in any order; no pre-determined sequence is dictated by the form of the web. In that respect, it is different from a flow chart, which has a linear temporal sequence built into it.

The Teacher's Topic Web

A web is a graphic mapping of the key ideas and concepts that a topic comprises and some of the major subtopics related to it. Teachers can of course work with a web designed by someone else. But the process of making a web in and of itself often helps teachers to become aware of their own knowledge and resources. Some teachers inexperienced in the project approach have reported to us that brain-storming a topic web increased their awareness of how much they did or did not know about a topic before they began searching information in a reference work. Teachers also often report a tendency to underestimate their own knowledge of a topic and how much young children can learn from objects, people, and places, as well as from books. The procedure outlined below is recommended for teachers who have had little or no experience in topic webbing.

Procedures for Creating a Topic Web

Five steps are suggested for generating a topic web:

1. Take one pack of small self-stick notes (1 inch x 1½ inches). Write down each idea related to the topic on a new piece of paper. For example, take the topic of "going to the hospital." The first succession of ideas might run as follows: ambulance, stretcher, doctor, ward, X-ray, nurse, waiting room, receptionist, bed, operating room, bandages, and syringes. Continue generating ideas in free-association fashion and writing them down on pieces of paper for about 10 minutes (Figure 6.2).

When this "brainstorming" exercise is conducted in a group, each person will probably produce the first set of ideas in a different order. Most of the participants will have the same ideas; but some ideas will be original, idiosyncratic, and in other ways, unique.

2. Move the pieces of paper around on a table so that related ideas are grouped together. Similar groups can be placed next to each other (Figure 6.3).
3. Take a few pieces of paper of a different color. Write a label that gives a heading to each group. If one group is very large, usually the ideas can be separated into two or three smaller subgroups under the main heading and each subgroup given a heading. For the hospital topic, the headings might include injuries, parts of a hospital, the ambulance, hospital workers, and treatment equipment.

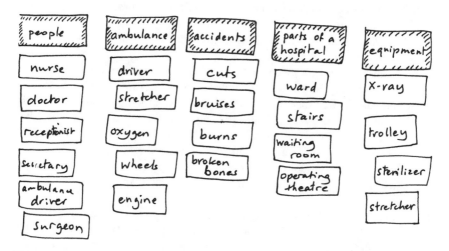

FIGURE 6.2.   Initial brainstorming

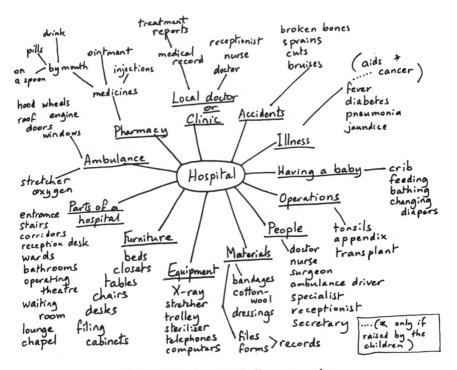

FIGURE 6.3. Ordering the items and labeling categories.

4. If a group of teachers is "brainstorming" a web together, this would be a good point at which they can examine each other's brainstorming for ideas with which to enrich one's own web. It is also interesting to observe the variety of ways others arrange ideas, yielding differences in focus or perspective on the same topic.

5. At this point, the ideas generated on the notes can be transferred to one sheet of paper for a more permanent, initial record. The most flexible way to do so is to take a large sheet of paper and begin with the title of the topic in the center. Then draw short lines radiating from the title and write the labels given to each group of items. Lines can then be drawn to other subheadings and eventually to lists of items in each group and subgroup (see Figure 6.1). Examples of webs for projects on "going shopping," "weather," and a "construction site" described in Chapter 3 are shown in Appendix E.

It is generally helpful at first to consider more ideas than could possibly be used in a single project. In the first place, not all of the ideas generated by brainstorming will be suitable as areas of investigation by the children. Second, if a teacher has considered a wide range of possibilities by herself, it will be easier for her later on to incorporate the ideas that children may offer in a preliminary discussion.

LINKING PROJECT TOPICS TO CURRICULUM AREAS

When the web is completed, it is useful to produce a second web that organizes the project ideas under curriculum subject area headings and the learning activities associated with them. Keep in mind, however, that the curriculum subject web should be developed only *after* the first kind of brainstorming has been completed. This sequence minimizes the likelihood of distorting the topic itself toward setting tasks within conventional subject boundaries.

Appropriate learning goals for children are more likely to be addressed by using the "brainstorming" web, which reflects relationships among the items of information about the topic itself. The curriculum subject web, on the other hand, reflects the teacher's purposes, which may or may not correspond to the web developed later with the children. For example, measuring the size of a vehicle involves exercising considerable mathematical skill. However, if the vehicle is measured only because the teacher wants the children to practice measurement, then it will be of much less value as a project activity than if the children do so in the course of planning to make a model of a vehicle to scale. Making a model to understand how the vehicle works provides opportunities for practicing measurement skills, rather than the other way around.

DECIDING ON THE SCOPE OF A PROJECT

The more general and abstract a topic, the more scope it has for subdividing the content. With each subdivision, topics become smaller until they are relatively microscopic. In the reverse direction, larger topics can be created by combining small, related topics. We suggest here that smaller and more specific topics are probably more suitable for younger children. As children get older, they can more easily see connections between subtopics within larger topics with a wider scope. Webs showing how the scope of a project on a school bus would vary for older and younger children are shown in Appendix F.

One technique that narrows the focus of a topic is what we call "zooming in" on a subtopic in the web. It is usually possible to focus on specific subtopics in the same way that a camera with a zoom lens can focus on a close-up view of part of a subject. The subtopic titles then become the center of a new web, which can be as elaborate as the previous one on the main topic. For example, in a hospital web, the ambulance can become a "zoom." At the center of a new web, the ambulance can give rise to subtopics, such as the motor, the wheels, emergency equipment, the siren, flashing lights, materials, the driver, emergencies, routes to the hospital, and shifts worked by the driver. An example of a "zoom" web for a project on "homes" is shown in Appendix G.

A second technique for narrowing or broadening the focus of a topic is to think in terms of its specificity or generality. Related topics can be located in a hierarchical classification, from the more specific to the more general. The more specific a topic, the more likely it is to be suitable for a project with younger children. Examples of hierarchically related topics that vary in scope are as follows:

1. hats, uniforms, clothes;
2. tortoises, reptiles, wild animals;
3. bedrooms, houses, villages, towns;
4. weather, seasons, climate.

The choice of project title as a focus for the work need not be limiting, however. In the case of the weather, no matter how young the children, the work can be extended to include the seasons or the climate. These more remote, abstract concepts would most likely not be as fully developed by the younger ones as by older children.

A third way of narrowing the scope of a topic, especially for children in the preschool period, is to predicate it in some way, as Blank (1985) suggests. Blank argues that the predication of a concept is vital to any dialogue about it. It is difficult to have a conversation about food, for example, until the word is predicated in some way that gives it a particular contextual meaning. Once it is known whether one is thinking about buying food, serving food, or preparing food, the word *food* takes on a significance that can generate conversation. Giving alternative perspectives to the topic of houses can indicate a direction for study: "building a house," "houses in our neighborhood," or "furnishing a house." A project about shops may have subthemes such as "going shopping," "stores on Main Street," or "setting up a store."

Predicates can be particularly useful in reflecting children's interests and ideas on a main topic. The three techniques discussed here for narrowing the scope of a topic for a project with younger children or for completing it in a shorter time have been found useful by teachers in adapting topics for particular groups of children.

FIVE PLANNING CRITERIA

In Chapter 4, we discussed *relevance* to the children's own experience as a principal criterion for selecting project topics. We return to this topic to consider five other criteria for selecting and focusing particular project topics that should also be considered: the activities that the children can undertake, applying skills, the availability of resources, the interest of the teacher, and the time of the school year.

Activities for the Children

No matter what the topic, certain kinds of worthwhile knowledge, skills, disposi-tions, and feelings are developed through project work. Although groups of children may undertake projects on different topics, much similar learning will take place. Whether the children study "birds feeding," "vehicles for cargo," or "clothes for cold weather," each topic offers opportunities for close observation, labeling of parts, counting and tallying (counting in groups), making bar charts, sorting accord-ing to different criteria, finding and recording information from books, negotiating with other children, and collaborating in group activities. The activities give chil-dren the occasion to observe, to reconstruct aspects of the environment, and to practice finding things out. These skills and processes are being learned and prac-ticed with every project undertaken, although the prominence given to particular skills and processes may vary from one topic to another.

During initial planning, the teacher develops a web to which the children's own ideas can be added. A familiar hospital in the neighborhood can be an important focal point in the web and project plans. Some of the children may have had rela-tives there or have been hospital patients themselves. It is likely that they and their siblings were born in the hospital. Some of the parents may work there. If so, one part of the web may be developed more fully to include resources well known to the children.

An understanding of hospitals might best be achieved by asking children to explore the common experiences they have had with local doctors. These experi-ences vary in different parts of the world. Children in rural areas of China are likely to be familiar with the barefoot doctor, her role in the community, and the instruments she uses. Children in rural India will probably be familiar with the primary health center in their community and its procedures and services. Many children in the Australian outback will have experience with visits of the flying doctor. Whatever the location, the doctor or district nurse might be willing to visit the school to talk to the children. Each culture offers different perspectives on the topic, and these can be reflected in the activities of the children as they develop the project.

Applying Skills

Project work gives children the opportunity to apply skills independently for pur-poses that they themselves have generated or helped to formulate. These purposes will arise from children's own experience. Even within one class, children show dif-ferent levels of competence and confidence in a variety of basic skills. Most children apply skills independently only when they feel confident and comfortable enough in the setting. They do so especially if the aim of the activities is learning rather than performance (see Chapter 2, p. 42).

The level of competence at which a child uses a skill unaided is not always related to the level of competence displayed during instruction or assessment. A quite able child may be reluctant, for example, to use a reference book to find out how water comes out of a bathroom faucet, whereas a much less able child may be eager to seek such a challenge (Dweck, 1987; Dweck & Leggett, 1988). In other words, just because a child has a competence does not mean he or she will use it. Children may be reluctant to look things up because their reading experiences have typically been with basal readers.

Besides competence, other important factors contribute to children's behavior. Feelings of self-efficacy, confidence, degree of interest based on prior knowledge or experience, learning style, and other individual attributes play a role in this variability of response to the challenge involved in applying skills independently.

Sometimes confident children, highly motivated to obtain information from a reference book, persist with reading the material, even though much of it is too difficult for them. Similarly, in adult life the same people may choose at times to attempt difficult tasks that stretch them almost beyond the limits of their ability. At other times, they may confidently prefer to work with more risk-taking and originality at something that is easy for them. So too in project work, children can choose from a variety of levels of challenge. This is another example of the way project work can bring activities in school closer to the quality of real-life experience, a major theme of the project approach. Projects offer tteachers opportunities to encourage children to work at an optimum level of confidence and to select different levels of challenge.

When children work independently, they might be expected to take more time at their tasks, to take risks, to be more exploratory and imaginative in their thinking than under conditions of direct instruction. For example, preschool children can learn about the purposes of reading and writing before they can actually read or write. In their play they can make shopping lists, "write" prescriptions, or follow recipes. Play or pretend writing may take the form of scribbling even after children are receiving writing instruction, just as there is a short overlap between a baby's crawling and walking when both methods of locomotion are practiced alternately. When writing comes to children easily, they use it with fluency and have no need for scribbling, just as infants drop the crawling when they become confident walkers.

The application of language skills is an important concern in the teacher planning of projects. Project work provides rich content for conversation not only on the topic itself, but also on the range of processes involved in the work, such as planning constructions, deciding on procedures and the materials to be used, and so forth. Project work offers children shared experiences of events to think about and discuss with one another. The experiences gained while working together on various aspects of the project become integrated with current understandings as children talk in a variety of situations. The dramatic play area (for example, housekeeping corner, domestic play space) can be equipped with props that stimulate conversation in roleplaying. When children not only dress up in nurses' and doctors' uniforms, but also have a stethoscope, syringes (with needles removed, of course), a thermometer, a sling, bandages, a blood pressure gauge, and empty medicine bottles, their play becomes considerably more focused on specific information. They can think about the diagnosis and treatment of illness and what medical personnel can do to help. Thus, many aspects of language development are stimulated and strengthened in the contexts provided by project work. As they involve themselves in the activities of planning, checking, collaborating, and coordinating their efforts, children use language purposefully and gain satisfaction from their own sense of effectiveness.

Language is the principal means by which young children can share, negotiate, and even create meaning. In the process of planning, the teacher can assess the potential of the project for adding to the children's growing store of words, expressions, and phrases. Children not only have to acquire new vocabulary. They also have to learn ways of using the words in scripts or basic sequences of related events leading to predictable outcomes in particular contexts and for particular purposes (see the discussion of event and script knowledge in Chapter 2).

While selecting and planning a suitable project, teachers can list the vocabulary, expressions, and concepts associated with different understandings. For example, diagnosis involves finding out what is wrong with a patient, where it hurts, how much it hurts, how hot she is, and how long she has been ill. Treatment, on the other hand, refers to what must be done to help the person feel better and recover from the illness or injury. The two concepts, diagnosis and treatment, are distinct; though similar vocabulary is used, diagnosis and treatment are terms used to talk and think about matters associated with different goals.

During planning, teachers can take into account the ways that children use their behavioral knowledge in developing their representational knowledge. When visiting the doctor, for example, children may exhibit the behavioral knowledge of being a patient: showing their tongue, coughing on request, and later taking medicine. The project activities help children develop representational knowledge that distinguishes behaviors related to diagnosis from those concerned with treatment.

Various cognitive processes are involved in the development of representational knowledge. Children actively engage in comparing and contrasting objects and events, note attributes of things, take them apart and reassemble them, group objects into classes, order them, and string them together in scripts. Hohmann, Banet, and Weikart (1983) offer a useful selection of "key experiences for cognitive development," tested and applied in the High/Scope curriculum for young children.

Appropriate communicative skills can be developed as children work cooperatively, questioning, speculating, reasoning, inferring, and arguing about and explaining their project-related work and actions. For the youngest children in the age range of concern here, communicative competence can be strengthened when they are encouraged to ask each other's advice, tell each other what they are planning to do, and ask each other questions about their work and progress in the project.

The basic academic skills of reading, writing, and mathematics can be employed when school-age children record observations, describe experiences, and note down what they have found out in books. Some projects offer greater opportunities than other projects for applying certain basic skills. In a store project with older children, there might be more opportunities for particular mathematical skills to be applied; in a study of the neighborhood, map reading and other graphic skills can be used. Most projects provide many varied opportunities for using skills in drawing, talking, writing, reading, mathematics, and science.

Some topics are particularly rich in potential for investigative activities, while others offer more opportunities for dramatic play. In their planning, teachers are generally concerned with achieving a long-term balance in the kinds of opportunities that the project is likely to provide for the children.

Accessing Resources

The term *resources* is used very broadly here to include any sources of information and experience, such as field trips and classroom visitors, as well as material resources, that contribute to the activities and learning of the children. The resources available for children's work and play are a major consideration for teachers when planning projects.

If, for example, the teacher introduces a project on "going to hospital," she might ask herself the following questions about resources: Where might the children visit (local clinic, doctor's office)? Who might be invited to talk to them in school (nurse, doctor)? Might this visitor have some discarded instruments, such as old X-ray pictures, to donate to the project? What resources does the school have from previous hospital projects (doctors' and nurses' coats and uniforms, charts, books)?

Teachers experienced in using the project approach often accumulate a personal collection of potentially useful items. In addition, parents may be requested to contribute to the school's collection by donating equipment and other items to exhibit, to work with, or to enrich play, for example, bandages, crutches, and empty medicine bottles.

Sources of information, experience, and resources can also be found beyond the school walls: the public library, local museum, businesses, factories, and educational resource centers. For example, children growing up in a fishing village can gain much knowledge from a project on "How do we get our fish?," as shown in the web in Appendix I. There is also a particular value in the children collecting resources from home, being given or loaned items, and collecting some on a visit they themselves have made. This initiative further illustrates the principle that young children's learning is maximized through effective interaction with their environment and the people in their community.

One of the most important aspects of good project work is that they are planned so as to include a significant proportion of firsthand and direct experience of real objects and people. The proportion of such experiences should be high in relation to secondhand information gained from books and visits to museums, where the information has already been experienced and presented by someone else.

If the project topic is about the neighborhood, local industry, or the surrounding natural environment, then resources may be plentiful and easy to obtain. Parents can be involved in the project, talking to the children about some special expertise, helping with field trips, and lending or giving objects, pictures, photographs, or other resources to the classroom. Topics that are distant in time (for example, Victorian England or castles) or distant in space (for example, Japan, or animals in the polar regions), only secondhand and indirect information would be available to the children, causing them to be very dependent on the teacher for their thinking, planning, and learning. Projects of this type are not suitable because they provide little or no personal experience and firsthand information on which children can base their contributions to the work of the project.

When children are older (from 8 to 12 years of age), they have enough general knowledge and awareness of learning strategies to learn a great deal from secondary sources. From 8 years of age on up, children can infer much information that is analogous to their own direct experience. They also share a set of public concepts that approximate or overlap those of the adult culture.

For young children, however, the availability of a store of general knowledge cannot be relied upon because their knowledge of the larger world is still being formed. When, for example, 9-year-olds study the Nile, some general knowledge about a local river can be relied upon. But young children acquire general knowledge about rivers most easily through studying a nearby river, one whose bridges they cross with their parents, or fish in, or walk beside. The teacher can share the children's experience of the river on a field trip and gain fuller insight into their interests and understanding.

Teacher Interest

It is also helpful if the teacher chooses a topic in which she herself has some personal interest and basic knowledge. In project work, the teacher is an important model to the children. She exemplifies the dispositions she wishes to strengthen by helping children with their explorations, by encouraging and acknowledging questions, discussing, and demonstrating an inquiring disposition. To do so, she uses books, pictures, charts, maps, and so forth to find out where the children can look for appropriate information.

Because there is a wide range of topics, teachers need not repeat the same projects every year or even every three or four years. Each year, they can usually plan some projects that are new, fresh, and personally challenging to the teacher as well as to the children. However, since the children have an important influence on the way projects develop, a responsive teacher seldom finds that even a repeated project takes the same course with a different class group.

Time of Year

When teachers first become acquainted with new classes of children, it is helpful to choose a topic that the children have experienced personally and are ready to share with others. For example, families, babies, or homes are topics that are very much a part of their everyday lives. The openness that can be fostered at the beginning of the academic year is well worth developing early, because it facilitates the teacher's understanding of individual children. Understanding is important for building relationships that help the children feel secure and through which they can be helped to explore their classroom environment with confidence.

Visits to Places of Interest

Some advance planning is desirable if it is appropriate to arrange a field trip to a place of interest, a walk around the school neighborhood, to a local store, or to a farm. It is usually a good idea for the teacher to visit a site before taking the children to it. Information obtained by phone or mail rarely provides enough detail to serve as a basis for preparing the children for a productive class visit. When the teacher makes an initial visit, she is likely to see points of interest in all kinds of unanticipated places. Consider, for example, visiting a park to gain firsthand appreciation of the opportunities it offers to people living in the neighborhood. In addition to what the teacher already knows about the park, a preliminary visit may yield useful information related to the interests of her own class. For instance, one group of children will appreciate the patterns in the wrought-iron gate at the entrance to the park; another group might prefer to read the signs on the trees and walls; and one or two individuals may want to spend most of the time studying the birds on the pond.

The staff of a department store, railway station, or clinic may find it difficult to visualize in advance the invasion of 20 young children. The teacher can help allay their anxiety and promote their understanding of what she hopes the children will gain from the experience. When a visitor comes to talk to the children in school, it may also be important for the teacher to explain in advance what she expects the children to gain and what they will be like. When given the opportunity to question a policeman who had finished speaking, one young child felt compelled to tell the man about his aunt's parrot that had just died, not quite appreciating the role of the police in relation to such small-scale disasters.

SUMMARY

Throughout the period of initial planning, teachers find it useful to identify the key events that might occur in the life of the project, for example, a visit, a speaker, displays, central activities to be undertaken by individuals or groups, products of the work undertaken, and a culminating event to draw the work to a close. These events are described in some detail in Chapters 6, 7, and 8. Once the preliminary planning has been undertaken, teachers can implement the project during the phase we call "Getting Projects Started: Phase I."

7

Phase I: Getting Projects Started

The organization of project work into three sequential phases helps teachers and children to identify the main tasks as they unfold, and to deepen the sense of direction and purposefulness of the work. In this way, projects can easily be thought of as having a beginning, middle, and ending phase—as do stories—with each having its own special value. As indicated in previous chapters, Phase I includes introducing and clarifying the topic and sub-topics to be investigated, sharing experiences and knowledge related to it, and specifying the list of questions to be investigated.

Some projects claim the children's interest from the first minutes; others require more effort from the teacher. Not all children will be equally interested in all topics. However, the way the teacher introduces the topic can be an important factor in determining how the project progresses and what is achieved. In this chapter, we discuss various ways of enlisting children's interest and participation when launching a project in Phase I. We begin by considering ways of involving children during the preliminary discussions in the earliest stages. Next, we describe types of activities that are particularly appropriate for getting projects started. These are followed by suggestions for involving parents.

ENGAGING CHILDREN'S INTEREST

Children's attention and interest are easily aroused by the new and the unexpected. This is especially true when they can relate the new to something they already know.

A brick, some mortar, a detached faucet, or a doorknob can raise interest immediately, because they look strange when detached from the houses in which children live and other familiar locations. Similarly, objects that children may have seen only from a distance, for instance, a wheelbarrow, a bicycle, or a sewing machine, can offer much to observe and talk about. Entirely new objects such as an oar from a rowboat, a beehive, or a blood-pressure gauge are also intriguing. The culture of the classroom where projects are undertaken encourages children to be curious about new things or familiar objects in new contexts.

Pictures can often provide a good stimulus for discussion and interest, especially if they are related to the objects presented. For instance, items of house construction might be accompanied by pictures of builders, plumbers, or electricians at work. Medical equipment might be shown in a picture-story sequence of a sick child going to a hospital for treatment and getting well again. A brief slide show can also be a good introductory stimulus, especially if there are plenty of opportunities to follow up on children's questions after the show.

When the project being introduced follows other previous projects, the children can be reminded of relevant events and experiences that had been particularly enjoyable. They might look forward to similar occasions in connection with the new project. The sense of a common group history strengthens the sense of community, and the teacher can do much to encourage this in simple, incidental ways. For example, a study of the neighborhood may include a walk around the streets close to the school. The teacher might remind the children how interesting they had found their walk to the supermarket earlier in the year during the project on buying food.

INTRODUCTORY DISCUSSION

The initial discussion should make a strong impression on the children. It is a good idea to present them with something arresting and engaging, arousing their curiosity and inviting interest. The teacher might tell a story from personal experience related to the topic, and one or more related objects might be displayed or passed around. Open discussion about the topic reveals the degree of familiarity the children already have with the topic. Their views, interests, and comments about particular items are welcomed.

In the early class discussions, teachers will find it useful to let children recount events in their own experience of the topic. For instance, in a hospital project, many of the children will be able to talk about their own accidents that resulted in a visit to the hospital. Helm, Beneke, and Steinheimer (1998) describe the beginning of an elaborate, indepth study of the mail system undertaken by a group of 3- and 4-year-olds arising from listening to a story entitled *A Letter to Amy* (Keats, 1968), which tells of a boy named Peter sending a letter to a girl named Amy. After having listened to the story several times, the teacher engaged the children in a discussion about how the letter might get from Peter to Amy. The discussion revealed to the teacher the extent of the children's knowledge, experience, understandings, and misunderstandings of the mail system and provoked their interest in learning more about it and developing one for their own school. The project involved all the children in the class over a period of six weeks (see Part III in Helm, Beneke, and Steinheimer [1998] for a full description of the project.)

The initial discussions of most topics usually generate script knowledge—knowledge about sequences of events leading to a goal—which many children will use spontaneously in their dramatic play. Children can also be encouraged to talk about their play and their use of the equipment. As they articulate their need for some new prop, such as a bag for the mailman to carry letters in, or a stethoscope or bandages in an investigation of the hospital, the teacher can encourage them to design and make what they need or to acquire real items.

At the beginning of a project, the children's enthusiasm is easily aroused. It is therefore important that enthusiasm be kept at an optimum level to avoid setting expectations that might not be met. Undertaking a project is a serious matter, and steady application on the children's part is required to achieve much of the work planned. Indeed, as we have suggested in Chapter 2, project work provides contexts for strengthening important intellectual dispositions, such as to become involved in sustained effort, to seek information, to make predictions, to test hypotheses, and to share findings.

In the initial discussion, the children should be invited to think about the project and aspects of the topic they want to explore and learn more about. The teacher and the children can think of items they might collect from home to display on walls and horizontal surfaces. Over the following few days, the children can be encouraged to volunteer or sign up for which parts of the work they would like to undertake.

During these early discussions, the teacher finds out the language and behavioral knowledge at the children's disposal for talking about relevant experiences. She learns what children can already say about the topic and where they might have difficulty expressing their ideas and questions. Sometimes clear misunderstandings and conflicting impressions are exposed, leading to animated exchanges among the children. The teacher should not be too ready to correct children in the group situation, since this may inhibit participation in the discussion. Instead, the teacher's approach at this point might be to draw their attention to the opportunities they will have to find out more and to clarify their understandings.

Throughout the first week or more of a project, the children can reflect on their experiences of the topic and share what they have experienced with the other members of the class. This sharing requires the children to first reflect on and represent their experiences in some way. They can tell stories, write, draw pictures, label drawings, make paintings or collages, make clay models, construct with blocks, roleplay, and so on.

Older children can also research each other's experience through interviewing each other and doing surveys to find out about each other's experiences. This research of their classmates involves children in rehearsing interview techniques, taking notes, data collection, and representation of the groups experience in graphs and charts of various kinds.

The teacher's role is to support the use of a variety of investigative and representational strategies. He or she also has a special responsibility to probe the children to reflect on their experiences and explain them. As children explain their experiences, they develop theories about how and why things are the way they remember them. Up to this point in a project a great deal of interest can be aroused in the topic because the children are the experts. They know what they have experienced and they reflect on what they know.

Throughout this process, they wonder about the different experiences and explanations their classmates offer. The teacher's ethnographer role extends to coordinating the work produced so that the children can all become aware of what has been learned and can appreciate a collective baseline understanding, which can be the foundation of the collaborative research process ahead of them in the second phase of the project. During the initial discussions, the teacher can suggest activities, some of them to be undertaken by individuals and others by small groups working together. Suitable activities are discussed below.

ACTIVITIES FOR EARLY STAGES OF EXTENDED PROJECTS

When a project with older children is planned to last for several weeks, there is time to allow for qualitative change in the activities as the work develops. For the younger children, relatively unstructured activities are most helpful to the teacher in assessing the children's prior understanding during Phase I. Dramatic play, painting, drawing, and, for older ones, writing from memory about personal experiences related to the topic are suggested activities. Each of these is discussed in turn below.

Dramatic Play

If the classroom does not have a dramatic play area, it would be a good idea to start one. A square of inexpensive carpet or matting can be laid in a corner of the room to delimit a small area. A three-sided screen with a door in one side and a window in another can also be placed there (Figure 7.1). Because it is flexible, this basic arrangement can become a farmhouse, a hospital, a hot-air balloon basket, a camper, or a boat. The teacher and children can discuss how to prepare the play area for a suitable topic related to dramatic play. The children are likely to be very interested in the transformation of the area from one project to the next. It is a good idea to encourage the children during these discussions to make suggestions to each other; not all the children's questions, comments, and suggestions have to be direct-

FIGURE 7.1.   Room arrangement options

ed to the teacher. Discussions involved in project work are ideal contexts in which to encourage the habit of child–child interaction; during group meetings, children learn to listen to each other's ideas and suggestions rather than just sit and wait until it is their turn to talk to the teacher, ignoring other children's contributions.

For the present discussion, the theater term *props* is used to refer to objects that the teacher introduces to enrich dramatic play. Dramatic play is particularly enhanced if the children have real objects as props. The children's understanding of events is reflected in the way they use the objects that are part of those events. Props also enable the children to replay the sequence of events that takes place in the real world, for example, to roleplay the scripts related to hospital events, shopping in a store, or buying stamps at the post office. It seems best to provide familiar props during the first phase of the project so that the children can easily explore their associations with the topic. As project work progresses, less familiar and completely novel objects can be added. To illustrate the points made above, let us look at the hospital project. The play area can become a hospital with a row of dolls in cribs, a child-sized cot, a chair, a dresser, and a sink. Props can include plastic medicine bottles, an arm sling, and bandages. It is a good idea to add steadily to the props throughout the life of the project. Later additions may include X-ray pictures displayed against a window, a sturdy thermometer, patient charts, a stopwatch, a bed pan, a wash basin, nurse and doctor uniforms, and various doctor's instruments. The quality of the play changes across the three phases of the project, and the functions fulfilled by the props become increasingly useful in refining and elaborating children's understanding.

From observations of children at play, the teacher can identify understandings and misunderstandings. The following examples of misunderstandings have been reported: "The doctor makes you better when he puts the thermometer in your mouth" and "I'm going to be a doctor when I grow up, because then I'll never get ill." Such revelations can provide information that can be used to clarify understandings in later group discussion.

Children have to accept certain conventions or precautionary rules about not putting things in their mouths, not using large instruments near their faces, having no more than six children playing in the hospital at one time, and the like. Such rules are usually readily accepted when the reasons for the precautions are given. Some rules can be generated by the children themselves to solve problems that emerge during their play.

Drawing, Painting, and Writing

Because various kinds of art media and writing are important ways of representing and communicating understandings, teachers can encourage children to apply these skills in project work. The effectiveness of communication can best be judged in relation to the people to whom the message is addressed. Project work can offer opportunities for children to communicate with their coworkers in small groups, with the whole class group, the teacher, parents, and with children in other classes.

Bulletin boards can be used to document different aspects of the project so that the children can see the story of their own work. The teacher can ask the children to suggest where and how their experience and their work should be displayed. She can also use many opportunities to draw children's attention to items on display. She can ensure that some aspects of the display change frequently so that the children continue to notice what is there (see Helm, Beneke, & Steinheimer, 1998).

Children can work individually or collaboratively in preparing documentation and reports of their work. For example, a group might construct a "wall story," which is an illustrated sequence of events depicted in paintings and writing. The story might be about a child who has an accident and goes to the hospital for treatment. This is another representation of a script. It can be displayed near the play area so that the children can refer to it in their dramatic play. For example, a dispute about the order of events arose among some children playing in the class hospital. Together they consulted the events depicted in the wall story to settle the dispute. In that case, the disposition to resolve disagreements by checking "the facts" can be expressed and satisfied.

Children will be able to draw and paint pictures of the events they remember from their own experience of an illness or an accident. In one class, the teacher found that all of the children had a story of some sort to tell about how they had hurt themselves. She suggested that they write and draw their stories and collect them in a book called "Accident Stories." In this way, children can read about the real things that have happened to them.

ENCOURAGING THE PARTICIPATION OF PARENTS

Parents can be involved in project work in at least four ways. First, because the topics of projects are likely to be familiar to the parents, they can easily discuss their own experience and knowledge with the children. For instance, children can ask their parents whether they have been to the hospital. A kindergarten class studying bicycles collected stories from their parents about bicycle accidents they recalled from their early experiences. In a study called "Water in Our Houses," kindergartners asked parents to show where the water is heated in their homes. Children and their parents can be encouraged to communicate about the real world. Some teachers particularly welcome the opportunity to speak to parents as a group about their intentions for children's project work during the year. In this way, they can prepare parents for the children's requests for information and other contributions to the project.

Second, parents can be encouraged to ask their children how the project is progressing, what activities they are undertaking, and about their findings so far. Often, parents find it difficult to obtain intelligible replies to questions about what their children are doing in school, especially in some areas of the curriculum. In project work, however, the teacher can help the children talk about their work at home by suggesting events and aspects of the work to discuss with their parents. In so doing, the teacher establishes communication and accountability with parents. Communication gives the children an additional opportunity to practice the new language they are learning in school. Parents also learn about aspects of the curriculum associated with the application of skills and the development of dispositions that are likely to help the child work well in school. Certain skills and dispositions in particular are generally less well understood, for example, the dispositions to persist in the face of difficulty and to vary the problem-solving strategies when first attempts fail. Documentation of such experiences can help further the parents' and community's appreciation for the role of dispositions in a wide variety of achievements.

Third, the parents can be very helpful in providing information, pictures, books, and objects to help the whole class in its pursuit of knowledge on the topic. Sometimes a parent who is a doctor or a nurse is willing to talk to the children during a health-related project. A father who is a mail carrier may come and talk about his work and bring some items from the post office. Parents can assist in arranging a visit to a factory, a farm, or a store. As part of project work, the children can write letters home asking for specific information such as common childhood diseases they have had and at what ages. For a project on babies, the children may find out when they cut their first teeth or learned to walk unaided.

Fourth, at a later stage of the project, parents might be invited to come and see the work the children have been doing. Each child can guide his or her parents around the display areas, and the class can perform a song or put on a small play on the topic that they have written about. Such visits help parents gain confidence in the school and in their own contribution to the child's continuing informal education at home. Parents can thus feel involved in an important part of their children's school life.

THE CLOSE OF PHASE I

The first phase usually ends with a clear and shared sense of what kinds of investigations are planned. This would include an agreed-upon set of initial questions that are going to be answered with a variety of strategies.

Many teachers learning to implement the project approach with young children have reported having difficulty getting the children to nominate research questions to be answered in Phase 2. Indeed, for many preschoolers and kindergartners, their most common school experience is of being asked questions rather than posing them—though throughout the second and third years of their lives, questioning adults and others is one of their common characteristics!

Teachers can help children regain their dispositions to pose questions by engaging them in discussions on the project topic by asking the children to talk about such things as:

a) what they want look at more closely;
b) what they want the visiting expert to talk about, tell them, or show them;
c) what they want to know more about; and
d) what parts of an object they want to draw in detail, or want photographed.

Discussions around these topics encourage children to discuss their questions and predictions. During such discussions, the teacher can then say something like "I see, so one question you want to get answers to is...," And thus rephrase the child's expressed interest in what she or he want the visitor to talk about.

One of the best ways to get questions asked is to explore current experience. Take the example of a project on the topic of the seashore. As teacher and children explore the things they have personally experienced, such as ocean beaches or creatures you can find on the beach or in rock pools, the teacher will find the children have gaps in their knowledge and some incomplete or erroneous ideas about crabs, shells, or fish. As these become apparent in the discussion, it is possible for the teacher to question the children with a view to helping them clarify their thinking on a topic.

It may be very important early on in a discussion not to tell the children they've got it wrong or to give them information. First comes a time of speculation and theory exploration. It is a time for the teacher to take an ethnographic role, with a genuine interest in finding out what is in the children's minds and helping them to construct a common or agreed basic understanding. This may be a very inadequate one. If you live in a landlocked state or province, the children will have even wilder or more primitive ideas about crabs. The topic in this case may not be such a useful choice. If you live near the ocean, however, some children will know a lot compared with others.

This early discussion can be livelier if the teacher, as the lead thinker, models how it is to think about and review past experience. The teacher might say how she found her first hermit crab and what she observed. Then there is usually a child who will want to join in and tell about his/her experience, then another child, and so on. The aim at first can be just to get the children keen to talking about the topic from their own experience or even from their own speculation. Then, as the discussion becomes more animated and richer in detail, the teacher can help the children formulate some questions about what they might need to know more about and who might be able to help them find out more.

If the teacher starts out questioning the class, it is easy for the children to think that the culture of the classroom is such that teachers question and children are supposed to answer. If, by contrast, you start by telling a personal experience, they will be drawn to share their personal experiences. Children need some modeling to follow at first. The teacher can also model "wondering." "When I think of that hermit crab I first saw I wonder if it was trying to get back into the water. I wonder how long they stay out on the sand. Perhaps I should ask someone who knows. I should ask a question." Then the teacher would make one up with the children. It may sound as though it could be a little laborious when described like this, but it isn't really. The children often all want to chip in and help with the discussion.

SUMMARY

Observation of children at play and at work can inform the teacher of their under-standings and misunderstandings. She can also learn about the children's preoccu-pations or concerns, such as mothers going into the hospital to have babies. Sometimes children play out anxieties that can be shared and alleviated. Children may also develop interests in some part of the topic through their play. An interest in the heart or bones can be followed up by reference to books, observations of a lamb's heart, pictures, X-rays, and so forth.

Toward the end of the first phase and the beginning of the second, the teacher can look back at her web plan of the project and evaluate different parts of it in light of what she has learned about the children so far. By the end of the first phase, a field trip will have been arranged or maybe a visitor planned. The teacher then can begin to prepare the children for this event by talking with them about the kinds of things they can expect to see and learn. The preparations should also include chil-dren volunteering or accepting responsibility for sketching particular aspects of the site to be visited, and for posing which questions on their list to which persons they will interview on the site.

8

Phase II:
Projects in Progress

The main thrust of the second phase of a project is field work, that is, seeking answers to the questions formulated at the end of Phase I. In this way, Phase II consists of a variety of ways of gathering data and gaining new information. In this chapter, we discuss preparations for field work and the types of activity typically included in Phase II to help obtain and organize the data gathered by the children. A selection of activities that children can undertake in pursuit of a fuller understanding of the topic is discussed, together with opportunities to practice skills and encourage desirable dispositions. The products of children's work are discussed and how they can be used to reflect learning and stimulate further questions. We also suggest ways the teacher might support the children's continued interest in the project, extend the challenges for more able children, and structure special opportunities for children with learning or motivational difficulties.

PREPARATIONS FOR FIELD WORK

When the children have agreed on the main research questions at the end of Phase I, a discussion about possible places to visit and visitors to invite begins the second phase. At this point, children can volunteer to work in small groups on specific subtopics. The teacher may then organize focal events such as a field trip or a number of appropriate visiting experts. These events can provide important sources of questions, information, and ideas of interest to the children. Group discussions are a valuable way to prepare children for a new experience and to debrief them afterward by helping them to share their understandings of new information.

Group Discussions

Discussions with the whole class and with smaller groups working on specified subtopics have both informative and motivational functions. At the beginning of the project, discussions enable the children to share what they as individuals know about the topic, and they enable the teacher to explore the children's present understandings. In the second phase, discussions have several additional functions: to prepare the children for field work, for classroom visitors, or other focal events; to help children refine their questions for investigations; to plan group learning activities; to evaluate what has been accomplished; to talk about the work being undertaken and how it is progressing; and to plan the next steps and other future work. In discussions, the teacher helps the children share the thoughts and experiences they are having, thus promoting the community ethos in which the work will thrive as she sets expectations and directs activities.

One of the most important aspects of preparation for field work is to come to a clear understanding and agreement concerning what the whole group and each of the subgroups want to find out about the topic. The teacher guides a discussion of the questions to be answered. Some teachers find it helpful to make a chart in which the agreed-upon questions are listed and the children's predictions of what the answers will be are also listed. A column is provided for them to fill in when they have collected their data. The children can be encouraged to challenge each other's predictions and indeed, to list a number of plausible predictions in the chart. As this discussion of questions and predictions proceeds, the teacher can ask those who offer predictions to share the bases on which they are making them. This kind of interested and positive probing can stimulate the disposition to reflect on the bases of one's own reasoning in general.

Young children's discussions are most likely to be fruitful when they have interesting and mind-engaging content. When they feel involved with the content, there is less need to repeat the rules of hand raising, turn taking, and careful listening. Children will listen to others because they want to hear what is being said. The teacher's talk can consist of comments as well as questions, and children can be encouraged to inter-

TABLE 8.1.
Questions, Predictions, and Findings about the Construction Site

Questions	Predictions	Findings
1. How long does it take to build a house?	2 weeks	3 or 4 months
2. How many doors will each house have?	5	13
3. How many bedrooms will the house have?	10	4

act with each other so that not all of the conversation directly involves the teacher. One way to encourage such "cross-child" discussion is for the teacher to ask the children to make suggestions to another group's plans, or to offer answers to classmates' questions. So, for example, in a class doing a project on a construction site, the group in the class that has elected to collect data on the types of building materials used, children in other groups studying other subtopics (for example, kinds of workers, types of rooms being built, and so on) can ask of them to be sure to include questions they also want answered. As the work in the second phase progresses and debriefing discussions of the progress being made are held, the teacher can take opportunities to encourage children pose questions to each other and to encourage, and even to congratulate, each other on what is being accomplished. If the teacher asks questions in turn of each group or of each child, and the children only answer her directly and are not encouraged to exchange questions and suggestions with each other, it is likely that they will tune out of the whole process as soon as their "turn" to talk is over.

The teacher can also take notes at these discussions and turn children's attention to their own earlier ideas and comments by rereading to them what they had said and ask them of their further thinking on the subject. In this way, the teacher can provide a model of an interested listener for the children. Her comments on the children's talk also model appropriate replies and reflections on what another person says in a conversation.

Some teachers report that they find it difficult to get young children to pose questions. It may be that asking the youngest children if they have any questions leaves them a bit confused about what is expected. However, if the teacher asks the children, for example, before a expert is due to visit their class, "What would you like the veterinarian to talk about?" or "What would you like the bicycle mechanic to tell you about or to show you?", then the children are more likely to come up with items that can be cast as research questions.

Sources of Information

In projects for the youngest children in our age range, the main field work is obtaining information by means of first hand, direct observation and experience. It also includes looking things up, gaining ideas, and copying words and diagrams from relevant books. With increasing age and the greater skillfulness in using various media, the sources of information can be expanded to include both direct primary sources as well as secondary ones. Primary sources include field work in real settings, observations of events and activities, work at an actual construction site to be observed, the operations of various machines related to the topic, or the goods delivery section of a supermarket. Interviewing people who have direct experience of aspects of the topic also provides information about other people's firsthand experiences. Secondary sources of information such as books, magazines, newspapers, relevant educational films, videotapes, brochures and pamphlets, and websites accessed via the Internet can be examined at this time as well.

FIELD TRIPS

Young children collectively can be interested in almost every imaginable aspect of a trip outside the school. Few details escape their notice if the teacher, together with the children, has made clear the expectations for the main purpose of the trip. The teacher can encourage awareness of the more routine aspects of the visit, such as arrangements for transport, meals, and groupings of children with particular adults. These routine aspects give the children practice in classifying, counting, and representing, pictorially and symbolically, the events of the day.

For example, older children can write descriptively in the following manner: "There were twenty-seven children and five adults on our bus. This was thirty-two people from our school and thirty-three people altogether with the driver. The bus had forty seats for passengers, so eight seats were empty." Inevitably, the children will be interested in the mode of transport and the food, and these interests can provide useful opportunities for teaching and learning. Of course, the teacher can also draw the children's attention to features of the trip that are pertinent to the main work of the project. The younger children can dictate their impressions for the teacher to record.

Some teachers find it useful to have the older children take notebooks or clipboards for making notes and sketching interesting items they see. Usually it is preferable to leave such on-the-spot recording open-ended. When the teacher supplies a checklist of items to look for or a list of questions to answer, children can be distracted by the "treasure hunt" quality in these activities. Instead, if she suggests only a few things to look for, the children can observe them closely and with interest rather than compete with each other to discover items on a common list.

Younger children's attention can be drawn to people or objects, their functions, how they work, and how they relate to other objects or people. The grouping of objects on the basis of common characteristics and their differentiation from other kinds of objects requires children to observe closely. Analytical discussion is encouraged, and later on in the classroom, the teacher can help the children represent their observations in various ways through pictures, charts, and writing.

Consider, for instance, a visit to a clinic. The children are likely to see a thermometer, blood-pressure gauge, and a stethoscope, all of which are instruments for diagnosing what is wrong with a sick person. The children are also likely to see surgical scissors, a hypodermic syringe, and forceps, which are used to treat a person once the problem is diagnosed. After the visit, a discussion can lead to the distinction between the two sets of instruments. The children's understandings of the two sets and how they overlap can be represented pictorially in a Venn diagram of two overlapping sets (Figure 8.1). The inclusive class of objects is labeled "instruments," and the distinction between the subsets is based on the difference between the functions of diagnosis and treatment. A small flashlight might be used for both. Children's labeled drawings can be grouped appropriately in the diagram, which can be displayed with a child's written commentary about the information summa-

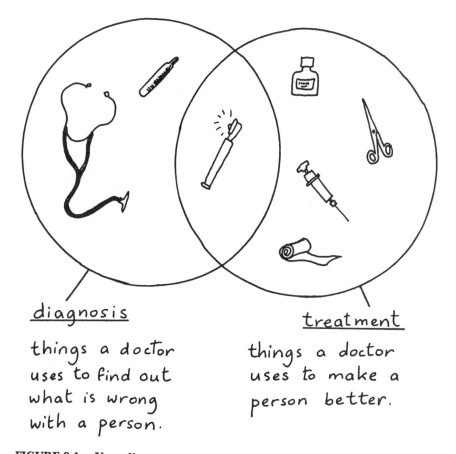

FIGURE 8.1. Venn diagram to represent two intersecting sets of objects.

rized in the diagram. Other children might write questions that can be answered by referring to the diagram: "Which instrument is used for both diagnosis and treatment?," "Which is the smallest instrument used for treatment?," or "Which instruments made of glass are used in diagnosis?"

If a museum is being visited, the children may be able to separate into groups, each with a particular interest to follow. Each group of maybe four or five children should be supervised by an adult who need not be a teacher. Parent volunteers can be briefed by the teacher to encourage observation and recording and to talk with the children about what they are seeing. Back at school, each group can report what they saw and noted. When children share with others who did not see the same things, there is a clear purpose to their communication, and the other children can be encouraged to ask questions to clarify their understanding.

Using illustrated books, the children can elaborate on their own sketches and fill out descriptions. More questions can be asked and answers sought. Often, new information leads children to ask more questions in school after the visit. If the museum is local, some children who visit it regularly with their families may be willing to make a weekend trip there to gather additional information needed. Otherwise, the children can write to the museum after a visit to clarify points that may arise back in the classroom.

Interest is strengthened when the topic is treated in the kind of depth made possible by direct experience of real-world settings. For instance, the mathematical skills of comparing, sorting, classifying, and ordering, which are often acquired and practiced in artificial and disembedded settings, can be applied to project work when the children study an item of real interest to them. Studying the parts of an ambulance, for instance, may lead to a comparison of the materials in it: metal, plastic, wood, and fabric. The substances that make the engine work—gasoline, oil, water, and air—can be compared in various ways according to their function.

If the teacher cannot take the children outside the school to visit an appropriate site, an expert may be invited to visit and bring objects or pictures to leave on loan to the class. Sometimes when it is impossible to go outside the school for direct firsthand experience, something can be arranged within the school building or on school grounds. In the walk around the school described in Appendix H, children can study the items they collect on the way. Another alternative is to ask the school janitor to accompany the children on a tour of the school, showing them where the materials and equipment used to clean and maintain the building are kept. They might then make a plan of the school building. If school meals are cooked on the premises, the children can see what is involved and observe the people who do the work. Above all, the point of a field trip is firsthand experience. If it can be provided any other way, it can compensate for not going out on a visit.

ACTIVITIES FOR LEARNING

As the project progresses, children can undertake a wide variety of activities, which are discussed here under three headings: construction, investigation, and dramatic play. We also discuss various ways that children can apply the basic academic skills of language (talking, reading, and writing), mathematics, and science to each of these types of activities.

Construction Activities

As children build models, they ask questions about design and construction. The models can be made of junk material, clay, and wood, as well as from construction toys, kits, or other materials. Children can talk about what to include in their model; for example, they can discuss the parts of the ambulance, both outside and inside.

They can talk about the problems they are solving as they construct the model—how to fasten the wheels on, the scale of the model, and how to fit all of the necessary items inside. Finally, they can discuss the finishing touches, such as the red cross and the lights, to complete the model to their satisfaction.

Basic skills, language arts, and mathematics are applied in activities related to the construction. These activities are enriched when the children can read about the ambulance, for instance, in books and study detailed pictures of it and its functioning. The writing of older children about the object they are constructing may be of two kinds. First, they can report how they made the model and describe the materials, strategies, and techniques that failed and succeeded. This writing might be collected in a class book about model construction or displayed alongside the model itself. Second, the children can write about events involving the ambulance: a journey to pick up a sick person in an emergency, an accident, or the life and work of an ambulance driver. This writing might form part of a display showing different aspects of the work of the hospital.

In mathematics, many activities related to the construction of the ambulance can be undertaken. Parts have to be measured to fit together, and relationships of width, length, and height can be considered. Some mathematical understanding can add depth to the construction of the dashboard, with its dials and gauges.

Investigation Activities

The primary purpose of investigation activities is to find out information. After being introduced to the topic, children who have gained confidence in what they already know about it can be encouraged to go further, in order to find out new information, to build on their basic understandings. New places and objects can be explored, and questions can be asked. The teacher can help extend the children's repertoire of active investigation strategies. In the classroom, children can hypothesize, estimate, and experiment. For example, in a study of the manufacture of clothing, children can find out about different fabrics by designing a test to compare fabrics for insulation or waterproofing efficiency. They can try to simulate some of the processes involved in producing fabric for clothing by growing, collecting, and cleaning cotton, wool, or linen. They can try spinning, dyeing, or weaving yarn or thread to make cloth.

Receptive strategies that children can use to investigate a topic include observing, listening to an expert, watching someone at work, and reading. Observation involves looking closely at objects, handling them, and maybe using other senses. Instruments used by doctors, tools used by builders or plumbers, and equipment used by cooks can all be studied closely, and the cause-and-effect relations implicit in their use can be noted—for example, the shape of the parts of a stethoscope for picking up and transmitting sounds, a syringe for injecting, and a hospital bed with mattress, pillows, headrest, and a progress chart for accommodating a patient.

Observations can be set up over a period of time so that changes can be noted, measured, and recorded. Growing plants in the classroom offers such opportunities, as do studies of the weather, animals, and birds outside the classroom window. Recording observations in drawings, writing, and tallies enables children to reflect on the learning involved in the observation. This can be further represented in mappings, charts, and graphs.

Investigation can often be motivated by construction activities. The older the children, the greater their concern with realism in their constructions; for example, the relative height, width, and length of the ambulance being built may become significant.

Dramatic Play

Dramatic play can be stimulated after a field trip by adding new props such as X-ray photographs and patients' progress charts. New scripts can be learned, such as visiting a sick friend in the hospital; going there to have a baby, an operation, or a broken bone set after an accident; and the roles of doctors and nurses in these scenarios. New understandings of the functions of objects and people are reflected, and new misunderstandings noticed and clarified.

Dramatic play in the second phase involves trying out new information in context. Children rehearse the new understandings embedded in situations, which they can be helped to imagine through accounts and stories, thus making their own best sense of the topic. Roleplaying activities can lead directly to questions. Children may want to know the journeys typically made by the ambulance in the area or in a given period of time. According to the age and understanding of the children, such investigation provides opportunities for work on direction, time, speed, and distance. In studying the work of the ambulance driver, the children might chart or map the places the driver goes in one day to pick people up or take them home or to another hospital. The ambulance driver may also have considerable training in first aid to offer emergency help such as giving oxygen or carefully positioning a person with a broken limb on a stretcher.

Products of Work

The work that the children produce may include pictures, pieces of writing, charts, graphs, models, and board games. These products can be stored in personal folders or mounted in individual books. They can be displayed in a class book focusing on one aspect of the project. They can be displayed on vertical and horizontal surfaces such as walls, windows, tables, and shelves. Children's work displayed under subthemes or particular aspects of the project serves various functions for the teacher and the individual child, as well as for the whole class.

The wide range of task complexity usually accompanying project work offers very able children an excellent opportunity to undertake challenging tasks suitable to their ability. Likewise, it offers an interesting selection of important but much simpler tasks for children who have learning difficulties. Teachers can help structure the tasks and advise individuals about how to apply their skills to maximum effect. This strategy is likely to strengthen children's motivation to collaborate with other children as they are able without fear of being shown less competent. The following example illustrates this point.

A small group of children were working together on a picture of an ambulance. They wanted to display it with strings running from different parts of the vehicle to word labels around the outside of the picture. Two children wrote the labels, one measured and cut suitable lengths of string, and the third pinned the strings in place. The child who pinned the strings would have had great difficulty writing the labels, but his contribution was valued because he performed a necessary task. At the same time, he improved his reading ability while matching the words and objects.

CLASSROOM DISPLAYS

Display areas devoted to the project can be major focal points for classroom-based activity as the work develops. During the first phase of the project, displays give children the opportunity to collect, sort, represent, and share current understandings of a limited range of relevant items. As the project progresses, the emphasis shifts to three other functions of display: (1) to provide information that the children can refer to in their work and play; (2) to reflect the children's growing experience of the project and show a developing record or diary of the work; and (3) to communicate the children's discoveries and achievements to particular audiences (their own teacher and classmates, other teachers and classes, the principal or head teacher, parents, or any other visitors to the school).

During the second phase of the project, these functions of display become still more important. Each function is discussed below.

Displays for Information

Displays are most informative when they include key words for children to use in their writing. In this way, they serve as a specialized glossary or word book. The children can compile an alphabetical list for reference, in addition to the easy-to-see labels of objects on display (all letters should be lowercase for young children). Pictures, photographs, reference books, maps, charts, and a small selection of commercially produced material can be displayed for information. Children's own pictures and writing can also be informative, as well as imaginative or reflective. Various pictorial and symbolic representations are undertaken specifically to present discoveries in an organized form that enables easy retrieval of facts by other children needing the information.

Bar graphs can present frequency information. Venn diagrams provide a mapping of information in sets of objects that have some similarity or are parts of wholes. The same set of objects that are parts of a thing can be classified into subsets according to different attributes. For instance, an ambulance has parts made of metal, rubber, glass, wood, plastic, and fabric. These same parts can be classified differently according to whether they are part of the transport function of the ambulance or the health emergency function of it. As the children gain experience in analyzing items in project work, they are more likely to suggest ways of their own for presenting information to others. When tasks differ from child to child, achievements should be shared so that the new understandings can benefit other members of the group. An informative display is particularly interesting when it depicts things that the onlookers have not personally experienced, but that they can easily assimilate in terms of what they already know.

Displays as a Record

The second function of displays during the second and third phases of the project is to provide a record of the life of the work as it develops. The contributions of individual children and cooperating groups provide a growing source of information about the achievement of the class. The teacher uses this record to reflect back to the children the progress they are making in their investigations. The children become familiar with the displays and take pride in their own and each other's work. In doing so, they are motivated to assimilate the new information where it enriches what they already know. They are also motivated to rework and accommodate their understanding to information that conflicts with their earlier concepts.

The shared and public meaning of things is given due status by display. The evidence of the children's work around the classroom is formally useful throughout the life of the project as a record of the achievement of the class for the teacher, the principal or head teacher, the parents, and other interested parties.

Displays to Communicate to Outsiders

The third function of displays is to offer children a place to communicate what they would like to tell others about their work. This function overlaps with the record-keeping function. It is, however, different in a very fundamental way. When displays are used as a record, some of the charts and observations children make are part of their investigation of an object or event. In contrast, when displays are intended for others, children sometimes write a description of their own work and what it adds to their personal understanding of the topic. They can write for older or younger children in another class. They may develop a quiz or a series of questions that can be answered by referring to a graph or to a mapping of groups of items.

To return to the ambulance example, a quiz for older children might include this question: "What is the largest thing that is made of rubber and is part of the health emergency function of an ambulance?" And for younger children: "What is the smallest metal instrument used by a doctor in finding out what is wrong with a patient?"

One of the best ways a person can be sure of understanding something is to try explaining it to someone else. When explaining things, we have to put ourselves in the mind of the other person and predict what we will need to say or write to ensure understanding (Benware & Deci, 1984). Children can write captions for graphs and diagrams that explain to other children how to extract information, or they can write or dictate to the teacher instructions for games. Children can also design and make simple board games for two players on some aspect of a project.

For the hospital project, they might design a dice and track game where some of the squares or positions on the track represent getting sick or having an accident, while other squares represent possible remedies or help from medical personnel. Setbacks for patients can be indicated by the instruction to "miss a turn" and positive gains by the instruction to "take another turn." On a different topic, one group of children explained their playground games in writing so that others who had never played these games could learn by following the rules. Another group tried them out and offered ideas for improving the instructions.

THE TEACHER'S ROLE

The scene is set for the project during the first phase, when the teacher evaluates the children's levels of understanding and interest in the project. In the second phase, the class revises and enriches their understandings on the basis of firsthand experience through visiting an appropriate location, looking closely at objects, discussing real events, and talking with people who are involved with the setting being studied. The teacher orchestrates the learning events, shaping the overall outcome of the project. Some of the activities the children can be engaged in are painstaking and slow-moving, others spontaneous and short-lived. Some play is open and free, other activity highly structured and focused.

In this second phase, the teacher is strengthening the children's dispositions to be resourceful, independent, imaginative, involved, cooperative, and productive. The timing of when to provide resources is related to activities the children can undertake, optimizing interest where possible. Timing is important in maintaining the momentum and depth of the work. The following is an example of judicious timing in a study of two tortoises.

During the project's first phase, lasting one week, the children observed and recorded the physical parts and attributes, activity, food intake, and behavior of one female tortoise. In the second phase, lasting two weeks, a male tortoise was introduced. The children then made a comparison study of the two animals, reviewing their understandings of the female and comparing in detail the female with the male. Thus, the study had two purposes: (1) finding out about one tortoise and (2) comparing two tortoises. Had the teacher introduced the two tortoises at the same time, the amount of interest would have been halved, since activities that were repeated with a new purpose would have been undertaken only once with both purposes lumped together. Repetition is a valuable way of learning, but its efficiency may be reduced by boredom when an experience is presented in the form of practice tasks.

We do not wish to suggest that the activities described in this chapter usually happen spontaneously in work on projects. They do not. However, the teacher can use many ways to help children pursue construction, investigation, and dramatic play. Children can be encouraged to ask questions and think about the possibility of alternative answers. They can be helped to see how observation can lead to questions, which in turn can lead to experiments. They can be taught how records of observations can be translated into reports of discovered information. Children can gain personal satisfaction from increasing their competence. They can appreciate the products of their efforts, as these contribute to a record of the learning of the whole class. The teacher is instrumental in promoting the classroom ethos, which enables children to cooperate, appreciate one another, and share the work of their class with others.

Compared with work produced through systematic instruction, the standards, complexity, length, level of difficulty, and precision in project work tend to vary considerably among the children's achievements because the children do not always work to the limits of their ability. Some will be free-wheeling, while others will be working at a level far beyond their customary performance, owing to some special interest in the activity. The teacher can be instrumental in ensuring that the more mature and more able children are sufficiently challenged by their work. She can also find many opportunities to motivate less able children in the varied classroom context that the project approach affords. Standards may vary among the different pieces of work produced by any one individual on the same project. The teacher notes these differences and monitors the general performance of individual children over time.

Although the teacher continues to have an active role in the second phase of the project, the orchestration of learning consists in her being responsive to children as they attempt to solve problems and to master tasks. They need encouragement when their confidence weakens, suggestions when they run out of ideas, answers to their questions, direction to other sources of information, or new objects to boost their interest. The excitement that accompanies the initial stages of the project should be replaced by a sustained interest and satisfaction in the work being accomplished.

SUMMARY

The second phase of a project is concerned mainly with providing children new firsthand experience and helping them think about it in many interesting ways that stimulate purposeful activity and involve the use of various skills.

In this phase of project work, children are learning to monitor and evaluate their own efforts and achievements. They are also being taught to respond to their own view of themselves, to trust their own judgment, to identify their uncertainties, to pose their own questions, and to risk trying when success is uncertain. The principle involved here is that children should be encouraged to rely on the database of their own personal experience. It is also important that teachers encourage children to share and appreciate the good work being done and to be helpful to one another in setting and achieving appropriate and satisfying standards. Children can learn to ask each other for advice, to discuss strategies, and to consult as they work together.

Field work. During Phase II, a field trip can be planned by the children and teacher together. Field trips do not have to be elaborate, involving expensive transportation to distant places. They can involve going to places close to their schools, such as shops, stores, parks, construction sites, or walks. With the use of teacher's aides, the children can go to these sites in small groups, enjoying the opportunity of having an adult to talk with about what they are observing.

The preparatory work completed before conducting field work includes identifying questions to be answered, people to talk to about their work, equipment, objects, and materials that can be observed closely. Children can carry simple clipboards (made with cardboard and paper clips) and sketch or write things of special interest to be used on return to the classroom. During the visit, children can also be encouraged to count, note the shapes and colors of things, learn any special words for things, figure out how things work, and use all their senses to deepen their knowledge of the phenomenon studied.

Back in the classroom. Upon return to the classroom the children can recall many details and represent them in increasingly elaborate ways as the children learn more about the topic. At this time, the children apply skills already learned: talking, drawing, dramatic play writing, simple mathematical notation, measurement, diagrams. If a field site is close by, such as a construction site in the vicinity of the school, it can be visited on several occasions and comparisons can be made between what was observed on one visit and on subsequent ones.

The children's work can be accumulated in individual project folders, on wall displays, and in group record books in which work is shared with others. Children can be fully involved in discussing and planning what will be displayed and how. The information collected from interviews can be represented in various similar ways. The work can also be stimulated and enriched by a variety of secondary source materials, books, charts, leaflets, maps, pamphlets, and pictures.

As the work progresses in Phase II, the children often develop a strong concern for realism and logic about the topic, and drawing real objects becomes an increasingly absorbing activity. In their observational drawing, young children can look closely at how the parts of a bicycle interconnect within the whole, note how the pattern inside a carrot dissected different ways indicates the way water and other nutrients contribute to its growth, and so on. Interest is stimulated by frequent recognition and review of the progress being made in the development of the project.

9

Phase III:
Concluding Projects

Sooner or later, projects in the classroom have to be concluded, even though children can be encouraged to recognize that learning on any topic is never really finished; there is always more to learn. A topic is merely set aside until the next time it is encountered, either within or outside the school context. Various approaches to concluding a project are discussed in this chapter.

CONCLUDING PROJECTS WITH YOUNGER CHILDREN

For a class of preschoolers the decision to end a project can be made by the teacher in consultation with the children. The teacher takes into account the play in and around the project constructions and materials. If the richness, frequency, and quality of play have declined to a low level, she may ask the children whether they are ready to dismantle the project or to set it aside in some special way. Similarly, if the play ceases to change, develop, or be elaborated after a week or two, the teacher can discuss with the children their readiness to end the project. If no new props are added or if constructions are not extended after a week or two, the children may have exploited the topic as much as they want to at that particular time.

The teacher may then suggest that the children contribute drawings, paintings, or dictate stories for a class book about their work. If the project included a large construction, the children may be interested in organizing guided tours to explain the construction and other aspects of the project to children in other classes. The children should discuss and agree in advance and in some detail what they will show and recount to the visiting children and parents. When the time comes to end the project, it is a good idea for the children to take responsibility for dismantling it themselves, preserving some elements and saving materials that can be used for subsequent projects.

If the teachers or participating parents have taken many photographs of the project in progress, they can be given to small groups of children to arrange in narrative sequence, to mount on background construction paper, and to dictate or write themselves the appropriate captions. In this way, the children participate in documenting their experience in the process of which they can achieve greater depth of understanding and clarity of what has been learned. The Phase III documentation processes provide a type of debriefing that can help children's mastery of information and concepts associated with the topic. In one classroom, the older, "buddy" class of fifth graders interviewed the kindergarten children on their work. They wrote down what the children said about photographs and self-selected drawings taken from their project folder.

The class can also invite parents and others in the community to listen to oral reports of the work of various groups on all the subtopics investigated, and to view their documentation and constructions (see a description of the documentation processes used with 3- and 4-year-olds in Part III of Helm, Beneke, and Steinheimer, 1998).

CONCLUDING PROJECTS WITH OLDER CHILDREN

Three aspects of the concluding phase of a project with older children are discussed in this chapter. First, children can usually gain a sense of closure if the teacher and the whole class together develop a shared view of what they have learned and achieved during the project. This can be done by arranging one or more culminating activities such as giving a presentation to other classes, to the whole school, or to parents and members of the community invited to an open house culminating activity.

Second, it is a good idea for the teacher to monitor the level of the children's interest to ensure that boredom does not become widespread—an indication that the time has come to call a halt to the project. Ideally, interest in the project activities should be sustained, and everyone should remain at least somewhat involved in project activities until a collective culminating activity has occurred. Many interesting ways can be used to encourage children to elaborate and consolidate their newly acquired knowledge and understandings. However, keep in mind that any topic, no matter how interesting it might be at the outset, can eventually be run into the ground.

Third, children should reflect on the work they have accomplished individually as well as in a group so as to appreciate their own growing competence. The teacher can help them evaluate the work accomplished and the evidence of progress as the project evolved. Individuals can take stock of what they have learned about their own learning. They have new strategies and skills, as well as new confidence to bring to *their study of the next topic.* An awareness of their corporate learning can help children value the collaboration involved in so many of their activities. The teacher's role is crucial in setting the tone of thoughtful self-assessment during the final weeks or days of work on a project.

During the first and second phases of a project with older children, much of the work should address the realities of the topic. The work should include observations, descriptions, experiments, and problem solving. The boundaries between the real and the imaginary, the probable and the fantastic, can be clarified in the course of working on a project.

Once the children have acquired an indepth understanding and relevant knowledge related to the main aspects of the topic, they are prepared to invent, create, and imagine characters and places for stories to write or plays to act. During the third and final phase of a project, activities that enable children to consolidate their understanding, applying newly acquired information in imaginary contexts, are appropriate. When these activities lose their appeal, the children are probably ready to move on to the next project.

CULMINATION OF A PROJECT

At all ages, the activities undertaken during the second phase of a project can generate interesting and informative products. As these accumulate in individual project folders, in class books, and on wall displays and constructions, they constitute a rich resource that serves as a communal record of the project's progress since its beginning. A different story can be told about each project. No two classes of children will ever develop quite the same ideas and interests, undertake the same tasks, or solve the same problems even if they investigate the same topics. The uniqueness of each project reflects the distinctive thinking of each class of children and their teacher. A school assembly, an open house, or an invitation to parents and administrators to visit the classroom offers the teacher and children the opportunity to give an account or tell the story of the project to interested outsiders. The displays show achievements of the children, and each child can talk about his or her own work and the work of others.

Presentations to Other Classes

In preschools and schools that offer regular assemblies, some assemblies can be set aside for individual classes to talk to the other children and the teachers about their work. Sometimes a class can talk to just one other class about its work. Such communications enhance the children's feelings of belonging to a larger social unit within their school. The spirit of caring about the learning and accomplishments throughout the school community helps to create an ethos in which the older and the younger children respect and support each other inside and outside the classrooms. The older children first listen to the achievements and efforts of the younger children and then present what they have been working on in a way that the younger children find interesting. In preparation for these presentations, the teacher can encourage the presenters to predict what elements of their experience and work are likely to be of greatest interest to others. They can also be encouraged to discuss and reflect on what might be the best ways to make their ideas, insights, and experiences clear to the intended audiences of older or younger schoolmates. The dispositions to anticipate others' interests and to strive to make oneself clear to them are among the valuable dispositions to be manifested during project work.

Some of the larger pieces of work such as paintings, murals, charts, and models can be shown at these meetings. Selected children can describe how these items were made, the materials used, the difficulties encountered and overcome, as well as what they represent. Individuals might read a description, a story, or a poem they have written. A small group might put on a brief play while the rest of the class acts as chorus, singing or playing incidental music on percussion instruments. Or the whole class might sing or play music together.

The teacher can coordinate the presentation of these products of project work, narrating the story from both the children's point of view and her own. Preparing for a presentation is usually enjoyable and energizing for the children and offers opportunities to formally summarize the highlights of the project for individuals and groups. Class discussion takes on a reflective, summarizing, and debriefing function, helping the children to appreciate their own and others' achievements.

We want to stress that a presentation is primarily a communication rather than a performance. A presentation offers the children the opportunity to represent and share their experience with interested others, and it offers the other children, teachers, and parents the opportunity to hear about the experience. Entertainment is not the main purpose, although these occasions often have entertaining features. Nor should the children construe the culminating events or displays as occasions for showing off. The event is intended to communicate learning, but it does not need to be a precisely learned, formally scripted and formally rehearsed occasion. Some spontaneity and improvisation should be permitted. The children themselves should take much of the responsibility for planning a culminating event. If children are accustomed to this kind of experience from an early age, most of them will not be overawed by an audience. The emphasis here, as in other aspects of project work, is on engaging children's minds in the processes of learning. Children talk as much about the activity and about how they worked as they do about the products of their work.

These learning processes involve making models, writing stories, designing and conducting experiments, recording observations, representing information in graphs, making books, and so forth. The emphasis is not primarily on the product, although the product is important as a record of the process. Children can learn to explain, describe, report, and record the way they worked. For example, if two previous versions of a drawing were instrumental in achieving quality in a third and final version, the child can show and report how she or he modified each drawing in each successive *effort*. First drafts are not described as "mistakes" or as evidence of "where I went wrong," but rather in terms of "when I realized" or "when I saw how I could do it differently" to achieve a desired effect. Children who describe their efforts in terms of trying out alternatives before attaining the most satisfying outcome are communicating the value of such an approach. They model an awareness of learning strategies for other children and show how their thoughtfulness contributed to the final work. Project work can thus strengthen dispositions to persist in the face of challenges and to strive toward learning and mastery.

Consolidation Activities

The process of consolidation involves applying the knowledge acquired in familiar situations to a range of other understandings and contexts. To illustrate the activities that facilitate this process, let us take a close look at a project on the weather. New knowledge is likely to have given children the sense that the weather is less arbitrary than they had previously believed. They may have come to understand better that many everyday happenings are directly related to the weather—the clothing they wear, gardening tasks, roof repairs before winter, the timing of a visit to the shops. Often, adults do not make their reasons for doing weather-related preparations explicit, even when questioned.

Consider this example. A sudden storm causes a father to rush out to close the windows of the car parked in the driveway. His 4-year-old child, standing somewhat in the way, asks, "Daddy, why are you running?" The father might give one of several possible answers: "The car will get wet inside"; "Mind, out of the way, I have to do this quickly!"; "It's going to rain any minute!"; "Look at those dark clouds over there!"; "Your mother is upstairs!"; or "Get your tricycle in before the rain comes!" A one-sentence answer to a child's question about an event presupposes that the child has the background understanding necessary to make sense of the answer (even if it is not a non sequitur). The child might be left wondering, "Why will the car get wet inside?" or "It isn't raining now; how does he know the rain is coming?" and so on. In their dramatic play and through writing poems, stories, or captions for paintings, children can give reasonable explanations for familiar events in the light of their new knowledge about how the weather affects our lives.

Sometimes consolidation activities allow children to elaborate peripheral interests in the project. In the school bus project, for example, older children might draw a map of an imaginary town with its school and children's homes. They might set and solve problems about the "best" routes a bus might take, given the location of the school and the homes. Not all of the ideas will come from the teacher; the children may have many ideas themselves. The displays remain a source of information, and various tasks connected with them can still be undertaken. Where appropriate, information on display can be used in connection with tasks that test children's understanding. The displays at this stage may be refined for public view during an open house. Most of the work products in the third phase can contribute to the children's own personal project folders, which form the records of individual progress.

Open House

Another form of a culminating activity is an open day or open house when the class can report on the project to parents, administrators, or other visitors. Children can give visitors a personal guided tour of the classroom, or they can make a more formal presentation along the lines described for the school meeting. It is a good idea to give parents the opportunity to see how their responses to the request of the teacher and of their own child have contributed to the project. If parents have been very involved, the visit will be especially interesting to them; if they have not been, it may suggest ways they can help in the future and may encourage them to do so the next time.

EVALUATING THE PROJECT

At the conclusion of any project, it is useful for the children and the teacher to reflect on the skills, techniques, strategies, dispositions, and processes of exploration that the children have used in the project work. All of these competencies can be applied with greater proficiency and confidence in the next project on a new topic.

Much evaluation can occur when planning a culminating presentation, for instance, when the teacher and class discuss the various special events or group and individual achievements. If each of the children has been keeping work in a project book or folder and the teacher has been monitoring their progress, she will know which children require help to complete work and which would benefit from supplementary activities to clarify limited or erroneous understanding. Some teachers also find it helpful to encourage children to look back at their own work during the course of the project. For example, during Phase I, when the direction of the investigation is being developed, the children can make predictions about what their findings can be. During Phase III, they can revisit these predictions and speculate about the bases upon which they made them, which predictions were close to the facts, which were not, and reasons for any errors.

Information on the bulletin boards can be used during this phase as a basis for formulating and responding to quiz questions. These can be a practical method of checking on the new knowledge that individual children have learned.

Children can also talk with each other and the teacher, either in a class group or individually, about the skills they have practiced in the project. The teacher can help to summarize these skills to ensure that they are more easily available when the children embark on the next project. For instance, if the children have counted frequencies for a survey, they may have tried alternative ways of recording items and counting them in groups or tallying them. They may have compared the efficiency of chunking the items in twos, threes, or fives. Discoveries about the most efficient way to count and record the results can be influential in similar situations in the next project. The skills can be practiced in subsequent surveys. The older the children, the more explicitly and deeply these evaluations can be discussed.

Teachers' records of individual progress throughout the project will vary in specificity according to the age of the children. With the youngest children, few records may be kept. With school-age children, some schools require more extensive records than others. In school systems that require extensive or detailed records of children's progress, the teacher can list all of the activities undertaken by each individual, some of the groups, or the whole class.

For each child, a record can be developed that notes which activities were undertaken and the level of proficiency achieved. One approach is to compile a matrix with curriculum competencies on one axis and the main project work activities on the other. When a competency is used in a particular activity, a check mark can be entered in the appropriate cell in the matrix. In this way, the project activities can be mapped onto the competencies. As each child works on an activity, the appropriate check on the matrix can be circled. Thus, the competencies practiced can easily be seen. Keeping precise records of achievement is more complex with project work than with worksheets and standard tests. Nevertheless, teachers should not be discouraged from incorporating the project approach into their curriculum.

In addition, records of what the whole class accomplished in the project can be useful for future reference. The web that was devised in the initial planning stages can provide a framework for this record. Using different-colored markers or some other method of marking, the teacher can note the activities accomplished, the visits made, the resources used, and the areas most fully investigated. She may also want to note aspects of the project that were least well developed. Activities or events that occurred but were not in the original plan can be added to the diagram.

An anecdotal account of how the web was expanded can serve as an additional evaluation of the project. A record of the whole project from the teacher's point of view is useful if she should wish to repeat a similar project and could be of interest to other teachers undertaking project work in a similar area. In some schools, records of this kind are kept on file as a planning resource. In this way, teachers can share ideas and make their experience available to each other.

WHAT HAPPENS NEXT

As the work of a project draws to a close, the teacher sometimes recognizes a strong new interest emerging for the children. In the bus project, the children's dramatic play might have led to play about the bus taking them on a vacation. They might have considered what it would be like to go to different places, and they might have talked about where they had been and where they were likely to go later on. If this would be an appropriate project to do next, then the teacher might encourage the idea. The children might set up a travel agency, collect brochures, and make tickets to sell. The school bus construction, if not too dilapidated by this time, might be repainted as a tour bus, or be converted into a ferryboat, or an airplane.

Or consider the school bus project of older children. Initially, they might have focused on the bus itself, making models, experimenting with wheels and motion, and graphing the time required by different children to ride to school. They might have become interested in the various routes. This interest might then lead appropriately into a project on making maps of the neighborhood, thereby extending the children's graphic skills and increasing their knowledge of their larger environment.

Sometimes the teacher has an idea about which area of the curriculum she wants to emphasize in the next project. If so, she can try sowing the seeds of new interests as she sees their potential for future project work develop out of the work now completed.

SUMMARY

The purposeful application of skills and dispositions in project work opens up many possibilities for children. The classroom offers more interesting activities than any one child can ever do. Children learn to be selective in pursuing their own intentions in an environment where learning opportunities abound. With the teacher's help, they learn to make responsible choices based on interest. The third phase of a project is a time for elaborating new knowledge introduced in the second phase. It is a time to reflect on and evaluate what has been learned. It is also a time to look forward to new ideas and to the application of skills in the study of a new topic.

At the end of the school year, the teacher and children together can recall the more memorable events in the projects undertaken and reflect on the greater facility the children have acquired during that long period. In one school, the teacher and children made a class book at the end of the prekindergarten year. The book included examples of individuals' work when they first started school. The children wrote about their early memories of school life and drew pictures of the events described. Each child could see how his or her own drawing and writing skills had advanced during the year. Through such activities, the children can become more fully aware of their increased competence and can be helped to look forward with confidence to the challenges in the year ahead.

10

Drawing in the
Context of a Project

Drawing can greatly enhance project work for children of any age. Most work products, whether they involve writing, diagrams, or other forms of representation, are more interesting and informative when accompanied by drawings. In addition, the process of drawing itself is instructive. Drawing in project work is mainly draughtsmanship, or technical drawing, done to convey factual information or sometimes children's theories of how things work. However, there are also opportunities for the more artistically expressive kinds of drawing. In the course of a project children can draw for a variety of different purposes throughout the three phases of the study.

This chapter is presented in three main sections. In the first section, the contribution of drawing to children's learning is discussed. Second, several different kinds of drawing and their purposes are examined in relation to the development of projects. The third section describes teaching strategies by which the teacher can encourage purposeful drawing in the context of a project. It will readily be seen that the contribution of drawing to children's learning is not limited to their use of it in project work but can add value to their work in many other aspects of the curriculum.

THE CONTRIBUTION OF DRAWING TO CHILDREN'S DEVELOPMENT AND LEARNING

Drawing in project work can contribute to all of the four kinds of learning goals mentioned in previous chapters: knowledge, skills, dispositions, and feelings.

Knowledge

Early in the life of the project investigation the processes of drawing help children recall the details of past experience relevant to the topic. Drawing enables children to retrieve and express relevant memories and gives them a focus for discussion with other children about the common as well as different experiences they have had. Once the children are learning from firsthand experience and from secondary sources of information about a topic, drawing enhances the examination of detail. Drawing from observation requires children to look closely and make frequent checks with the real phenomena they are observing. In so doing, they discover detailed information about objects, events, people's roles and the relationships of parts to wholes.

Skills

Drawing also provides children with an ideal "language" for representing complex ideas. In order to represent reality in the form of a drawing, some data reduction is necessary. Only the most salient details can be represented. This data reduction involves children in sifting through visual clues and selecting those that will best reduce the information to its essentials. This selection process can guide children's choice of words for oral or written language. Thus, drawing can help children with various aspects of linguistic as well as visual expression.

Drawing involves a kind of problem solving as the three dimensions of the reality are reduced to two dimensions on the paper. Drawings can also be revisited, modified, elaborated, and labeled. This process of revisiting is a reflective one helping to make experience memorable and deepen the learning.

Dispositions

Drawing is a pleasant and intrinsically satisfying activity for most young children. The desire to draw can energize children's work and provide opportunities to strengthen several dispositions of particular value to teachers. Five examples of such opportunities afforded by drawing are worthy of special mention here.

First, high-quality illustrations can contribute to the attractiveness and personal significance of project work. Children's experience of ownership of their project work is enhanced by drawing because it allows for individual expression in representational work. Second, since children value the results of skillful drawing, they will usually apply themselves willingly to practicing their drawing skills and techniques. Practice at drawing can be shown to produce small increments of improvement, which children can readily appreciate. Third, when children encounter problems in their drawing, they are often persistent and resourceful in solving them. Fourth, when children are in the process of drawing, their attention is most often particularly focused. The resulting concentration often shows itself in children as a deep, calm absorption. Another explanation of this quiet absorption is that it is very difficult for anyone to draw and talk at the same time, perhaps because these activities make simultaneously competing demands on different functions of the brain (Edwards, 1979).

Fifth, the disposition to work hard at personal strengths is strong in those children who draw well since project work offers many different opportunities for drawing to be appreciated. Competence in drawing can be especially valuable to some children with difficulties in other parts of their achievement profiles. These children are helped in all areas when they can see their skillfulness in drawing contributing to the collaborative effort of a team or small group to the project as a whole.

Feelings

Drawing can build feelings of confidence and self-esteem, as it features children's strengths and encourages them to persist in following up their own ideas in the exploratory climate of the project. Drawing is another form of communication, and one that opens new opportunities for children's ideas to be expressed and appreciated. There is also an aesthetic dimension to drawing, enabling the development of sensitivity to pattern and structure. In the classroom, many teachers have remarked on the power of drawing to help very active and impulsive children to focus their attention in a calming way. "Children who learn to look, learn to question, to discover and to understand.... Looking absorbs, engages, calms and sensitizes the learner" (Sedgwick & Sedgwick, 1993, p. 18).

THE CONTRIBUTIONS OF DRAWING TO THE DEVELOPMENT OF A PROJECT

Drawing can facilitate and elaborate the development of a project from its beginning to its conclusion. Children can apply drawing skills in projects to extend and enrich their work and give it a particularly personal quality. Whereas the systematic instruction of older elementary school children in art can help them to acquire new skills and extend their drawing activity, the application of drawing skills to project work makes very different demands on the children compared to the requirement to follow instructions in an art class. In an art class, the teacher may expect all the children to work on the same particular drawing skills (for example, perspective) at the same time. The enrichment of project work through a variety of different kinds of drawing at any time can be combined with other forms of representation to give the work a particularly personal quality. A discussion of different kinds of drawing tasks in each of the three phases of a project is presented to show how they can enrich children's project work.

Phase I: Beginning a Project

In the first phase of a project when the children are discussing their own experiences, the representations that they draw can provide the teacher with information about the children's personal experiences. The experiences they represent may be as recent as last week's shopping trip, or as distant as an airplane journey two years earlier. Drawing from memory often lacks specific detail, is simple, impressionistic, and approximate. Whatever the memory, many children may have difficulty recalling details to represent. It is usually easier to draw an item or detailed process from observation than from memory. However, the data reduction involved in representing a memory can still serve the child and teacher well in reflecting the child's initial knowledge and experience with the topic of the investigation.

Paradoxically, however, drawing from memory can help many young children articulate complex ideas. For example, in the first phase of a project on pets, one child drew two people, a car, and a cat in a box. He was able to explain the events depicted through his drawing. He described how the family cat was being taken to the vet for shots and his father asked him to come along and talk to the cat on the way to comfort it because it was usually unhappy in the car. The drawing greatly helped the teacher and child together to reconstruct the scene in words. This helped the child share his experience with the other children and write a suitable caption for his drawing. It is only when the details of such a story are clear that the teacher can gain insight into how much the child understands about the topic as a result of the experience.

Rich discussions occur when children are encouraged to share their experiences in detail. As the teacher invites children to explain the details of experiences represented in their drawings, he or she provides an active model of the careful and interested listener. This model helps the children learn to question each other in a similar way. The process of oral sharing has also been described by Gallas (1994), as contributing to "the complex process that teachers go through to build a powerful, inclusive classroom community" (pp. 15–16). This community-building is an essential aspect of good project work. Our experience is that children talk about the project topic among themselves in the class, at recess, after school, and at home with their parents as they become more and more interested in it. The more details in drawings are discussed at "sharing times" in the classroom, the easier it is for the teacher to help the children identify and discuss areas of confusion or gaps in their understanding. These discussions then provide the basis for formulating questions for follow-up investigation.

The drawings completed in the early stages of a project represent children's early understanding of the topic. Early drawings can be compared with the much more detailed ones achieved later in the study. Both teachers and children can appreciate the evidence of progress made in understanding. A sequence of drawings completed at different times during the project can give children props or cues to help them discuss their learning in conferences with teachers and parents. An example of a sequence of drawings from observation of a car wheel by a 4-year-old girl involved in a project on cars is shown in Figure 10.1 (from Beneke, 1998).

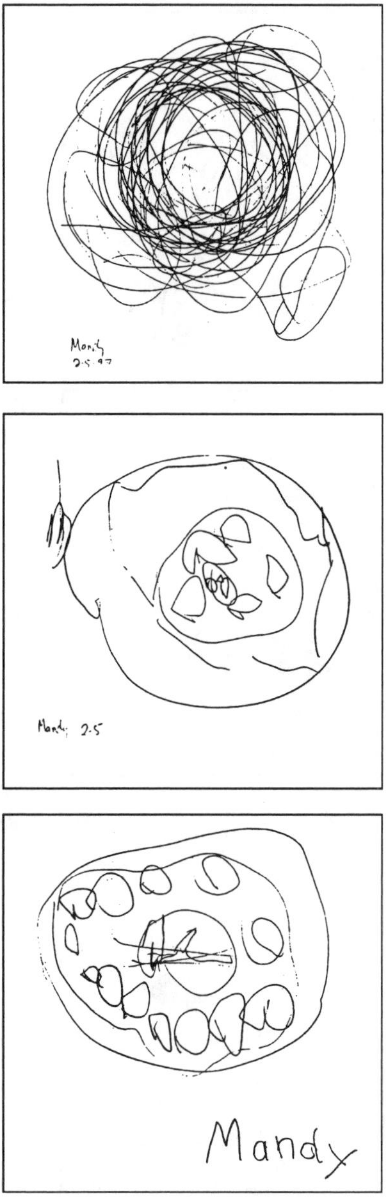

TIME 1

TIME 2

TIME 3

FIGURE 10.1. A sequence of observational drawings of a wheel by a 4-year-old participating in a project on cars. Times 1, 2, and 3 were interspersed with tactile exploration and discussion. All three drawings were done on the same day.
Source: Reprinted by permission from Beneke (1998).

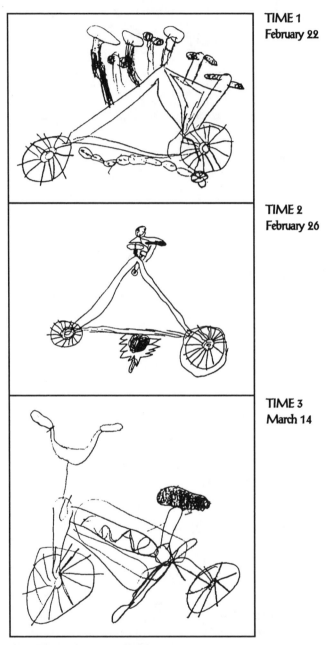

TIME 1
February 22

TIME 2
February 26

TIME 3
March 14

FIGURE 10.2. A sequence of drawings of a bicycle by a first grader participating in a project on bicycles.
Source: Reprinted by permission from the Peoria School District, Peoria, Illinois.

142

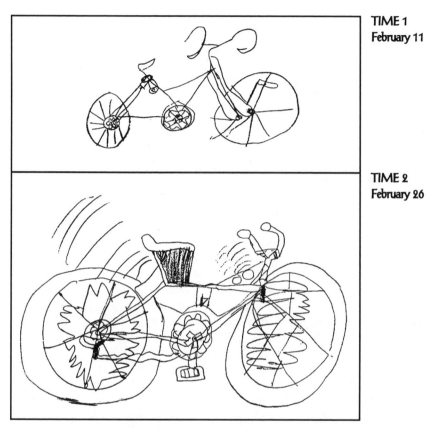

TIME 1
February 11

TIME 2
February 26

FIGURE 10.3. **Another sequence of drawings of a bicycle by a first grader participating in a project on bicycles.**
Source: Reprinted by permission from the Peoria School District, Peoria, Illinois.

Two other examples of sequences of drawings from observation by first graders involved in a project on bicycles in Figures 10.2 and 10.3 were made available by their teacher, Jolyn Blank.

Phase II: Developing the Project

In the second phase of the project, the children are extending and deepening their knowledge of the topic with a shared perspective from primary and secondary sources of information. During Phase II, their greater experience with real objects, events, processes and roles is the major source of information for drawing. On field visits, the children can make sketches to remind them later of what they have seen. Sketches focus children's attention at the field site and facilitate discussion on return to the classroom. Children can use the sketches as bases for further illustrations of the phenomena being studied. Because of time constraints in the field, these sketches are usually drawn economically including only the most salient and significant details. Field sketches involve looking closely at the objects and people studied and making judgments about the parts of an object, the stages in a process, or the sequence of actions taken by a person.

Back in the classroom, the children can elaborate their drawings with reference to photographs and secondary sources of information. They can undertake sustained observational drawing of artifacts collected during Phase II. Increasingly, detailed knowledge can be represented as it is collected. Sustained drawing enables children to study the nature of things, shapes, colors, textures, and other attributes. It encourages children to examine the relationship of parts to the whole of objects. "Close observation—mixed with wonder—is essential for the development of artist, scientist, writer, as well as mathematician, humorist, inventor, and more" (Ruef, 1994, p. 22).

In a video, George Forman (1993) describes how his son, Jed, learns about how a bicycle works through the process of drawing it in detail. In turn, Jed talks about his drawing, revisits the bicycle itself, talks about what he observes, and resumes his drawing. By these means, Jed corrects his early impressions of how the pedals, chain, and wheels are connected and improves his understanding of how the bicycle moves. Another example shows how children themselves can appreciate the value of drawing to learn. A teacher in South Carolina told us about a kindergarten child who discovered for the first time that he could draw in the context of a project on the seashore. He developed a strong interest in crabs and drew many of them with increasing attention to detail. At the end of the project, the teacher was reviewing this boy's portfolio of project work. Looking at his drawings of crabs, she asked him to tell her about them. After a while, she exclaimed, "Sammy, how did you get to know so much about crabs?" Sammy replied, "Well, you see, the more I drew, the more I learned."

Processes and roles can be represented in an "event map" (see Figure 10.4 and Hinchman, 1997, p. 156), or in a drawing in which time and location are identified and labeled with words and measures. The sketches of the same object or event in the field made by several children can lead to animated discussion and argument about what was actually observed. In such cases, the teacher can encourage children's dispositions to be empirical by suggesting that they take opportunities to revisit the site or look again at the objects or photographs of them to ascertain the actual facts.

Interdisciplinary links can be facilitated as drawings and captions are prepared to enhance a composite representation such as a poster, class museum exhibit, or book. Drawings can also be included in representations of phenomena prepared by a group. The drawings can often help to clarify the connections between different parts of the work contributed by the individual children within it. For example, in the development of a classroom museum, rocks and shells could be classified and labeled for display, their frequency counted and represented in a chart or graph, and the locations at which they were found could be mapped. Depending on the maturity of the children, the labels might include the age of the rocks and timelines might be used to

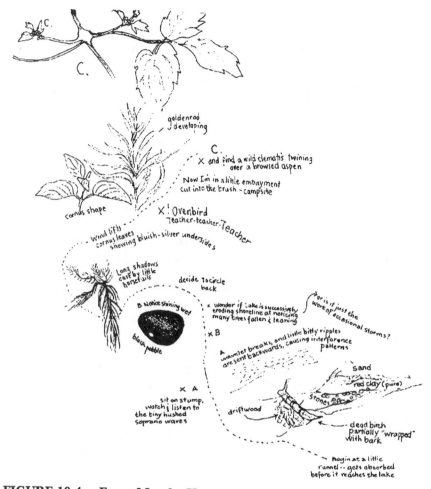

goldenrod developing

C.

X and find a wild clematis twining over a browsed aspen

Now I'm in a little embayment cut into the brush ~ campsite

cornus shape

X! Ovenbird Teacher-teacher. Teacher

Wind lifts cornus leaves showing bluish-silver undersides

Long shadows cast by little horsetails

decide to circle back

B Notice shining wet

x wonder if lake is successively eroding shoreline at noticing many trees fallen & leaning

or is it just the work of occasional storms?

x B

A wavelet breaks, and little bitty ripples are sent backwards, causing interference patterns

black pebble

sand

red clay (pure)

stones

x A

sit on stump, watch & listen to the tiny hushed soprano waves

driftwood

dead birch partially "wrapped" with bark

begin at a little runnel -- gets absorbed before it reaches the lake

FIGURE 10.4. Event Map by Hannah Hinchman.
Source: personal communication with Hannah Hinchman.

show their respective ages. Drawings could include the terrain in which different types of rocks were found, the shore location of different kinds of shells, and the location of the co-occurrence of different kinds of rocks or shells. Language and math skills can combine with social studies and science concepts and representations to enable the children to develop a sound, balanced understanding of the topic.

Multistage work, such as the construction of a building or making a model village, requires drawing for the processes of planning and drafting the evolution of the ideas as the work progresses. Field sketches can serve as the basis for such work. Other kinds of multistage work include presenting a dramatic performance with appropriate scenery; making a complex model of, for example, a farm, a factory, or a town; or making a simulation game featuring the main cause-and-effect relations associated with a topic.

Drawings of many different kinds can be included in project work. Sometimes a drawing can be executed simply at one sitting, at other times, it may be revisited and indeed, added to several times before it is complete. In the case of a revisited drawing, it may be of interest to the teacher as documentation of the progress made by a child or a group of them. Photocopies made at different times in the drawing process can record the progressive addition of detail leading to the finished product. Such documentation is helpful to other children interested in this kind of long-term work.

Sometimes a drawing may stand alone with only a brief caption to indicate its significance to the study. At other times, there may be word labels added to a drawing indicating the technical terms for the parts of the object, time taken for processes depicted, or weights to indicate amounts of material shown, and so on. In project work, there are many opportunities to mix media and means of communication to render a more accurate, detailed, and informative representation. As the children grow older, they can undertake increasingly complex combinations of representational strategies.

Most of the drawing in the second phase of a project is observational. However, it is important to note that younger children will mix observational drawing with memory or symbolic drawing, adding in figures or objects that they would like represented there as well. For example, several 5-year-old children who drew a bicycle in their classroom added drawings of the sun to their pictures and people riding the bicycles. To judge from the children's conversation at the time, the tendency to provide these additions was probably provoked by the power of their association of bicycles with the outdoors and being with other people. The difference between the quality of the drawing of the bicycles and the quality of the added information was marked. The suns and added people tended to be more symbolic representations than realistic ones, for example, a typical circle with rays for the sun and primitive "hairpin" or "sausage" figures for the people, in sharp contrast to the more mature and informative drawing of the bicycles themselves (see Figure 10.5).

Drawing from observation is informative for the child. Close observation leads the child to notice details and discover relationships. London (1989) writes about this kind of engagement:

> We have the responsibility to see for ourselves and not to settle for hearsay. If we live our lives in rumor and hearsay, who we are and what we do will reflect not the world of our own experience but the diluted, inaccurate reflections cast by others. Seeing something is to meet the thing. (p. 53)

Drawing can be further encouraged to increase analytical thinking. Throughout the range of different kinds of drawing, from drawings labeled with words to structural analyses labeled with short paragraphs and exploded drawings (drawings in which parts of an object are separated and enlarged), there are many ways for children to learn about the function of the parts of an object, the role of a person, the sequence of stages in a process, the layers in a cross-section, and so forth. Technical drawing of this kind is used in science textbooks, for example, in engineering or medicine, at any level of study in these subjects because words and numbers alone are insufficient for conveying detailed and complex information. Even where an entity is too small to see with a microscope scientists still speculate about structure in drawings and three dimensional models. Moline (1995) makes the point that

> [r]eading and writing visual texts is not merely a transitional phase which is later discarded in favor of reading and writing words: visual text elements can be highly complex and are used extensively at all levels of learning through to university text books and post graduate research papers. Visual texts are therefore not an academically "soft option" to verbal texts, since they can be equally demanding to produce. (p. 2)

Drawing can also be decorative or abstract. It is helpful to have folders in which children can keep their individual pieces of project work, both for completed items and for pieces that are still being worked on. The outside fronts and backs of these folders can be illustrated with pictures of items of particular interest to the children. Sometimes, children's work can be specially featured on paper with illuminated borders made up of miniature drawings in which the children depict details referred to in the text. This kind of drawing makes the material more memorable to the child as well as making the content of the work more accessible to other children. Illuminated borders are sometimes designed by teachers for children's work; but in the context of a project, the process of designing and making the border can itself be an important opportunity for the child to consolidate his or her own learning.

Creative written work, such as poems or descriptive prose essays, can sometimes benefit from an accompanying piece of art. This may involve the kind of drawing that is less informative or decorative than it is abstract and impressionistic. Such art may be primarily expressive of personal feelings or impressions rather than representing information.

Phase III: Concluding a Project

In the third phase of a project, most of the questions asked earlier in the study will have been answered in the course of field work or research with secondary sources of information. Although the time must come to bring the work of a project to a close, it is not because every question will have been answered and every research avenue exhausted. The reasons for finishing a project have more to do with other aspects of work to be included in the school year and the need to move on to other studies. In fact it is important for children not to think that they know everything there is to know about a topic by the end of a project. On the contrary, from project work, children learn how the answer to any question provokes us to ask questions at a new level of inquiry and understanding.

In the third phase of a project, some particularly interested children may want to speculate on what the answers to some of their new questions might be. An investigation of stores and markets today may give rise to questions about other kinds of buy-

FIGURE 10.5. Observational drawings of a bicycle by six 5-year-olds on the same occasion.

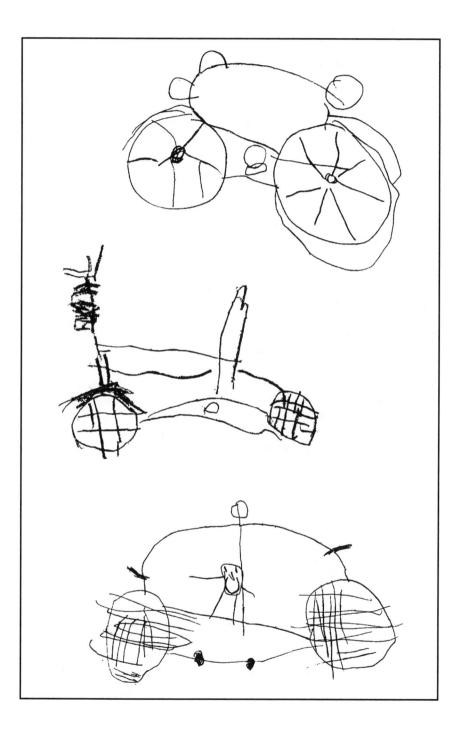

ing and selling in the future. A study of rapid change over time lends itself naturally to speculation about the future. Predictions can be well expressed in speculative drawings. Depending on the ages of the children, the study of a building, newspaper, or business may prompt designs of how things might look in a future time or other place.

At this time, the teacher can assess how well the children have learned the main ideas that emerged from the study of the topic. Planning for the culminating event to share the work with others can involve considerable discussion. This discussion will provide useful opportunities for review and evaluation of what has been accomplished. There are other opportunities for review involving drawing. The main information learned in the project can be applied by children in the design of a simulation in a board, track, or card game. The imaginative activity involved in such work helps children to personalize their new knowledge, making the project even more memorable.

Drawings, especially for the younger children, can be very helpful in enabling them to represent what they have learned in the course of the work in a way that others not involved can appreciate their experiences and efforts. In one kindergarten class, the children paired up with their 5th-grade buddies (ages 10–11) and shared three pictures they had selected from their project folders to explain what they had learned through their project work. The older children were to write what the younger children told them about the items in the pictures. Elsewhere, in a first-grade class, the children were invited to draw and label as much as possible about what they had learned in a picture to present to others.

In summary, project work drawings may be of many different kinds: rough sketches, plans for future work, parts of larger composite pieces of work, or scenery for a dramatic presentation. A few drawings may be discarded, having served their purpose (like rough drafts or "scratch" notes). Many drawings will be intended for worthier final destinations, taking their place in a book or report, on a poster, or in the child's individual project folder. They may be given to informants in recognition and appreciation for their help, or displayed in the library for others to learn from and enjoy. Above all, drawing for projects should be regarded as important school work, not taken home each day to disappear from the learning environment of the classroom. The third section of this chapter is devoted to discussion of strategies for the teacher to encourage purposeful drawing in the context of project work.

TEACHING STRATEGIES THAT ENCOURAGE DRAWING

The value placed on drawing is one of the characteristics of the culture of an early childhood or elementary classroom where projects are a regular part of the work. In this section, we address some of the issues teachers have raised with regard to encouraging drawing in their classrooms. These issues fall into three main categories: encouraging children to draw, building a drawing community in the classroom, and setting expectations and standards for children's drawing.

Encouraging Children to Draw

Teachers sometimes describe children as resistant to drawing and cite this observation as a reason not to insist upon it in their classrooms, perhaps because many children, by the age of 5, assert that they cannot draw. However, teachers rarely, if ever, decline to teach or encourage reading on the grounds that the children in their class don't want to read. Our experience suggests that the desire to engage in almost any activity in a social setting is a function, to some extent, of cultural expectations. When children have the opportunity to observe respected peers or adults deeply engaged in an activity, it is likely to be valued by most children and they will strive to engage in it themselves.

In the matter of reading, writing, and other academic tasks, evidence that a child dislikes the work is not a reason to omit it from the child's schedule. On the contrary, required tasks are insisted upon and many teachers go to great lengths to make all required activities interesting and desirable to children. The same can apply to drawing.

Further evidence for the social origin of attitudes to drawing can be found in the response of many teachers to a child's apparent reluctance to draw as compared to his or her response to a child's reluctance to read. When a child in our culture complains because she "can't draw," the adult tends to offer sympathy and reassurance. The adult may say that he too cannot draw very well and that has not handicapped him too much in life. Sometimes, the adult goes on to say drawing is one of those things that some people can do and others can't, and that people are just born with or without the ability to draw. However, adults' responses to young children who complain of not being able to read, for instance, are often quite different. They usually explain to such children that reading is very difficult, but you learn it gradually over a long period of time with lots of practice and help from the teacher and everyone around you, and that in time you will learn to read, just like everyone else. Younger children, those around age 3, rarely resist drawing because they have not yet learned to believe that they cannot do so! Thus, it is a good idea to introduce purposeful drawing alongside expressive drawing as early as 3 years of age.

If drawing is to be perceived by children as valued in the culture of the classroom, the teacher must respond in similar ways to both the children's reluctance to draw and their reluctance to read. Teachers must show children that they value drawing as an essential form of representation and show many examples of how drawings can enhance text, diagrams, or mathematical statements as well as express feelings.

Building a Drawing Community

One requirement for making a classroom an environment in which drawing is encouraged is that children be invited to explore the processes of drawing without fear of rebuke or ridicule when their efforts turn out to be less than effective. Drawing tends to be quite a public activity in a classroom. Unlike writing, drawing is more easily seen by others: it is hard to hide drawings you are working on. A gradually developing skillfulness in draughtsmanship thrives in a classroom culture in which drawing is a valued means of communication for all. Such a culture is appreciative of open communication, expressiveness, originality, trial and error, and honors children's intentions and the process of working on successive approximations toward their intended goal. Adults should resist the temptation to infer children's intentions and offer adult solutions to the drawing problems young children encounter. As Goodnow (1977) has noted in a report of her research on children's drawing, "The apparent disorder in children's behavior—its apparent lack of principles or rules—is due to our own ignorance of the principles they work by" (p. 60). Children must feel genuinely safe and free to make tentative and repeated tries and to talk openly with others about their work.

Explicit Expectations

Creating a culture in the classroom that encourages drawing involves making clear how drawing is regarded by the adults and their expectations of children's attention to it. One basic characteristic of this culture would be the expectation that students would continuously be improving their drawing and using it to communicate what they are learning. An expectation at first grade (children that are 6–7 years of age) and beyond would be that each child would draw at some time within the school day, in the same way that writing is normally required everyday. The drawing required for project work, however, would be different for each child and not all of it would be destined for sharing or public display.

The Classroom Environment

Making provision for daily drawing involves preparing space and time and real objects to draw. It also means teaching children to manage a variety of drawing materials, mark-making tools, paint, and paper. Children can be expected to select media and materials for their needs, prepare space in which to work, mix paint, clean up when their work is completed, and account in some way for how they have used their time and what they have accomplished. All project work involves children in managing transitions between different tasks; but drawing especially may involve some specific housekeeping strategies.

Through their management of the physical preparation for drawing activity, the children can learn respect for the tools and materials. The teacher takes responsibility for training the children, even the young ones, in the care of materials by calm but persistent reminders and insistence on good practices. However, such insistence should be accompanied by the communication of values in respect of efficiency and economy. Scarce resources have to be safeguarded to avoid waste and ensure that they are maintained in good condition. Children can be particularly vigilant in developing a collective responsibility in areas of work for which they have a personal appreciation.

Noncompetitive Climate

Some classroom climates, intentionally or not, encourage children to be competitive and to compare their work to that of others. Such comparisons do not help the development of a community culture that encourages drawing. Take, for example, the common practice of putting artwork depicting the same objects or ideas by every child on a bulletin board or in the hallway. When every child's work on the same subject is displayed, each product can be compared with every other one. This means that a few children may judge—sometimes correctly—that their work is less "good" than that of most other children. In order to avoid such disparaging and irrelevant comparisons, teachers have resorted to giving instructions to ensure that every child can achieve the same standard. The consequence is often a sacrifice of individuality for the sake of uniformity.

Standardizing work products is inappropriate and irrelevant for project work. For example, informative drawing is a specially valuable means of representation precisely because it enables children to show a personal perspective that can enrich everyone's interest in the topic (see bicycle drawings in Figure 10.2). In a project, so many different kinds of drawing can represent different aspects of the topic; there will be no "class sets" of the same work to display. Instead, each final draft picture can make a unique contribution to some part of the project work. Taken together, the different findings help to explain how a bicycle moves and what parts it needs to have in order to work.

CHOOSING APPROPRIATE LEVELS OF CHALLENGE

Group discussion of the demands of various drawing tasks and activities, sketching, drafting, elaborating, and so on help children to elect to draw at different levels of formality and complexity. One child may want to contribute a drawing for the cover of a class book. Another, a drawing to be included in the book, and yet another may rarely elect to make drawings available for public display. These preferences for the final destination of drawings can be respected without negative effects on any child's progress in developing his or her drawing skill. If every child is expected to draw everyday, every child is likely to make progress, albeit at different rates and at different levels. As even the child who is least competent at drawing gains confidence, the whole class can expect to develop considerable facility in representational drawing.

Exercising Choice in Drawing

Opportunity to make choices can often improve children's motivation to participate in an activity. Children can exercise choice of media and subject matter when it comes to drawing. They can also choose among many different kinds of drawing in project work. In addition, they can choose to take on levels of challenge in their drawing, which are appropriate to their current levels of achievement. The choice of level of challenge particularly facilitates the development of self-assessment strategies and understandings about the demands of particular kinds of drawing. In some classrooms, suggestions are made by the teacher to invite drawings for a specific display or for scenery for a play, or for a poster or game. These may be requested over several days. In that time, the children come to understand the complexities of the task. Consider the following example.

In one classroom where checkered flags were required for a play, the teacher invited the children to paint these over the course of a week. Eight children in a class of 30 responded to this challenge. The first flags were painted by children to whom the idea had immediate appeal and who were not afraid to work with little direction as to the form of the finished product. By the third day, the discussions of the first drawings had generated some key information about the nature of a checker pattern. Those children who subsequently undertook this painting task were able to build into their work an appreciation of the "horizontal and vertical," the "equidistant parallel lines," and the "black and white squares," which "touched at the corners" in parts of the rather impressionistic flags completed earlier. The problem solving became increasingly sophisticated with each day's discussion throughout the week. Children who completed flags earlier also had a chance to paint another flag if they wished.

SETTING EXPECTATIONS AND STANDARDS FOR CHILDREN'S DRAWING

It is likely that children see the teacher valuing drawing when she makes it clear that it is expected as a regular and significant part of their project work. Both explicit expectations and the support and encouragement of the community culture in the classroom are important if confident drawing is to become part of every child's project work. We now discuss the strategies teachers can use to help children develop their drawing skills. This is important because children gain confidence in their ability to draw when they experience success in developing their own competence in graphic representation.

BECOMING A TEACHER WHO DRAWS

Unfortunately, many teachers have little confidence in their abilities to help children to improve their drawing. Indeed, many teachers in the North American culture do not themselves draw or use the activity of drawing in their own lives. For those in this position, we recommend Edwards's book *Drawing on the Right Side of the Brain* (1979) or Hinchman's *A Life in Hand* (1991) and *A Trail Through Leaves* (1997). However, even if you are a teacher who does not draw, or who has not done so for a very long time, but who wants to help children to develop their drawing skills, there are several ways to do so without a great deal of specialist knowledge of art education, desirable though this may be.

PEER MODELING

Much can be accomplished through peer modeling by which children learn from each other. The impulse to draw is likely to flourish in a classroom where a variety of examples of drawings done by peers are on display on bulletin boards or available in class

book collections. Peer modeling is a particularly powerful influence on children's drawing when work products are discussed by children and teachers in the class group. The
work is most usefully selected by the teacher for the purpose of discussing drawing strategies and effects. In a brief discussion of the positive features of a few drawings each day,
much can be done to sensitize the children to the advantages of different techniques.

A LANGUAGE TO TALK ABOUT DRAWING

Children can draw intentionally and thoughtfully when they work in an environment in which words are frequently used to describe different kinds of visual images
and graphic effects. In the early childhood classroom, for example, there are many
opportunities to talk about the kinds of illustrations found in children's books. For
younger children, illustrations are often more accessible aids to understanding the
stories than text. Children can acquire through such talk a vocabulary for describing line, shape, color, tone, value, and texture.

In addition to words used to describe particular effects in finished drawings, there
are words that can be used to describe the techniques and strategies for achieving
those effects. Children themselves can share successes and challenges arising in their
use of particular techniques. Skillful drawing involves the development of abilities.
Discussion of techniques should be straightforward, direct, matter-of-fact, and
open. Teachers can add their own suggestions if they are familiar with the issues discussed. There is no need for the reverence or mystique that sometimes obscures discussions about young children's "art." No more place needs to be accorded
self-deprecation or self-aggrandizement in the discussion of drawing than there
would be in discussions of writing or math skills.

The description of drawing conveyed above may suggest that there are sub-
skills to be learned similar to those for writing and math. However, we think it is
important to recognize some important differences between conventional academic skills and the representational skills involved in drawing. The purpose is not
that children should develop a convergent style in drawing, such as they would in
writing or computation. Rather, the variety of possibilities for drawing can open
up ways for children to explore and develop their drawing ability on a daily basis
as part of life in the classroom. With these differences in mind, there are three
messages to be conveyed by the teacher to help children willingly strive to improve
their drawing.

The first message concerns the value of originality in drawing. Originality, difference, and variety are to be valued. Originality is usually achieved quite easily
when children draw freehand. It is to be expected that different children may have
different thoughts to convey in their representational drawings. These differences
can be explored in the children's discussions about the subject of their drawing and
the processes of freehand drawing.

With respect to the value of originality, then, it is important to caution against the use of templates, stencils, tracing or coloring in predrawn outlines, which can suggest the opposite value. The use of these techniques suggests that there is one right way to draw and some intermediary object between the brain and the fingers can enable you to do it right (that is, like everyone else who uses the same object). Using such drawing "aids" is actually more difficult for young children than freehand drawing. Some teachers mistakenly believe that they are helping children through these intermediary objects and gadgets. In fact, training children to use them may seriously inhibit the development of freehand drawing skills. These convergent production techniques intervene between intentional thought and mark-making, between the intention to represent in drawing and the freehand drawing process itself.

The second message to be conveyed to children is that they will inevitably find themselves at very different levels of competence in drawing compared with others in the class. This is an important message to combine with the earlier expectation that they will progress beyond their current level of ability in the direction of greater competence. Whatever level of competence children may judge themselves to have, they will nonetheless all be equally able to contribute to any group discussion of representation in drawing. Some more primitive levels of technique have particular understandings to convey about the nature of objects or processes. Children are helped when they come to see that there is no intrinsic value in one kind of drawing as compared with another kind, for example, the execution of a simple line drawing compared with a detailed rendering of a tree with every leaf drawn on every twig. The decision between these alternatives would depend on the visual information or sensation that the person doing the drawing wanted to represent.

The third message to give children concerns cultural conventions. For instance, there is a convention that the distant background of a scene should be portrayed behind the main items in the foreground; the sky should come down to meet the ground at the horizon in the picture rather than be represented as a blue bar at the top and a green bar at the bottom of the picture. Such conventions can be seen for what they are: cultural conventions. They need not be suggested to children who show no desire to explore the advantages of those conventions for themselves. Especially damaging to some children's drawing development can be the rote learning of "how to draw" particular objects, such as dogs or houses. Hinchman (1997) tells how she learned to draw horses from a book as a child. She describes how this continues to have an inhibiting effect on her drawing of the horses she can see from the windows of her home. Teachers can best encourage children in their drawing if they can recognize the intrinsic merit in any form of representation young children choose for themselves. Their choices will be made on the basis of their appreciation of pictures drawn by others, adults or children. Dissatisfaction with his or her own level of skill when expressed by a child can be countered with suggestions of alternative strategies to try out or other children with whom to talk to seek advice and assistance.

These three messages will help teachers to encourage successive attempts by children to apply their drawing skills to exploring alternative effects in the representation of people, objects, events, or processes of interest to themselves and to their classmates.

SUMMARY

In the context of a project, children can be encouraged and supported in their desire to find out about the world around them. We suggest that drawing can offer children an especially valuable and satisfying means of investigating and representing important features of a topic of study. There are opportunities for children to engage in many different kinds of drawing for a variety of different purposes. Drawing provides for a wide variety of individual ideas to be shared and project work thrives on the consideration of a rich body of information about a topic. Finally, it is important for teachers to be confident in their encouragement and support of children as they develop their ability to draw. Through their own confidence, teachers can inspire children to enliven and personalize their project work with drawing and thereby achieve the appropriate depth of learning.

11

The Project Approach
in Perspective

The project approach is one of many responses to the challenge of engaging the minds of young children. Our experience supports our view that good project work stimulates the intellectual, social, and emotional dispositions that can contribute to the capacity to lead a satisfying life—in the present and in the future. Because this approach to learning is so flexible, our introduction to it is intended to serve as a guide. We know of no single way to implement project work. More detailed suggestions on how to implement each phase can be found in two practical guides by Chard (1998a, 1998b).

We want to emphasize that projects are indepth investigations of phenomena or events within children's direct experience. Not all the things that are important for young children to know about and to learn are best treated as projects. Especially in the early primary years, some topics are prescribed by school authorities and must be "covered." Projects, on the other hand, are ways that topics can be "uncovered" as the investigation proceeds and takes various directions, depending on the interests and ideas of the particular group of children involved.

We have also suggested that project work is *part* of the curriculum—sometimes a large part, and sometimes a small part, depending on a variety of time, space, and curriculum constraints and opportunities. In other words, we see it as a vital part of a *balanced* curriculum. As indicated in Chapter 1, we see the project approach as complementary and supplementary to other aspects of the curriculum for young children.

Early childhood educators and parents are not and should not feel that they are caught between the choice of curricula that offer *either* mainly play plus arts and crafts *or* mainly formal lessons, drills, and worksheets, for neither type of activity by itself sufficiently challenges young minds. Nor do we suggest that all conventional activities commonly provided for children be set aside. Some time should be available for spontaneous play for all young children. Similarly, a sound curriculum offers ample opportunity for a range of physical activities, experience of good literature, music, and many other commonly available experiences.

In addition, many young children will also need carefully implemented, individual, systematic instruction to ease their way into the processes of acquiring the basic, complex skills required for competent functioning in the later school years.

Many parents and commentators who address educational issues seem to believe that unless children are engaged in formal instruction or in early literacy and numeracy exercises, they are occupied primarily by frivolous, fanciful, or mindless activities. *In general, such views are related to a common tendency to overestimate children academically and underestimate them intellectually.*

Our advocacy of the project approach is based on the assumption that when well done, it provides ample contexts, pre-texts, and texts that support, stimulate, and deepen children's important *intellectual* dispositions—dispositions that are typically inborn, and may be undermined by excessive and premature exposure to academic instruction and exercises.

Webb (1974) long ago framed these issues by suggesting that education must address two types of aims: *instrumental* and *intrinsic*. Instrumental aims, she suggested, assume that children are an "instrument" of society and that schooling is "an 'instrument' for purposes outside the school," such as preparing children for future occupations and other utilitarian and technical objectives. Intrinsic aims deal with those learnings that benefit children themselves. These aims include valuing knowledge for its own sake, aesthetic awareness, appreciation and sensibilities, and confidence in one's own intellectual powers. To these aims we would also add the intellectual dispositions, such as to be experimental, reflective, analytical, and critical when confronted with a range of problems and issues. Clearly, all schools are obliged to address both the instrumental and intrinsic aims of education. In our view, the project approach allows both kinds of aims to be addressed equally well.

Only a few of the topics that might be of value and interest to young children are presented in this book. By definition, the project approach can encompass a wide range of topics that are locally suitable and culturally relevant to the participants. One of the challenges of incorporating projects into the curriculum is to identify topics that are appropriate for each group of children and are responsive and sensitive to features of their environment. For example, project work based on a variety of topics and conducted in diverse locations are described by the teachers in two catalogues of the exhibits of project work shown at the 1996 and 1998 annual national conferences of the National Association for the Education of Young Children (Helm, 1996, 1998).

In Chapter 2, we presented the case for project work, using research evidence to support our position. Abundant evidence can certainly be marshaled to support other views. A curriculum that directly instructs children in the skills usually assessed on standardized achievements tests clearly has an edge in producing the kind of success such tests indicate. However, as we indicated in Chapter 2, there is research to suggest that these early successes are overshadowed *in the long term*—not in the short term—by the benefits of early childhood curriculum models, which give children ample opportunity to be interactive and proactive in their early childhood classes (Consortium for Longitudinal Studies, 1983; Marcon, 1992, 1995; Miller & Bizzell, 1983; Schweinhart, 1997).

Early childhood education has a long-standing tradition of placing high priority on supporting the development of social competence (Biber, 1984; Isaacs, 1933; Katz & McClellan, 1997). Recent insights into this aspect of children's growth confirm the wisdom of this tradition. Current research confirms the notion that the groundwork for the development of social competence is laid down in the very early years. Virtually everything of importance in our lives involves interaction with others; most of what adults do requires interpersonal competence. Indeed, the major problems we face locally and worldwide are not simply technological, scientific, mathematical, or logical ones; they are primarily problems of a social nature. The quest for solutions to these socially based problems will undoubtedly continue for decades to come—when today's children have become tomorrow's adults.

The project approach, as we see it, gives teachers the opportunity to attend equally to social *and* intellectual development. Decisionmakers who are intent upon school reform rarely hesitate to cry out that improvements in education are necessary to cope with the economic and technological exigencies of the future. Early experience in working cooperatively on mind-engaging tasks may also improve the chances of being able to cope with the complex social issues of today and those that are likely to face our children as they grow up and grow old.

It may be a propitious moment in time to return to the proverbial drawing board and develop methods for assessing the potential benefits of good project work. Assessment of practices that help develop desirable dispositions, such as children's eagerness to work, to persist and overcome setbacks as they proceed with their work, to proceed without rewards, their level of interest in their projects, their willingness to come to school, their general cooperativeness, and peer interactive competence, as well as their developing competence in literacy and numeracy skills should be closely observed and help us learn to improve our methods.

To date, the evidence of the benefits of the project approach is primarily indirect rather than careful systematic and controlled comparative longitudinal studies. However, like every curriculum approach, the project approach can be implemented at various levels of effectiveness. When well done, we suggest that the project approach can address all aspects of children's development and learning. Until such evidence is available, we suggest that teachers themselves experiment with the project approach. We are eager to hear about these experiments. From them, we hope to learn more about providing the education that best serves the long-term developmental and learning needs of young children.

In the past few years since the publication of the first edition of this book, we have already been privileged to learn a great deal from firsthand accounts of teachers' professional development as they have communicated with us about first-time and subsequent projects undertaken with children throughout the early childhood and elementary years. For many teachers, the project approach can seem to be a complex way to teach. It does not claim to offer panaceas for teachers that teach children with learning or motivational difficulties. Projects are easier for some teachers to implement than for others for a variety of reasons. These individual differences may be related to teachers' prior teaching philosophies, practices and experiences, or to the institutional, collegial or administrative contexts in which they work.

SUMMARY

We have learned that both teachers and children take time to learn the strategies and skills necessary to develop productive projects. We have learned that it helps teachers just embarking on the project approach to begin slowly, to investigate smaller-scale topics, sometimes referred to as "mini-projects," on topics such as "sunflowers," "the backyard," or "the people in our class." It has been reported to us that many teachers find it helpful when their pupils acquire cooperative learning strategies and gradually develop ways to be proactive and to take initiative and responsibility in developing their project work. Some teachers seem to find it easier in some ways to guide younger than older children in developing their projects. Older children often appear to have already learned to be passive in the class, at first are challenged when a teacher begins to involve them more directly in planning, developing, and evaluating their own work. On the other hand, because most older children have more representational skills available than younger ones to apply to their project work and potentially greater communicative competence, it does not take long before they "take over" the project.

Our aim continues to be to help teachers embarking on the project approach to have access to the problem solving experiences of teachers who have already become skilled in developing successful projects. Two practical guides to the project approach, published in 1992 and 1994, are now available from Scholastic (Chard, 1998a, 1998b). A listserv has been provided by the ERIC Clearinghouse on Elementary and Early Childhood Education at the University of Illinois (PRO-JECTS-L@postoffice.cso.uiuc.edu), where some 500 teachers from all over the world currently exchange ideas and experiences by e-mail. A website (http://www.ualberta.ca/~schard/projects.htm) has also been developed that features examples of projects and serves as the resource base for an online course for teachers. It is our intention to continue to provide such assistance to teachers as is made possible by the latest communication technology.

We look forward to continuing to hear from teachers who are personally experiencing the very real and direct advantages of projects to the children they work with. We also hope to be able to offer support to teachers experiencing doubts or difficulties. We have learned that sometimes the most important help can be given by teachers to other teachers, as we know children can often provide the most significant support to other children in their learning.

Our extensive experience of teaching and working with teachers who are implementing the project approach supports our conviction that when it is well done, it engages the growing minds of young children in ways that develop and strengthen the most important dispositions and feelings. In addition, good projects on worthwhile topics provide contexts for the construction and acquisition of knowledge, and for strengthening basic and important social and academic skills. We look forward to learning more from this work, and sharing that learning in as many ways as we can.

Appendix A:

Houses: How Are They Built?

The web and journal excerpts that follow were adapted with the authors' permission from a project proposal written by Angela G. Andrews and Helen L. Hocking, kindergarten teachers at Scott School, in Naperville, Illinois.

EXCERPTS FROM THE TEACHERS' HOUSE
PROJECT JOURNAL

Visit #1

Today we visited the construction site. There are five houses, each one in a different stage of construction. One is just a hole in the ground, and one is a model home with a "For Sale" sign on it.

"Look at this big pile of dirt," said Tommy. "It's for the swimming pool," said Jimmy.

"It's a basement hole," corrected Michael. "We had one."

Some boys were looking at the sewer cover. "It says 'water' on it."

"I know about sewers. There's alligators down there," said Steven.

Some girls were wondering about the plastic on the outside. They couldn't figure out why it was there. "What color is this house gonna be?" they asked.

"Does this house say 'for sale'?" asked Justin. "I don't think so. There's no *S* on it," answered Heather.

Some men were carrying long pieces of board into the house. "Those boards are very longer," said Tommy.

A generator was running and there was lots of hammering noise and sawing noise. The children could identify these sounds.

Some men working on the roof waved to us. "Be careful!" yelled the girls. The men were listening to music and it was turned up loud. "They must like that station," the children agreed.

"I see some stairs in there," said Jessica. "We have some at home."

On the way back to the school, Michael pointed to the sign. "That says 'Hunter's Woods.' I see the *H* and the *W*." I asked why did the children think it was called that. "Maybe somebody used to hunt here a long ago time," guessed Erin. "A man named Mr. Hunter used to live here," stated Michael. I don't know if that is true but the children seemed to accept his answer as truth.

Visit #2

We went back to the house. The masons were putting a brick facade on one of the houses. One of the children asked them what the silver tanks in the garage were for. After telling them the reason, the worker invited us in. I hesitated only for a minute, thinking about liability [insurance] and safety, sized up the group and my control of it, and we went inside!

"There's going to be a basement!" said Steven.

"There's going to be an upstairs!" said Michael.

"I have tile like this on my floor," said Mary Ella.

"Where is the kitchen?" asked Tyler. The appliances and cabinets were not in yet.

"It's pretty big inside here," commented Jason.

"The lights will go in that hole up there—right?" said Meredith.

"That is called scaffolding," reported Mary Ella. "We had that in our house a lot."

"Look at all the doors in here. How many are there?" said Tyler. The doors were stored in the garage.

"We like your house!" the children yelled to the masons as we left.

Visit #3

On our third visit, the builder dropped by. We told him we were watching his house being built. He smiled and watched us for a while. We were very careful as we looked at the window wells.

(Back at school one of the boys went over to the [paper] cups, picked one up and looked at it a long time. "Can I cut this up for a window well?" I saw that the middle part is ridged very much like the wells [we saw on the houses being constructed]. Soon an assembly line of window-well cutters was begun. The class decided that only the cracked cups should be cut up.)

We see a pile of gravel by the foundation site. The second house has a new tar driveway and is roped off. The sidewalk is being completed near the third house.

Some boys wanted to know how the window wells are attached [to the building] and they spent a long time looking at this.

"There's a pole across today!" notices Michael as we approach the foundation. A builder nearby tells us it is an *I* beam.

"What are these?" the children asked about the bolts protruding from the foundation. "That is how the decking will be attached," says the builder. Back at school the boys pour over my book that has a picture of this.

Visit #4

On our fourth visit, the children notice that the foundation has been sprayed black. I ask them why.

"Maybe they like that color," guess some of them.

"No. That's waterproof paint. It will keep the basement from leaking," states Michael.

A garbage truck drives up and takes away the scraps from in front of the house. The children watch this process but make no comment.

Visit #5

"There's a problem at the house. Want to go see what it is?" I ask on Monday. I have now got the habit of driving by and checking the house each day for signs of change. The children are eager to see.

"I told you it was a swimming pool!" said Jimmy. The basement is flooding. (Justin loves to say things are history).

The next day we went back to the site. A man was using a sump pump to get the water out. The pipe has been fixed. The water is going out into the street near a gutter. The children are fascinated by this sight.

"How long will it take to get the water out of there?" asked the class. "I don't know," said the worker.

There is a lock on the door of the house we went in one day. "That's to keep the robbers out," said Evan. "No, we had a lock like that on my house. It means the house is for sale," said Erin.

We walk around the outside, counting the window wells. Later I see them doing the same thing with their models. "Oh, look—a deck is going to be here!" states Heather. "We have one of those."

Back at school, I noticed that children are building foundations with the blocks instead of their usual building [piling] up [blocks from the ground]. Matt wanted to draw plans for the foundation. He laid some paper on the floor and began to sketch it out. The other boys began to build on his plan. They roll their plans up and put them in the cubbies. I made a note to bring a tube to school and let them store them in there, the way my dad, an architect, used to store his plans.

Visit #6

"It's a blue house!" reported Erin. "I saw it on my way to school."

Of course we have to go and see it. One of the houses has some blue siding on it now.

"I knew it would be blue," said Justin.

"Look at that hole in the side," points Shannon. "That's going to be a door." (It is for the fireplace.)

We notice that the driveway has been plowed up at one of the houses. We wonder why. "They just didn't do it right," says Michael.

Back at school I notice more evidence of carryover. I overheard Tommy, who was drinking from a cup with a straw, say "That's how they got the water out" to no one in particular. I see that the boys are taping their plans together now.

"What can we use for the *I* beam?" asks Nathan. They decide on a ruler. "We can use these for the joists," says Michael, indicating the unifix cubes. There is much measuring and comparing as they make the necessary boards.

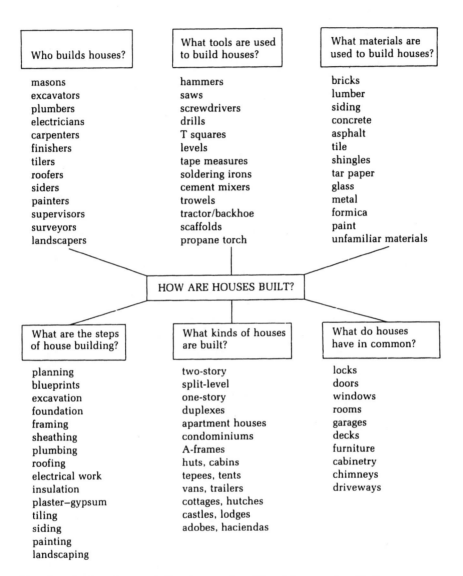

Who builds houses?	What tools are used to build houses?	What materials are used to build houses?
masons	hammers	bricks
excavators	saws	lumber
plumbers	screwdrivers	siding
electricians	drills	concrete
carpenters	T squares	asphalt
finishers	levels	tile
tilers	tape measures	shingles
roofers	soldering irons	tar paper
siders	cement mixers	glass
painters	trowels	metal
supervisors	tractor/backhoe	formica
surveyors	scaffolds	paint
landscapers	propane torch	unfamiliar materials

HOW ARE HOUSES BUILT?

What are the steps of house building?	What kinds of houses are built?	What do houses have in common?
planning	two-story	locks
blueprints	split-level	doors
excavation	one-story	windows
foundation	duplexes	rooms
framing	apartment houses	garages
sheathing	condominiums	decks
plumbing	A-frames	furniture
roofing	huts, cabins	cabinetry
electrical work	tepees, tents	chimneys
insulation	vans, trailers	driveways
plaster–gypsum	cottages, hutches	
tiling	castles, lodges	
siding	adobes, haciendas	
painting		
landscaping		

Teachers' planning web for the project How Houses Are Built.

Appendix B:

Guidelines for a Project on Seedpods

Particularly in tropical regions around the world, many varieties of trees, bushes, and plants bear their seeds in podlike structures (leguminosae). These pods can be collected as part of the children's school activities as well as afterschool hours. No field trips and special equipment are required.

Pods that individuals collect can be examined separately or pooled for sorting and examination in small or large groups. Some preliminary suggestions are listed below:

1. Identify the common and scientific names for the plants or trees the pods come from.
2. Sort and describe them by length—from shortest to longest; and by size—largest, smallest, widest, thinnest, thickest, and number of seeds in them. Measure actual length in inches or centimeters, and determine how many short pods equal one long pod.
3. Sort and describe by shape—flat, round, straight, curved, bulbous, tubular, cylindrical.
4. Sort and describe by color, hue, and luster.
5. Sort and describe by texture—smooth, rough, prickly, oily, ribbed.
6. Sort and compare by weight. Test to see how many small pods weigh as much as a large one.
7. Describe by source—tree, bush, plant, flower.
8. Sort by vegetable, fruit, and decorative.
9. Note whether they grow in clusters, groups, or singly, and whether they are

symmetrical when opened. Note how the seeds are arranged inside the pod, whether it is transparent, and whether the number of seeds can be detected without opening the pod. Determine the largest and the smallest number of seeds found in each species, whether the seeds rattle when the pod is shaken, and how the pods change over time as the seasons change.

10. Other activities: make musical instrument with the pods that rattle, or draw and paint how favorite pods look on the plants.

11. Drawing, painting, sketching, and tracing can be used to record observations, depending on the ages of the children.

Appendix C:

Dramatic Play in the Hospital

The following is a transcript of a recording of seven 5-year-olds playing in the class hospital. The comments in brackets are those of Sylvia Chard, who observed the children.

Dr = doctor; N = nurse; V = visitor (mother of patient); P = patient.

[10.07 a.m. Children just settling, getting used to me. I bandaged a boy's finger on request, fearing that might have been the wrong thing to do, but he went away and busied himself very soon as Dr2.]

    N1: Does she feel all right? Poor thing.
     V: What room is she in?
   Dr1: That's not how to do it.
    N1: Lee, I do all the things.
     P: I feel sick.
    N1: Where's the medicine? I need some medicine.
    N2: Give her some medicine.
   Dr1: No you can't open that bottle. It's childproof.
    N2: Where's that little white pot? Thank you.
    N1: Go to sleep.
    N2: She doesn't want to.

[Both nurses are being very attentive to the patient; one is sitting on the bed]

> *P:* Why are you sitting on me?
> *N2:* People have to sit on beds.{\dia}

[10.12 a.m. Dr1 bandages patient's finger carefully, first with a tubular cotton-knit dressing, then with a gauze bandage also using surgical scissors. N2 goes out of the room with a tray of cups. I later learned that she regularly takes a cup of tea to the teacher. N2 reenters half a minute later with the tray of cups. Dr2 gives the patient medicine with a tin of Andrews Liver Salts and a plastic spoon. N1 telephones the patient's mother, V, who has gone out of the room to receive the call from home.]

> *N1:* She's getting better now.
> *V:* All right, I'll come.
> *Dr2:* You'll like this, you've got to have this medicine today, it's nice, it's fizzy medicine.

[N3 has been spending most of the time so far arranging a variety of surgical instruments, medicine bottles, boxes, bandages, and cups and saucers on the shelves and in the cupboard at the side of the little room. Dr2 is mixing medicines in different jars from different bottles.]

> *Dr1:* Here you are, this will make it better.

[He is sponging the patient's forehead very gently with a little white sponge, putting disinfectant on the sponge from a tiny bottle. The bottle is emptied and he says to the patient, "Here you are, you can keep it." Patient plays with the bottle. N3 is still arranging and rearranging items on the shelf.]

N1 (to patient): You're a teenager and you're having a baby. Now you've had your
baby—she's broken her leg.

[10:17 a.m. She picks up a baby doll with a missing leg out of one of the three cribs in a row on the other side of the small room. Patient winces.]

> *N2:* Go to sleep. I'll put your blankets on, or you might get a cold.
> *Dr1:* She doesn't feel very well.
> *N1:* She's having a baby.
> *Dr1* (trying to step out of the corner): Can I come out please?

[N2 talks sweetly with patient, covers her up, and kisses her goodnight.]

> *Dr2:* I've got some medicine to give her.
> *P:* I want to kiss her (indicates V).
> *Dr2:* I'm the doctor.

    V: I'm her Mum.

 Dr2: You're not allowed to … it's cough medicine to make the baby come out.

[After some moments of confusion, the patient becomes the baby and acts with much less restraint than hitherto; she cries, indicates she wants to get out of bed.]

  N1: No you can't go out.

  N2: Doctor, she wants you.

 Dr2: This will keep her quiet.

 Dr1: I'm back again.

   V: Your doctor's here.

 Dr1: You're not going to like this. [Gives her medicine.] It's so we can give her an operation. So that's that done. I hope she doesn't wake up. [To patient] You're having your operation.

 Dr2 [advancing with forceps]: I'm going to take your heart out with these scissors.

[10.22 a.m.]

  N1: And that'll make you stay asleep a long time.

  N2: That's got her asleep!

 Dr1: Look what's in her heart!

 Dr2: Some brown stuff.

   P [wakes up expressively].

 Dr1 [To nurse]: Can you turn her face over please?

   V: That's the new doctor you like.

 Dr1: Can I have a look at your teeth? [Pretends to probe in her mouth with instrument.] I've got one of her teeth! It's got all blood over it.

  N1: It's got all blood over it [echo].

[Patient tries to crawl out of bed and is put back by V and N2; Dr1 starts work at the foot of the bed.]

 Dr2: I've got to check her hair [moves away].

  N1: I'm checking her hair.

  N2: The doctor's got to do that.

   P: Ow, ow!

   V [to Dr1, who is working on the patient's foot]: Stop it, Doctor, she's crying!

 Dr1: I have to do it.

   V: Stop crying … you can have a sugar lump if you be a good girl!

 Dr1 [businesslike]: Right! That's it; finished.

N1: I'll get the injection.

P: Ow, she's hurting me with her pin....

V [tickles patient]: I'm making her laugh.

[10.27 a.m. Dr2 works with concentration, putting medicines together for several minutes.]

N2: Doctor, she won't...

Dr1: Have your sugar lump. I can see your baby coming out... here's your baby.... I'm going to have to pinch her baby out [waves his forceps].

Teacher: Could you finish your game and tidy up your hospital now? Babies need to be covered up; you must make them as comfortable as possible. Make sure all the medicines are on the shelf.

Child: She's bleeding!

Teacher: Make her as comfortable as possible. Put all the bandages in the box.

Appendix D:

Instructions for Children:
How to Make Your Own Book

HOW TO MAKE YOUR OWN BOOK

Planning

Decide:

1. What is it about?
2. How big is it?
3. What shape is it?
4. How many pages does it have?

Work To Do on the Book

1. Think of a title.
2. Design the cover.
3. Do the writing (stories, poems, facts, or descriptions).
4. Draw the pictures.
5. Make any moving parts (fold-out, pop-up, or pull-along).
6. Number the pages.
7. Write the table of contents (front).
8. Write the index (back).

9. Make any other additions you want (dedications, acknowledgments, "The End" page, decorations for first letters or words, patterns in page margins).
10. Don't forget the name of the author and the date you finish it.

Appendix E:

Project Webs for Going Shopping, Weather, and a Construction Site

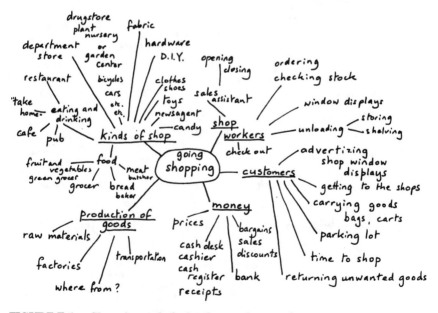

FIGURE E.1. Shopping web design by another teacher.

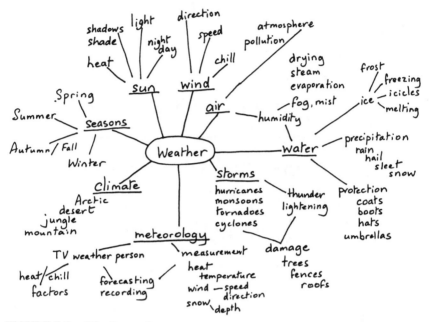

FIGURE E.2. Weather web.

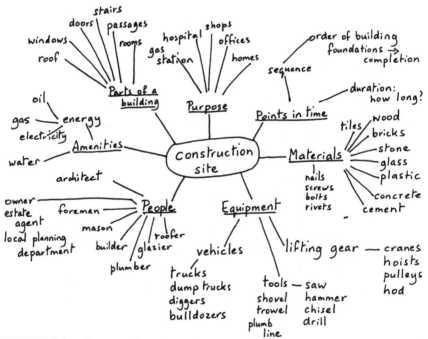

FIGURE E.3. Construction site web.

Appendix F:

School Bus Webs for Younger and Older Children

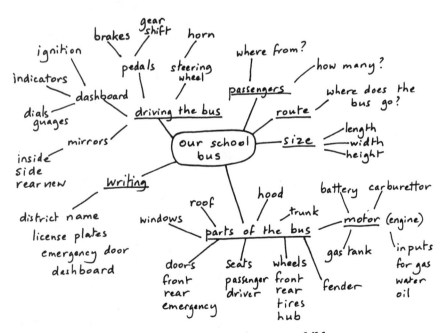

FIGURE F.1. School bus web for a class of younger children.

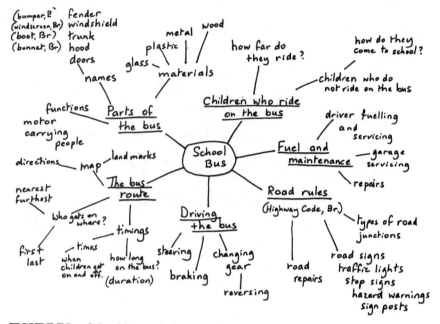

FIGURE F.2.   School bus web for a class of older children.

Appendix G:

Zoom Web on Homes

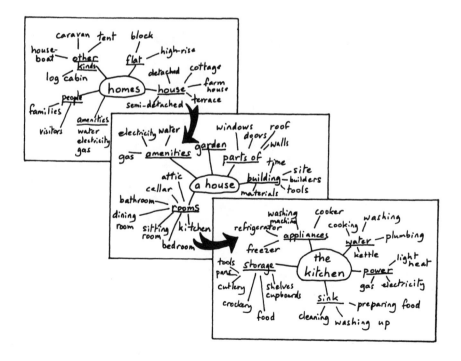

Appendix H:

A Walk Around the School*

Teachers can use a walk around the school, or any nature walk, to obtain readily accessible learning materials. Walks can help children take the first important step in learning, once they express curiosity. The activities outlined below are not exhaustive. However, they illustrate the principle of relating objects that the children are curious about to the organized disciplines that they should begin to master in the school years. The activities are appropriate for children 4 to 8 years of age, although some activities are more appropriate for the older ones.

WHAT TO TAKE ALONG

Be sure to take sturdy paper bags so that children can collect rocks, stones, sticks, plants, feathers, bones, insects, or anything else they would like to bring back to look at more closely. In the classroom, some children may wish to pool their collections and work in small groups, while others may prefer to work alone.

The materials collected can be organized to suit various ways of grouping topics and skills. Unlike the way projects are organized in the main part of the book, this outline groups the activities under traditional subject headings, reflecting conventional disciplines.

---

* Adapted from Chard, 1971. Reprinted in Katz & Chard, 1989.

TEACHING MATHEMATICS WITH ROCKS AND STONES

Mathematics is a good subject to begin with, since there are many ways of using rocks and stones to illustrate or strengthen mathematical concepts. Here are a few starters:

Seriation. Have the children lay out the stones in order of size (for example, smallest to largest), weight (lightest to heaviest), color (lightest to darkest), shape (flattest to roundest, thinnest to thickest).

Counting. Separate stones into sets by color or size, and put each set on separate paper plates. Count the number of stones on each plate, and make a card for each plate showing the number of stones. Talk about how shepherds used "counting stones" to keep track of their sheep.

Weighing. Compare the weight of rocks or stones to other ones and to materials such as wood, sand, water, or metal objects. Determine how many smaller stones or rocks it will take to balance a larger one.

Estimating. Try to guess or predict from their size how many stones it might take to fill up a glass jar or to make a stone "path" from one corner of the room to the other. Have the children check their estimates with the facts.

Measuring. Use a tape measure to determine the length, breadth, and circumference of different rocks. Talk about the "stone" as an old unit of measurement. Make a crayon mark on a large stone, roll it along the floor, and count the number of times the mark reappears as a way of describing and measuring the distance covered.

TEACHING SCIENCE WITH STONES

The study of stones and rocks is a natural jumping-off place for introducing the natural and life sciences. Here are some preliminary suggestions:

Identification. Look up the names of rocks and stones in a rock book. Make labels when identification has been successful.

Rocks and water. Suggest some of the following questions for children to explore: Do rocks sink or float? Which rocks will sink, which will float?

Have the children predict and then test their predictions in answering these questions: How much water does a rock displace? Measure the spillover. Compare the weight of a cup of sand and a rock that displaces an amount of water equal to that displaced by the sand.

Notice how shiny the wet rocks are. Why is that so? How does wetness change the color of stones and rocks? How does water change the shape of stones (as in erosion)?

Rocks and fire. With tongs, hold a rock in a candle flame. Ask the children beforehand whether some rocks will burn, what color the flame might be, and whether they will turn black and crumble. Experiment with different rocks and note the differences among them.

Rocks and Motion. Discuss ways of moving large rocks (lever, crane, pulley, and so on). Talk about how the pyramids and other ancient buildings were constructed and contrast them with modern building materials and methods. Take opportunities to observe large mechanical cranes and earth-moving equipment.

Geography and geology. Suggest some of the following points for discussion: What is the earth made of? Talk about different kinds of rocks and how they were formed; how valleys, riverbeds, waterfalls, and mountains are created; what causes landslides, erosion; how rocks can give clues about the past (fossils, arrowheads, and so on).

Human uses for rocks. Talk about (or suggest projects involving) stone-age tools, making fire with flint, weapons (throwing rocks, arrowheads, slingshots, catapults), building shelters and houses, extracting metals from rocks, coal for power and heat, sand and gravel for roads, precious gems for decoration and jewelry, sculptures, stone fences, chalkboards, stones in fish tanks, plumb line with a stone.

TEACHING LANGUAGE ARTS WITH STONES

Expressions involving stones. Start with some of the following expressions, and encourage the children to think of other sayings, stories, and poems about stones and rocks and to make some up:

"A rolling stone gathers no moss."
"People who live in glass houses shouldn't throw stones."
"A stone's throw from here."
"Rock bottom," "stone cold," "stone deaf," "heart of stone," "stoned."
Kidney stones, gravel-voiced

Tell the story of "Stone Soup," tell how the little red hen filled the bag with stones to fool the fox, tell about the Gorgon's head, and tell about David and Goliath.

Famous rocks. Discuss Plymouth Rock, the Rock of Gibraltar, Stonehenge, Mount Rushmore and the presidents' faces carved in stone, "Rock of Ages," prehistoric cave paintings.

Creative activities. Encourage the children to write poems and stories about some aspect of rocks. Make a rock collage (glue the small stones to a background painting), paint stones in bright colors, use colored stones as paper weights. Make beetles, ladybugs, or animals from stones with paper, pipe cleaners, and so on. Paint faces on stones, make stone prints.

Vocabulary enrichment. Inspection and comparison of stones provide a good opportunity to increase vocabulary. Describe:

Shape: round, flat, square, angular, triangular, pointed, top, bottom, wide, long.
Color: pale, light, dark, speckled, striped.
Size: small, tiny, minute, miniscule, big, large, giant-size, wide.
Weight: heavy, light, hefty.
Comparatives: heavier, longer, lighter than.
Texture: hard, soft, rough, smooth, sharp, flakey, crumbly, rounded, jagged.

Encourage the children to feel the rocks in a bag and guess the color as you say, "Find me the white, rough rock; a yellow, sharp, pointed rock; a black, smooth rock," and so forth.

Movement. Children will generally enjoy these pantomimes:

- falling like a rock
- carrying a heavy bucket of rocks
- moving a big rock by rocking it back and forth
- walking on a rocky riverbed through the water
- walking with rocks in your shoes
- stumbling, slipping, stubbing your toe
- climbing a rock face and feeling for handholds and footholds.

LEARNING WITH STICKS

The same sorts of activities can be planned around collections of sticks and plants. The brief outlines that follow present only a few suggestions to serve as starting points.

Sticks and Mathematics

Sorting: Lay out sticks according to length, thickness, color, roughness, alive or dead, kind of bush, tree, or plant.
   Seriation: Lay out according to length, such as stick, rod, pole, log, stakes.
   Counting: Make groups and sets by number.
   Weigh and measure: Estimate lengths of various sticks; talk about use of rods and poles as measuring tools.
   Shapes: Make geometric shapes with sticks and lumps of clay.

Sticks and Science

Identify the source of sticks and twigs in a tree book. Suggest questions for the children to explore: Do sticks burn; green ones too; both when wet and dry? Do sticks float or sink? Does weight make any difference in ability to float? What are the differences between green and dead sticks? What are some different qualities of various woods? What happens to trees in winter? Note the way some insects are camouflaged to look like the plants and trees they inhabit. Take a field trip to a tree nursery.

Human Uses for Sticks, Poles, Logs

Many uses can be discussed, such as starting fires by rubbing sticks together; burning in fires for heat, power, cooking; early writing by making pictures in the sand and dirt; fishing rod, bow and arrow, boomerang, spear, house frames, teepee, hammock, boar, birch canoe, propulsion of boats with oars and poles, mast, raft, fence, stilts, flagpole, totem pole, handles of tools, brooms as little sticks fastened to a big one, divining rod for water detection, beating drums.

Sticks and Art

Use sticks to apply paint or scratch designs in paint or crayon. Use in printing; make collages; make models with sticks and clay, sticks and paper (kites), sticks and cloth (teepee, hammock, wagon cover), sticks and sand (walls of a fort). Draw stick men and women.

Sticks and Music

Sticks can be struck against one another, used for drumsticks, hollowed for pipes, used to clean flutes. Sounds that sticks make include scraping, grating, creaking, snapping, cracking.

Similar activities can be developed with other materials gathered on the walk. For example, with leaves and flowers, the teacher can develop groups of activities and explorations under the general headings of language arts, mathematics, science, human uses, art, music, movement, and creative writing.

Appendix I:

Project Web for "How We Get Our Fish"

References

Alexander, P. A., Murphy, K., & Woods, B. S. (1996, April). Of squalls and fathoms: Navigating the seas of educational innovation. *Educational Researcher, 23*(3), 31–39.

Ames, C., & Ames, R. (1984, August). Systems of student and teacher motivation: Toward a qualitative definition. *Journal of Educational Psychology, 76*(4), 535–556.

Azmitia, M. (1988). Peer interaction and problem solving: When are two heads better than one? *Child Development, 59*(1), 87–96.

Beneke, S. (1998). *Rearview mirror: Reflections on a preschool car project.* Champaign, IL: ERIC Clearinghouse on Elementary and Early Childhood Education.

Bennett, N., Desforges, C., Cockburn, A., & Wilkinson, B. (1984). *The quality of pupil learning experiences.* Hillsdale, NJ: Lawrence Erlbaum.

Benware, C. A., & Deci, E. L. (1984). Quality of learning with an active versus passive motivational set. *American Educational Research Journal, 21l*(4), 755–765.

Bereiter, C. (1986). Does direct instruction cause delinquency? *Early Childhood Research Quarterly, 1*(3), 289–292.

Berk, L. E., & Winsler, A. (1995). *Scaffolding children's learning: Vygotsky and early childhood education.* Washington, DC: National Association for the Education of Young Children.

Biber, B. (1984). *Early education and psychological development.* New Haven, CT: Yale University Press.

Blank, M. (1985). Classroom discourse: The neglected topic of the topic. In M. M. Clark (Ed.), *Helping communication in early education* (pp 13–20). Education Review Occasional Publication No. 11. Birmingham, England: University of Birmingham.

Blyth, J. (1984). *Place and time with children five to nine.* Kent, England: Croom Helm.

Blyth, W. A. L. (1984). *Development, experience and curriculum in primary education.* London: Croom Helm.

Bodrova, E., & Leong, D. J. (1996). *Tools of the mind: The Vygotskian approach to early childhood education.* Englewood Cliffs, NJ: Merrill.

Boggiano, A. K., & Main, D. S. (1986). Enhancing children's interest in activities used as a reward: The bonus effect. *Journal of Personality and Social Psychology, 51*(6), 1116–1126.

Brandt, R. (1997). On using knowledge about our brain. A conversation with Bob Sylwester. *Educational Leadership, 54*(8), 16–19.

Bredekamp, S., & Copple, C. (Eds.). (1997). *Developmentally appropriate practice in early childhood programs* (Rev. ed). Washington, DC: National Association for the Education of Young Children.

Bretherton, I. (1984). (Ed.). *Symbolic play: The development of social understanding.* New York: Academic Press.

Brown, A., & Campione, J. (1984). Three faces of transfer. In. M. E. Lamb, A. L. Brown, & B. Rogoff (Eds.), *Advances in developmental psychology* (Vol. 2, pp. 143–192). Hillsdale, NJ: Lawrence Erlbaum.

Bruner, J. (1980). *Under fives in Britain.* Ypsilanti, MI: High/Scope Foundation.

Bruner, J. (1985). Vygotsky: A historical and conceptual perspective. In J. V. Wertsch (Ed.), *Culture, communication, and cognition: Vygotskian perspectives* (pp. 21–34). New York: Cambridge University Press.

Buss, D. M., & Craik, K. H. (1983). The act frequency approach to personality. *Psychological Review, 90*(2), 105–126.

Carey, S. (1986). Cognitive science and science education. *American Psychologist, 41*(10), 1123–1130.

Chard, S. C. (1970). *Opening up the classroom: A walk around the school.* Urbana, IL: ERIC Clearinghouse on Elementary and Early Childhood Education.

Chard, S. C. (1998a). *Book 1. The project approach: Making curriculum come alive.* New York: Scholastic.

Chard, S.C. (1998b). *Book 2. The project approach: Managing successful projects.* New York: Scholastic.

Clark, M. M., & Wade, B. (1983). Early childhood education [Special issue]. *Educational Review, 35*(2).

Consortium for Longitudinal Studies. (1983). *As the twig is bent.* Hillsdale, NJ: Lawrence Erlbaum.

Dearden, R. F. (1984). *Theory and practice in education.* London: Routledge & Kegan Paul.

deCharms, R. (1983). Intrinsic motivation, peer tutoring, and cooperative learning: Practical maxims. In J. M. Levine & M. C. Wang (Eds.), *Teacher and student perceptions: Implications for learning* (pp. 391–398). Hillsdale, NJ: Lawrence Erlbaum.

Deci, E. L., & Ryan, R. M. (1982). Curiosity and self-directed learning. In L. G. Katz (Ed.), *Current topics in early childhood education* (Vol. 4, pp. 71–86). Norwood, NJ: Ablex.

Deci, E. L., & Ryan, R. M. (1985). *Intrinsic motivation and self-determination in human behavior.* New York: Plenum Press.

Department of Education and Science. (1978). *Primary education in England.* London: Author.

Donaldson, M. (1978). *Children's minds.* Glasgow, Scotland: Fontana.

Donaldson, M. (1983). Children's reasoning. In M. Donaldson, R. Grieve, & C. Pratt (Eds.), *Early childhood development and education.* London: The Guilford Press.

Durkin, D. (1980). *Is kindergarten reading instruction really desirable?* Evanston, IL: National College of Education.

Dweck, C. S. (1991). Self-theories and goals: Their role in motivation, personality, and development. In R. A. Dienstbier (Ed.), *Perspectives on motivation* (pp. 199–236). Lincoln, NE: University of Nebraska Press.

Dweck, C. S. (1986). Motivational processes affecting learning. *American Psychologist, 41*(10), 1040–1048.

Dweck, C. S. (1987, April). *Children's conceptions of intelligence.* Paper presented at the annual conference of the American Educational Research Association, Washington, DC.

Dweck, C. S., & Leggett, E. L. (1988). A social-cognitive approach to motivation and personality. *Psychological Review, 95*(2), 256–273.

Edwards, B. (1979). *Drawing on the right side of the brain: A course enhancing creativity and artistic confidence.* Los Angeles: J.P. Tarcher; New York: St. Martin's Press.

Edwards, C. P., & Springate, K. (1993, Fall). Inviting children into project work. *Dimensions of Early Childhood, 22*(91), 9–12, 40.

Edwards, C. P., Gandini, L., & Forman, G. (1998). *The hundred languages of children: The Reggio Emilia approach—advanced reflections* (2nd ed.). Stamford, CT: Ablex.

Fein, G., & Rivkin, M. (1986). *The young child at play: Reviews of research* (Vol. 4). Washington, DC: National Association for the Education of Young Children.

Forman, G. E. (1993). *Jed draws his bicycle: A case of drawing-to-learn* [Videotape]. (Available from Performanetics, 19 The Hollow, Amherst, MA 01002)

French, L. A. (1985). Real-world knowledge as the basis for social and cognitive development. In J. B. Pryor & J. D. Day (Eds.), *The development of social cognition* (pp. 179–210). New York: Springer-Verlag.

Fry, P. S., & Addington, J. (1984). Comparison of social problem solving of children from open and traditional classrooms: A two-year longitudinal study. *Journal of Educational Psychology, 76*(1), 318–329.

Gallas, K. (1994). *The languages of learning: How children talk, write, dance, draw, and sing their understanding of the world.* New York: Teacher's College Press.

Garvey, C. (1983). Some properties of social play. In M. Donaldson, R. Grieve, & C. Pratt (Eds.), *Early childhood development* (pp. 11–24). Oxford, England: Basil Blackwell.

Gersten, R. (1986). Response to "Consequences of Three Preschool Curriculum Models through Age 15." *Early Childhood Research Quarterly, 1*(3), 293–302.

Glaser, R. (1984). Education and thinking: The role of knowledge. *American Psychologist, 39*(2), 93–104.

Goodnow, J. (1977). *Children's drawing.* Isle of Man, UK: Fontana/Open Books.

Greenberg, P. (1987). Lucy Sprague Mitchell: A major missing link between early childhood education in the 1980s and progressive education in the 1890s–1930s. *Young Children, 42*(5), 70–84.

Grolnick, W. S., & Ryan, R. M. (1987). Autonomy in children's learning: An experimental and individual difference investigation. *Journal of Personality and Social Psycholgoy, 52*(5), 890–898.

Gross, N., Gianquinta, J. D., Bernstein, M. (1975). Failure to implement a major organizational innovation. In J. V. Baldridge & T. E. Deal (Eds.), *Managing change in educational organizations: Sociological perspectives, strategies, and case studies* (pp. 409–426). Berkeley, CA: McCutchan.

Groves, M. M., Sawyers, J. K., & Moran, J. D. (1987). Reward and ideational fluency in preschool children. *Early Childhood Research Quarterly, 2*(4), 335–340.

Grusec, J. E., & Arnason, L. (1982) Considerations for others: Approaches to enhancing altruism. In S. Moore & C. Cooper (Eds.), *The young child: Reviews of research* (Vol. 3, pp. 159–174). Washington, DC: National Association for the Education of Young Children.

Harkema, R. (1999). The school bus project. *Early Childhood Research & Practice* [Online journal], *1*(2). Available: http://ecrp.uiuc.edu/v1n2/harkema.html [November 1, 1999].

Harrison, C. (1980). *Readability in the classroom.* Cambridge, England: Cambridge University Press.

Hatch, T. (1997). Getting specific about multiple intelligences. *Educational Leadership, 54*(8), 26–29.

Heath, S. B. (1987, April). *The quest for uncertainty.* Paper presented at the annual conference of the American Educational Research Association, Washington, DC.

Helm, J. H. (Ed.). (1996). *The project approach catalog.* Urbana, IL: ERIC Clearinghouse on Elementary and Early Childhood Education.

Helm, J. H. (Ed.). (1998). *The project approach catalog 2.* Champaign, IL: ERIC Clearinghouse on Elementary and Early Childhood Education.

Helm, J. H., Beneke, S., & Steinheimer, K. (1998). *Windows on learning: Documenting young children's work.* New York: Teacher's College Press.

Hohmann, M., Banet, B., & Weikart, D. P. (1983) *Young children in action.* Ypsilanti, MI: High/Scope Foundation.

Hinchman, H. (1991). *A life in hand: Creating the illuminated journal.* Salt Lake City, UT: Peregrine Smith Books.

Hinchman, H. (1997). *A trail through leaves: The journal as a path to place.* New York: W.W. Norton.

Hughes, M., & Grieve, R. (1983). On asking children bizzare questions. In M. Donaldson, R. Grieve, & C. Pratt. (Eds.), *Early childhood development and education* (pp. 104–114). Oxford: Basil Blackwell.

Hunter, M., & Barker, G. (1987, October). "If at first...":Attribution theory in the classroom. *Educational Leadership,* 50–53.

Isaacs, S. (1933). *Social development in young children.* London: Routledge.

Isaacs, S. (1966). *Intellectual growth in young children.* New York: Schocken Books.

Johnson, D. W., Johnson, R. T., Holubec, E. J., & Roy, P. (1984). *Circles of learning: Cooperation in the classroom.* Arlington, VA: The Association for Supervision and Curriculum Development.

Johnson, R. T., & Johnson, D. W. (1985, July/August). Student–student interaction: Ignored but powerful. *Journal of Teacher Education, 36*(4), 22–26.

Julyan, C., & Duckworth, E. (1996). A constructivist perspective on teaching and learning science. In C. T. Fosnot (Ed.), *Constructivism: Theory, perspectives, and practice* (pp. 55–72). New York: Teacher's College Press.

Kamii, C., & Ewing, J. K. (1996). Basing teaching on Piaget's constructivism. *Childhood Education, 72*(5), 260–264.

Karmiloff-Smith, A. (1984). Children's problem solving. In M. Lamb, A. Brown, & B. Rogoff (Eds.), *Advances in developmental psychology* (Vol. 3, pp. 39–89). Hillsdale, NJ: Lawrence Erlbaum.

Karnes, M. B., Schwedel, A. M., & Williams, M. B. (1983). A comparison of five approaches for educating young children from low-income homes. In Consortium for Longitudinal Studies (Ed.), *As the twig is bent ... lasting effects of preschool programs* (pp. 133–170). Hillsdale, NJ: Lawrence Erlbaum.

Katz, L. G. (1995). *Talks with teachers of young children: A collection.* Norwood, NJ: Ablex.

Katz, L. G. (1996). Child development knowledge and teacher preparation: Confronting assumptions. *Early Childhood Research Quarterly, 11*(2), 135–146.

Katz, L. G, & Cesarone, B. (Eds.). (1994). *Reflections on the Reggio Emilia approach.* Urbana, IL: ERIC Clearinghouse on Elementary and Early Childhood Education.

Katz, L. G., & Chard, S. C. (1989). *Engaging children's minds: The project approach.* Norwood, NJ: Ablex.

Katz, L. G., Evangelou, D., & Hartman, J. A. (1990). *The case for mixed-age grouping in the early years.* Washington, DC: National Association for the Education of Young Children.

Katz, L. G., & McClellan, D. (1997). *Fostering children's social competence: The teacher's role.* Washington, DC: National Association for the Education of Young Children.

Katz, L. G., & Raths, J. D. (1985). Dispositions as goals for teacher education. *Teaching and Teacher Education, 1*(4), 301–307.

Keats, E. J. (1968). *A letter to Amy.* New York: Harper & Row.

Kliebard, H. M. (1985). What happened to american schooling in the first part of the twentieth century? In E. Eisner (Ed.), *Learning and teaching the ways of knowing* (pp. 1–22). Chicago: University of Chicago Press.

Koester, L. S., & Farley, F. (1982). Psychophysical characteristics and school performance of children in open and traditional classrooms. *Journal of Educational Psychology, 74*(2), 254–263.

Kohn, A. (1993). *Punished by rewards: The trouble with gold stars, incentive plans, A's, praise, and other bribes.* Boston: Houghton Mifflin.

Kohn, A. (1994). *The risks of rewards.* Urbana, IL: ERIC Clearinghouse on Elementary and Early Childhood Education.

Krathwohl, D. (1985, March). Cooerative learning: A research success story. *Educational Researcher*, 28–29.

Lepper, M. R. (1981). Intrinsic and extrinsic motivation in children: Detrimental effects of superfluous social controls. *Aspects of the Development of Competence: Minnesota Symposia on Child Psychology, 14*, 155–214.

London, P. (1989). *No more second hand art: Awakening the artist within.* Boston: Shambhala.

Lougee, M. D., & Graziano, W. G. (n.d.). *Children's relationships with non-agemate peers.* Unpublished manuscript.

Maccoby, E. E. (1984). Socialization and developmental change. *Child Development, 55*(2), 317–328.

Maccoby, E. E., & Zellner, M. (1970). *Experiments in primary education: Aspects of project follow-through.* New York: Harcourt Brace.

Maehr, M. L. (1982). *Motivational factors in school achievement.* Washington, DC: National Commission on Excellence in Education. (ERIC Document Reproduction Service No. ED 227 095)

Marcon, R. A. (1992). Differential effects of three preschool models on inner-city 4-year-olds. *Early Childhood Research Quarterly, 7*(4), 517–530.

Marcon, R. A. (1995, May). Fourth-grade slump: The cause and cure. *Principal*, 17–20.

McClellan, D. E., & Kinsey, S. J. (1999, Spring). Children's social behavior in relation to participation in mixed-age or same-age classrooms. *Early Childhood Research & Practice* [Online journal], *1*(1). Available: http://ecrp.uiuc.edu/v1n1/index.html [June 1, 1999].

McCullers, J. C., Fabes, R. A., & Moran, J. D. (1987). Does instrinsic motivation theory explain the adverse effects of rewards on immediate task performance? *Journal of Personality and Social Psychology, 52*(5), 1027–1033.

Miller, L. B., & Bizzell, R. P. (1983). Long-term effects of four preschool programs: Sixth, seventh, and eight grades. *Child Development, 54*(3), 727–741.

Moline, S. (1995). *I see what you mean: Children at work with visual information.* York, ME: Stenhouse.

Morgan, M. (1984). Reward-induced decrements and increments in instrinsic motivation. *Review of Education Research, 54*(1), 5–30.

Mounts, N. S., & Roopnarine, J. (1987). Social-cognitive play patterns in same-age and mixed age preschool classrooms. *American Educational Research Journal, 24*(3), 463–476.

Nelson, K. (1985). *Making sense: The acquisition of shared meaning.* New York: Academic Press.

Nelson, K. (1986). *Event knowledge.* Hillsdale, NJ: Lawrence Erlbaum.

Nelson, K., & Seidman, S. (1984). Playing with scripts. In I. Bretherton (Ed.), *Symbolic play: The development of social understanding* (pp. 45–72). New York: Academic Press.

Parker, J., & Asher, S. (1987). Peer relations and later personal adjustment: Are low-accepted children at risk? *Psychological Bulletin, 102*(3), 357–389.

Pinard, A. (1986). "Prise de conscience" and taking charge of one's own cognitive functioning. *Human Development, 29*(6), 342–354.

Plowden Committee Report. (1967). *Children and their primary schools*. London: Her Majesty's Stationery Office.

Prawat, R. S. (1995). Misreading Dewey: Reform, projects, and the language game. *Educational Researcher, 24*(7), 13–22.

Radke-Yarrow, M. (1987, April). *A developmental and contextual analysis of continuity*. Paper presented at the biennial conference of the Society for Research in Child Development, Baltimore, MD.

Reggio Children. (1997). *Shoe and meter. Children and measurement: First approaches to the discovery, function, and use of measurement*. Reggio Emilia, Italy: Author.

Rogoff, B. (1982). Integrating context and cognitive development. In M. E. Lamb, A. L. Brown, B. Rogoff. (Eds.), *Advances in developmental psychology* (Vol. 2, pp. 125–170). Hillsdale, NJ: Lawrence Erlbaum.

Rosenfield, D., Folger, R., & Adelman, H. F. (1980). When rewards reflect competence: a qualification of the overjustification effect. *Journal of Personality and Social Psychology, 39*(3), 368–376.

Ruef, K. (1994). *The private eye (5X) looking: Thinking by analogy—A guide to developing the interdisciplinary mind*. Seattle, WA: The Private Eye Project.

Ryan, R. M., Connell, J. P., & Deci, E. L. (1985). A motivational analysis of self-determination and self-regulation in education. In C. Ames & R. E. Ames (Eds.), *Research on motivation: The classroom milieu* (pp. 13–51). New York. Academic Press.

Sanderson, M. (1999, Spring). Reaping the rewards of project work with infants and toddlers: *Innovations in Early Education: The International Reggio Exchange*, 5–8.

Schank, R. C., & Abelson, R. P. (1977). *Scripts, plans, goals, and understanding*. Hillsdale, NJ: Lawrence Erlbaum.

Schickedanz, J. A. (1999). *Much more than the ABC's*. Washington, DC: National Association for the Education of Young Children.

Schweinhart, L. J. (1997). *Child-initiated Learning activities for young children living in poverty*. Champaign, IL: ERIC Clearinghouse on Elementary and Early Childhood Education.

Schweinhart, L. J., & Weikart, D. P. (1997). The High/Scope preschool curriculum comparison study through age 23. *Early Childhood Research Quarterly, 12*(2), 117–143.

Schweinhart, L. J., Weikart, D. P., & Larner, M. B. (1986a). Consequences of Three preschool curriculum models through age 15. *Early Childhood Research Quarterly, 1*(1), 15–46.

Schweinhart, L. J., Weikart, D. P., & Larner, M. B. (1986b). Child-initiated activities in early childhood programs may help prevent delinquency. *Early Childhood Research Quarterly, 1*(3), 303–312.

Sedgwick, D., & Sedgwick, F. (1993). *Drawing to learn*. Sevenoaks, UK: Hodder and Stoughton.

Sfard, A. (1998). On two metaphors for learning and the dangers of choosing just one. *Educational Researcher, 27*(2), 4–13.

Shuell, T. J. (1986). Cognitive conceptions of learning. *Review of Educational Research, 56*(4), 411–436.

Slavin, R. E. (1983). *Cooperative learning*. New York: Longman.

Slavin, R. E. (1987a, Spring). A theory of school and classroom organization. *Educational Psychologist, 22*(2), 89–108.

Slavin, R. E. (1987b). Developmental and motivational perspectives on cooperative learning. *Child Development, 58*(5), 1161–1167.

Slavin, R. E. (1987c). *Grouping for instruction: Equity and effectiveness.* Baltimore, MD: Center for Research on Elementary and Middle Schools.

Skinner, E. A., Zimmer-Gembeck, M. J., & Connell, J. P. (1998). Individual differences and the development of perceived control. *Monographs of the Society for Research in Child Development, 63*(2–3, Serial No. 254).

Smagorinsky, P. (1995). The social construction of data: Methodological problems of investigating learning in the ZPD. *Review of Educational Research, 65*(3), 191–212.

Smiley, P. A., & Dweck, C. S. (1994). Individual differences in Achievement goals among young children. *Child Development, 65,* 1723–1743.

Spodek, B. (1987). *Knowledge and the kindergarten curriculum.* Paper presented at the Annual Conference of the American Educational Research Association, Washington, DC.

Stevahn, L., Johnson, D. W., Johnson, R. T., & Real, D. (1996, Winter). The impact of a cooperative or individualistic context on the effectiveness of conflict resolution training. *American Educational Research Journal, 33,* 801–823.

Stewart, J. (1986). *The making of the primary school.* Milton Keynes, England: Open University Press.

Taylor, J. (1983). *Organising and integrating the first school day.* London: Allen and Unwin.

Tudge, J. (1986, May). *Beyond conflict: The role of reasoning in collaborative problem solving.* Paper presented at the Annual Symposium of the Jean Piaget Society, Philadelphia.

Van Ausdal, S. J. (1988). William Heard Kilpatrick: Philosopher and teacher. *Childhood Education, 68*(3), 164–168.

Walberg, H. (1984). Improving the productivity of America's schools. *Educational Leadership, 41*(8), 19–30.

Webb, L. (1974). *Purpose and practice in nursery education.* Oxford, England: Basil Blackwell.

Wells, G. (1983). Talking with children: The complementary roles of parents and teachers. In M. Donaldson, R. Grieve, & C. Pratt (Eds.), *Early childhood development and education* (pp. 127–150). London: The Guilford Press.

Wells, G. (1986). *The meaning makers: Children learning language and using language to learn.* Cambridge, England: Cambridge University Press

Willes, M. J. (1983). *Children into pupils.* London: Routledge & Kegan Paul.

Williams, D. A. (1998). *Documenting children's learning: Assessment and evaluation in the project approach.* Unpublished master's thesis, University of Alberta, Edmonton, Alberta, Canada.

Wilson, P. S. (1971). *Interests and the discipline of education.* London: Routledge & Kegan Paul.

Wisconsin Center for Educational Research. (1984, Summer). Ability grouping can hurt achievement. Madison, WI: Author.

Wood, D., & Wood, H. (1983). Questioning the preschool child. *Educational Review, 35*(2), 148–162.

Zimiles, H. (1987). The Bank Street approach. In J. L. Roopnarine & E. Johnson (Eds.), *Approaches to early childhood education* (pp. 163–178). Columbus, OH: Merrill.

Author Index

A

Abelson, R. P., 30, *198*
Adelman, H. F., 41, *198*
Addington, J., 52, *195*
Alexander, P. A., 19, *193*
Ames, C., 44, 48, *193*
Ames, R., 44, 48, *193*
Asher, S., 32, *198*
Azmitia, M., 47, 52, *193*

B

Banet, B., 99, *196*
Barker, G., 39, *196*
Beneke, S., 10, 47, 55, 106, 107, 110, 130, 140, 141, *193, 196*
Bennett, N., 45, 46, *193*
Benware, C. A., 38, 52, 125, *193*
Bereiter, C., 35, *193*
Berk, L. E., xv, 14, 27, *193*
Bernstein, M., 19, *195*
Biber, B., 161, *193*
Bizzell, R. P., 37, 161, *197*
Blank, M., 33, 96, *193*
Blyth, J., 24, *193*
Blyth, W. A. L., 28, *193*
Bodrova, E., xv, 27, *193*
Boggiano, A. K., 39, *193*
Brandt, R., xv, *193*
Bredekamp, S., xv, 35, *193*
Bretherton, I., 50, *194*
Brown, A., 14, 47, *194*
Bruner, J., 33, 47, *194*
Buss, D. M., 34, *194*

C

Campione, J., 14, 47, *194*
Carey, S., 48, *194*
Cesarone, B., 7, *196*
Chard, S. C., 159, 162, 185, *194, 196*
Clark, M. M., 33, *194*
Cockburn, A., 45, 46, *193*
Connell, J. P., 38, 45, *198, 199*
Consortium for Longitudinal Studies, 37, 161, *194*
Copple, C., xv, 35, *193*
Craik, K. H., 34, *194*

D

deCharms, R., 40, *194*
Deci, E. L., 38, 52, 125, *193, 194, 198*
Department of Education and Science, 12, 19, *194*
Desforges, C., 45, 46, *193*
Donaldson, M., 28, 46, *194*
Duckworth, E., 27, *196*
Durkin, D., 51, *194*
Dweck, C. S., 42, 43, 46, 48, 98, *194, 199*

E

Edwards, B., 139, 154, *194*
Edwards, C. P., xv, 3, 7, 17, *195*
Evangelou, D., xv, 18, 51, 53, *196*
Ewing, J. K., 26, *196*

F

Fabes, R. A., 40, *197*
Farley, F., 53, *197*
Fein, G., 50, *195*
Folger, R., 41, *198*
Forman, G., xv, 3, 7, 144, *195*

French, L. A., 16, 30, 32, *195*
Fry, P. S., 52, *195*

G

Gallas, K., 74, 140, *195*
Gandini, L., xv, 3, 7, *195*
Garvey, C., 50, *195*
Gersten, R., 35, *195*
Giancquinta, J. D., 19, *195*
Glaser, R., 47, *195*
Goodnow, J., 151, *195*
Graziano, W. G., 51, *197*
Greenberg, P., 22, *195*
Grieve, R., 28, *196*
Grolnick, W. S., 40, *195*
Gross, N., 19, *195*
Groves, M. M., 39, *195*

H

Harkema, R., 72, *195*
Harrison, C., 14, *195*
Hartman, J. A., xv, 18, 51, 53, *196*
Hatch, T., xv, *195*
Heath, S. B., 29, *195*
Helm, J. H., 10, 47, 55, 67, 106, 107, 110, 130, 160, *196*
Hinchmann, H., 144, 154, 156, *196*
Hohmann, M., 99, *196*
Holubec, E. J., 53, *196*
Hughes, M., 28, *196*
Hunter, M., 39, *196*

I

Isaacs, S., 18, 161, *196*

J

Johnson, D. W., 9, 53, *196, 199*
Johnson, R. T., 9, 53, *196, 199*
Julyan, C., 27, *196*

K

Kamii, C., 26, *196*
Karmiloff-Smith, A., 47, *196*
Karnes, M. B., 36, *196*
Katz, L. G., xv, 7, 18, 19, 22, 26, 28, 32, 34, 36, 41, 51, 53, 161, 185, *196*
Keats, E. J., 106, *197*
Kinsey, S. J., 51, *197*
Kliebard, H. M., 19, *197*
Koester, L. S., 53, *197*
Kohn, A., 13, 23, 44, *197*
Krathwohl, D., 53, *197*

L

Larner, M. B., 35, 37, *198*
Leggett, E. L., 42, 98, *194*
Leong, D. J., xv, 27, *193*
Lepper, M. R., 38, *197*
London, P., 148, *197*
Lougee, M. D. R., 51, *197*

M

Maccoby, E. E., 22, 35, *197*
Maehr, M. L., 38, *197*
Main, D. S., 39, *193*
Marcon, R. A., 35, 37, 41, 161, *197*
McClellan, D., 32, 51, 161, *196, 197*
McCullers, J. C., 40, *197*
Miller, L. B., 37, 161, *197*
Moline, S., 148, *197*
Moran, J. D., 39, 40, *195, 197*
Morgan, M., 38, *197*
Mounts, N. S., 51, 52, *197*
Murphy, K., 19, *193*

N

Nelson, K., 30, 31, 33, 47, 51, *197*

P

Parker, J., 32, *198*
Pinard, A., 28, *198*
Plowden Committee Report, 19, *198*
Prawat, R. S., 18, *198*

R

Radke-Yarrow, M., 22, *198*
Raths, J. D., 34, *196*
Real, D., 9, *199*
Reggio Children, 30, *198*
Rivkin, M., 50, *195*
Rogoff, B., 47, *198*
Roopnarine, J., 51, 52, *197*
Rosenfield, D., 41, *198*
Roy, P., 53, *196*
Ruef, K., 144, *198*
Ryan, R. M., 38, 39, 40, *194, 195, 198*

S

Sanderson, M., 64, *198*
Sawyers, J. K., 39, *195*
Schank, R. C., 30, *198*
Schickedanz, J. A., 35, *198*
Schwedel, A. M., 36, *196*
Schweinhart, L. J., 35, 37, *198*
Sedgwick, D., 139, *198*

Sedgwick, F., 139, *198*
Seidman, S., 30, 51, *197*
Sfard, A., 26, *198*
Shuell, T. J., 28, *198*
Skinner, E. A., 45, *199*
Slavin, R. E., 47, 51, 53, *198, 199*
Smagorinsky, P., 25, *199*
Smiley, P. A., 42, *199*
Spodek, B., 26, *199*
Springate, K., 17, *195*
Steinheimer, K., 106, 107, 110, 130, *196*
Stevahn, L., 9, *199*
Stewart, J., 18, *199*

T
Taylor, J., 81, *199*
Tudge, J., 52, *199*

V
Van Ausdal, S. J., 18, *199*

W
Wade, B., 33, *194*
Walberg, H., 37, 52, *199*
Webb, L., 160, *199*
Weikart, D. P., 35, 37, 99, *196, 198*
Wells, G., 33, *199*
Wilkinson, B., 45, 46, *193*
Willes, M. J., 48, 199
Williams, D. A., 17, *199*
Williams, M. B., 17, 36, *196*
Wilson, P. S., 84, *199*
Wisconsin Center for Educational Research, 51, *199*
Wood, D., 33, *199*
Wood, H., 33, *199*
Woods, B. S., 19, *193*

Z
Zellner, M., 35, *197*
Zimilies, H., 18, 53, *199*
Zimmer-Cembeck, M. J., 45, *199*

Subject Index

A

abilities
 age as predictor of, 17–18, 51–52
 drawing, 150–151, 154
 grouping by, 51–52
 mismatched with tasks, 45–46
 perceptions regarding children's, 7
 performance goals and perception of, 42–44
abstract representational knowledge, 28–30
academic goals *vs.* intellectual goals, 34–35
accomplishment, sense of, 130–134, 136
accountability
 project work *vs.* systematic instruction, 16–17
 topic selection and, 89
activities
 active *vs.* passive, 47–48, 52
 appropriateness of, 23–25, 35–36
 avoidance of, 78, 150–151
 choice, opportunities for, 14–15, 77–78, 136
 consolidation activities, 133–134
 construction activities, 120–121, 129–130
 corresponding competencies, 135
 dramatic play, 57–58, 66, 98–99, 108–110, 122
 drawing, 137–157
 for early stages of extended projects, 108–110
 investigation activities, 121–122
 as planning criterion, 97
 products of, 122–123, 131–134
ADHD (attention deficit and hyperactivity disorder), 53
affective development, 5–6, 22–23
 see also feelings
after-school programs, *xvi*

age norms, 22
age ranges, 17–18
 content of interaction, 48
 teaching methods and, 50–53
aims of education, 160
analysis
 disposition toward, 35
 drawing and increase in, 148
animals, 63
 family pets, 71
 research ethics, 75
anxiety and performance goals, 42
approaches. *See* project approach, systematic instruction, traditional education
art
 media, 110–111, 189
 as contingent reward , 40
 see also drawing
assessment and evaluation
 accountability and, 16–17
 competencies checklists, 135
 diagnostic responsibilities of teacher, 14
 discussions as method of, 135
 of displays, 134–135
 of learner's progress, 48–50
 of projects, 134–136
 of resources, 100–101
 self-evaluation, 15, 49, 130–131
 standards for children's drawings, 154
 teacher as evaluator, 14, 135, 149
attention
 drawing and focus, 138–139
 guiding learner's, 118
attention deficit and hyperactivity disorder (ADHD), 53

B

Bank Street curriculum model, 18
bar graphs, 124
basic skills
  in construction activities, 121
  in curricula, 6, 8, 161
  damaged disposition hypothesis, 36–38
  drill and practice, 31
  preschool instruction in, 35–36
  project planning and, 89, 100
behavioral knowledge, 16, 28–30
  project planning and, 99
  revealed in discussions, 107
benefits of project work, 1–20
bonus effect, 39
books
  class books as concluding phase, 129–130
  documenting projects, 59, 64, 77
  Drawing on the Right Side of the Brain, 154
  illustrations as information sources, 120
  instructions for making, 177–178
  A Life in Hand, 154
  A Trail Through Leaves, 154
boredom, task difficulty and, 15
brainstorming topics, 93–95
building sites, projects about, 64–66
burnout, academic, 46
  rewards and, 41

C

calendar rituals, 23–25
capabilities, age as predictor of, 17–18
catalog of successful projects, 67
cause and effect, 121, 198
challenge-seeking behaviors
  choice and, 153
  damaged by rewards, 40
  intellectual disposition toward, 42–44
change, aspect of dynamic development, 22
chaos, avoiding, 49
choice
  activities selection, 14–15
  drawing and, 153
  level of challenge, 153
  opportunities for, 6, 10, 76–81, 136
  reminders and suggestions, 81–82
civics, competencies, 197–198
classification, data
  practice in, 56
  Venn diagrams for, 118–119, 124
classroom culture
  community ethos, 9, 131–133

drawing and, 140, 150–152
  optimal informality in, 48–49
  questions and, 113
climate. *See* weather
cognitive development. *See* development
coherence and continuity in learning, 8
communication
  conversations, 33–34
  drawing as, 139
  observation and purposeful exchange, 119
  in project work, 110–111
  via presentation, 131–133
  see also discussions; questions
communicative competence, 33–34
community
  community ethos, 9, 131–133
  democracy and topic selection, 87
  drawing and, 140, 151
  sense of common history and, 106
competencies checklists, 135
competitive learning environments, 9, 44
  detrimental to drawing, 152
  interaction and, 48
concluding phase (III) of projects
  closure, 130
  community ethos, 130
  consolidation activities, 133–134
  construction activities, 129–130
  debriefings, 49–50, 130
  dramatic play during, 72–73
  drawing and, 149–150
  emerging interests, 136
  interest, 130
  open houses, 134
  project evaluation, 134–136
  reflection during 72–73
  self-assessment and confidence, 131
  webs, graphic maps, 135
confidence of learners, 4, 7
  drawing, 139
  inappropriate, confusing activities and, 23–24
  performance goals and erosion of, 42–43
  self-assessment, 49, 131
  skills application and, 98
  see also self-esteem
confusion, strategies for learners, 23–24, 49
consolidation activities, 133–134
construction activities, 120–121
  as concluding phase, 129–130
construction site projects
  description of, 11, 64–66
  "Houses: How Are They Built?", 165–169

webs, graphic maps, 180
constructivist theory, 26–28
  zone of proximal development (ZPD), 14, 45
content
  conversations and communicative competence, 33–34
  sustaining interaction, 48
  see also topics
conversations, as specialized interactions, 33–34
cooperative learning environments, 9, 44, 53
  choosing co-workers, 80–81
  concluding phase of projects, 131
counting, 186, 188
co-workers, choosing, 80–81
creativity
  damaged by extrinsic rewards, 39
  disposition toward synthesis, 35
  expressive vs. receptive activities, 47–48
  ideational fluency as index of, 39
  originality in drawing, 155
  rocks as inspiration, 187
criteria
  for project planning, 96–102
  for topic evaluation, 89–90
culture
  classroom culture, 9, 48–49, 113, 131–133, 150–152
  conventions in drawing, 156
  cultural relevance, xv, 53
  vs. heritage, 86–87
cumulative effects, aspect of dynamic development, 23
curricula
  balanced activities in, xv, 7–8, 159–163
  competencies and project activities, 135
  curriculum models research, 52–53
  desirable intellectual dispositions and, 36
  effects on development and learning, 47–50
  feelings and academic orientation of, 45
  integrating project approach, 3
  narrow teaching methods and restricted, 50–53
  project topics and curriculum areas, 95
  requirements of and topic selection, 87
  restrictions and topic selection, 89
  units and, 5

D
damaged disposition hypothesis, 36–38
data
  collecting, 5, 115, 118
  drawing and detail selection, 138

recording observations, 60–61, 122
debriefings, 49–50, 130
decontextualization and cognitive development, 16
delayed impact, aspect of dynamic development, 22–23
democracy
  education and, 9–10
  topic selection and, 87
development
  concepts of, 21–25
  drawing and, 137–139
  individual idiosyncrasies, 17–18
  knowledge and understanding, 26
  language and secondary knowledge sources, 31
  responses to bizarre questions, 28
  role of spontaneous play, 50
discouragement and stress, 15
discussions, 66, 69
  cross-child discussions, 117
  drawing and, 140, 154–156
  evaluation of projects, 135
  functions of, 74
  introductory, 106–108
  as motivation, 116
  planning phase, 70
  preparation for field work, 115–117
  project as context for, 74
  questions and investigations, 112–113
displays
  bulletin boards, 110–111
  communication function of, 124–125
  in conclusion phase, 130
  consolidation activities, 133–134
  evaluating projects, 134–135
  for information, 75–76, 123–124
  presentations, 131–133
  as a record and documentation, 124
  of work products, 75–76, 110–111, 122, 127, 131–133
dispositions
  academic skills and intellectual dispositions, 35–38
  children's desire to understand the world, 28
  damaged disposition hypothesis, 36–38
  defined, 26
  desirable dispositions, 36
  development of, 34–44, 161
  drawing and, 138–139
  as learning goal, 26
  maladaptive (i.e., helplessness), 42

mastery, desire for, 42–44
social dispositions, 44
strengthening, 41, 125
teacher's role, 37–38, 101
see also interest, capacity for
diversity
cultural, 86–87
enrichment of knowledge sources, 31
originality and, 155
of personal experiences, 86
teaching methods and, 50–53
topics selection and concerns about, 86–87
as value, 9–10
documentation
books, 59, 64
bulletin boards, 110–111
displays as record of project, 124
multi-stage work and drawing, 146
photographs, 130
representation of learner's experiences, 75
dramatic play, 57–58, 66, 122
in early stages of extended projects, 108–110
hospital transcript, 173–176
project planning and, 98–99
props for, 109–110, 122
reflection and conclusion phase of project,
72–73
drawing
abilities, 150–151, 154
abstract or decorative, 148
analysis improved by, 148
assessment and evaluation standards for, 154
books about, 154
as communication, 139
community and, 140, 151–152
concluding phase of project, 149–150
cultural conventions, 156
development and, 137–139
discussions about, 140, 154–156
disposition toward, 138–139
documenting multi-stage work, 146
in early stages of extended projects, 110–111
encouraging students in, 150–152
environment and resources, 152
explicit expectations, 151
language to describe, 154–156
noncompetitive climate for, 152
observation and, 128, 138, 146–148
originality as value, 155–156
peer modeling and, 154
in progress phase, 143–148
self-esteem and, 139

symbolic representations in , 146
teacher's ability for, 154
understanding represented by, 140–143
Drawing on the Right Side of the Brain, 154
drill and practice
damaged disposition hypothesis, 36–38
skills practice, 31
dynamic development, 22–25

E
economics, 197
effort
associated with low ability by learners, 43
intellectual disposition toward, 42–44
emotional learning. *See* feelings
empiricism, 10
event maps and, 144
engagement of learner, 5–6
environment
choosing where to work, 79–80
source of topics, 4
errors, as learning opportunities, 15, 133
estimating, 186
ethnographers, teachers as, 108
evaluation
comparison and competition, 152
competencies checklists, 135
of individual progress, 135
of projects, 134–135
self-assessment and responsibility, 15, 17, 49
standards for children's drawings, 154
topic evaluation criteria, 89–90
evaluation of projects, 134–135
event knowledge, 30–31
events
defined, 30
event maps, 144
focal events for projects, 115
exhibits, 62
see also displays
exotic topics, 85
experiences, resources to provide, 100
experiments
insulation properties, 65
investigational strategies, 75
shopping bags tests, 59
expertise, learner *vs.* teacher as expert, 15–16
experts
interviewing, 56, 65
learners as, 15–16
visitors as, 71–72, 111–112, 120
expressions / sayings, 63–64, 187

expressive *vs.* receptive activities, 47–48
expressive work
    display of, 122
    drawing, painting and writing, 110–111
    reflection and conclusion phase of project,
      72–73
extrinsic motivation, 13–14

F
failure, feelings and consequences of, 45
features of project approach, 69–90
feedback
    productivity and, 40
    tributes *vs.* inducements, 40
feelings
    affective development, 5–6, 22–23
    defined as learning goal, 26
    development of as learning goal, 45–47
    drawing, 139
field work, 74–75
    alternatives to site visits, 120
    discussions and, 115–117
    drawing and, 143–148
    interest and, 118, 120
    preparation for, 115–120, 127
    in progress phase (II) of projects, 71, 74–75,
      127
    as project strategy, 74–75
    trips and visits, 56–57, 64, 102, 118–120, 127
fire and rocks, 186–187
formal academic instruction
    emphasis of, 29
    inappropriate for younger children, 53
    procedural interaction emphasized in, 48
    see also systematic instruction
fourth-grade slump, 40–41
free association for topic development, 93–95
French, L.A., 16
frustration level, reading, 14

G
games, 125, 149
geography and geology, 187, 197
goal structures, 44
goals
    academic *vs.* intellectual goals, 34–35
    aims of education, 4, 160
    intellectual goals of project approach, 6–7
    performance goals, 42–44
    of project approach, 6–7
    topics and, 87–88
    see also learning goals

government, 197
graphic languages, *xv–xvi*
groups
    choosing co-workers, 80–81
    communicative skills and, 33–34
    mixed age and project work, 18, 53
    risks of ability grouping, 51

H
heritage *vs.* culture, 86–87
historical perspectives, 18–20
history, 198
horizontal *vs.* vertical relevance, 4, 6
houses, construction projects, 64–66, 165–169
The Hundred Languages of Children, 62
hyperactivity, 53
hypotheses, 116, 186
    disposition toward forming, 35

I
ice, 61
ideational fluency, 39
identification, practice in, 186
illuminations, 148
images, engaging interest with, 106
imagination *vs.* fancy, 85
incompetence, feelings of, 45–46
independent learning, 14, 72
independent work
    devices to encourage, 82
    displays of information and, 75–76
    skills application and, 98
individualistic learning environments, 9, 44
individualized learning, 3–4
inducements, 40
information
    displays as reference tools, 75–76, 123–124
    drawing and discovery, 148
    first hand observation, 117
    investigation activities, 121–122
    secondary sources, 31, 101, 117
initiative for learning, 4–5
innate intellectual dispositions, 34–35
instructional level, reading, 14
integrated curriculum, 19
    appropriateness for younger children, 53
intellectual dispositions. *See* dispositions
interactions
    procedural *vs.* substantive, 48–49
    role in learning, 47–48
interest, capacity for, 38–41
    assessing educational value of, 84

concluding phase (II) and, 130–131
defined, 38
drawing, 150–151
feedback and rewards, 38–40
field work and, 118, 120
interaction and, 48
motivation source, 13–14
peripheral interests, 133–134
planning phase (I) of project, 105–106
stimulation of, 41, 85–86, 136
teacher's interest in topic, 101
topic selection and, 41, 83–86
Internet resources, xvi, 117
interrogation-type questions, 33–34
interviews
    debriefing for learners, 130
    as information sources, 117
    peers and personal experiences, 108
intrinsic motivation. *See* interest, capacity for
investigation
    activities for, 121–122
    drawing as means of, 137–157
    projects as research, 2–3, 75
    questions and planning, 112–113

K

kindergarten. *See* preschool education
knowledge
    abstract representational knowledge, 28–30
    acquisition and construction of, 26–31
    behavioral knowledge, 16, 28–30, 99, 107
    as construct of learner, 26–28
    core knowledge, 7
    defined as learning goal, 25
    diversity and enrichment of, 31
    drawing and, 138
    event and script knowledge, 30–31
    project planning and, 99
    secondary sources of, 31

L

language arts
    competencies, 196
    in construction activities, 121
    sayings and myths, 63–64, 187
    skills application and project planning, 98–99
    stones used to teach, 187–188
lead thinker, role of teacher, 113
leadership in projects, 3
learners
    accountability and, 16–17, 39
    choice opportunities and, 76–81

engagement of, 5–6
expertise of, 15–16
teacher as guide for, 118
see also confidence of learners; self-esteem
learning centers, 3
learning goals
    categories of, 25–47
    drawing and, 137–139
    vs. performance goals, 42–43
    topics and, 87–88
life, school as, 8–9
A Life in Hand, 154
life skills, 32
light, shade and shadow studies, 62
listening, 32, 117, 140, 196
listserv addresses, 67
literacy, preschool interest in, 35–36
literature project work and integration of, 59, 60

M

marbles, teaching quantitative information with, 16
mastery, desire for
    academic exercises and drills, 41
    intellectual disposition toward, 42–44
mathematics
    competencies, 196
    in construction activities, 121
    marbles to teach, 16
    rocks and stones to teach, 186
    sticks to teach, 188
measuring, 186, 188
media
    primary and secondary sources of information, 31, 101, 117
    tape recording sessions, 56
memory
    drawing as access to, 138, 140
    knowledge and, 26
    scripts and, 30
methods, teaching, 50–53
    see also project approach; systematic instruction; traditional education
mind, defined, 5–6
mini-projects, 162
mixed-age and mixed-ability groups, 51
models, constructing, 120–121
Montessori, Maria, 50
motion, 187, 188
motivation
    cooperative learning environments and, 53
    discussions as motivation, 116
    extrinsic, 13–14

positive feedback and rewards, 38–41
  see also interest, capacity for
music, 189

N
nature walks, 185–189
negative attitudes, reinforced by teaching strategies, 39
networking, resources for, *xvi*
normative development, 22
novelty, children's interest and, 105

O
objectives, in project documentation, 5
observation
  children's aptitude for, 118
  drawing, 128, 140–143
  as information source, 117
  as investigation, 121
open education, 19–20, 52–53
open houses, 134
optimal informality, 48–50
Organizing and Integrating the First School Day, 81
originality, value in drawing, 155
overjustification effect, 38

P
parents
  audience for reports, 130
  communication with, 111
  encouraging participation of, 111–112
  as expert visitors, 65, 111–112
  as information sources, 74
  open houses for, 134
  pressure to succeed academically, 19
  role in knowledge construction, 28
passive *vs.* active activities, 47–48, 52
performance goals, 42–43
personal experiences
  introductory discussions and, 106–108
  planning phase of projects, 70–71
personality traits. *See* dispositions
pets, 71
phases. *See* concluding phase (III) of projects;
    planning phase (I) of projects; progress
    phase (II) of projects)
photographs, 130
Piaget, Jean, 27
pictures, engaging interest with, 106
planning, teacher's preparatory, 70–71, 91–103
planning phase (I) of projects, 105–114
  discussions during, 106–108, 111–112

dramatic play during, 108–110
drawing during, 110–111, 140–143
engaging children's interest, 105–106
parental participation and, 111–112
roles of teacher, 70–71, 112
writing during, 110–111
play
  complexity and mixed age grouping, 52
  contribution to development, 50
  in project context, 73
  vs. projects, 3
  spontaneous play, 6–7
  see also dramatic play
Plowden Report, 19
portfolios, 49, 127, 149–150
predicates, topics and, 96
predictions, 85–86, 116, 186
preschool education
  calendar rituals, 23–25
  project work in curriculum, 12
  traditional nursery/kindergarten approach,
    6–7
presentations, 131–133
problem solving
  drawing and, 138–139
  open/informal education and, 52
  teachers and challenges, 10–11
problematic situations and creative solutions,
    10–11
procedures, optimal informality, 48–50
products of work, 75–76, 122, 127, 131–133
progress phase (II) of projects
  activities for, 120–123
  construction activities during, 120–121
  displays during, 123–125
  dramatic play during, 122
  drawing, 143–148
  investigation activities during, 121–122
  field work during, 71, 74–75, 115–120, 127
  products of work, 122–123
  teacher's role during, 72, 125–126
project approach
  aims of, 5–11
  balanced curriculum and, 7–8,
    50–53159–163
  choice making, 76–81
  community ethos fostered by, 9
  current interest in, 19–20
  democracy and education, 9–10
  features of, 69–82
  teaching and learning, 3–4
  teaching style and, 3

see also project work; projects
project work
  ability and age grouping, 51–52
  accountability in, 16–17
  activities selection, 14–15
  choice opportunities in, 76–81
  coherence and continuity of, 8
  contrasted to systematic instruction, 12–17
  defined, *xii*
  democracy and, 87
  drawing in context of, 137–157
  evaluation of progress, 48–50
  examples and illustrations of, 55–67
  feelings of competence and, 47
  historical and international perspectives on,
    18–20
  imagination stimulated by, 85–86
  interdisciplinary nature of, 8–9
  intrinsic motivation and, 13–14
  learning goals and, 25–54
  location of expertise, 15–16
  phases of, 70–73, 105–114
  portfolios and, 49
  purpose of, 47
  skills application and, 13
  social competence skills developed by, 32
  strategic features of, 73–76
  sustained effort and interest, 41
  systematic curriculum as context for, 11–17
  topic selection, 83–90
  see also project approach; projects
projects
  catalog of, 67
  concluding phase of, 129–136
  defined and described, 2–3, 5
  discussion in context of, 74
  duration of, 3
  evaluation of, 134–136
  field work as strategy, 74–75
  guidelines, example, 171–172
  mini-projects, 162
  objectives in documentation, 5
  planning, 91–103
  play in context of, 73
  reflection and conclusion phase, 72–73
  representation of experiences, 75
  research question development, 112–113
  scope of, 95
  vs. spontaneous play, 3
  temporal structure or phases of, 70–73
  vs. themes and units, 4–5
  website addresses, 67

see also project approach; projects
props
  defined and described, 109–110
  to stimulate dramatic play, 122

Q
questions
  bizarre or silly questions, 28
  chart for documenting, 116
  classroom culture and, 113
  in conversations, 33–34
  eliciting from children, 49, 117
  research questions for projects, 112–113
  roleplay and, 122

R
rain, 62
reading
  competencies, 196
  effect of contingent demands, 39
  levels of difficulty, 14
realia
  displays of, 75–76
  engaging interest with, 105–106
  props for dramatic play, 109–110
receptive strategies, 121
record keeping, cross with documentation, 124
recurring innovation, 19
Reggio Emilia, Italy, 7, *xv*
  behavioral and representational knowledge,
    29–30
  The Hundred Languages of Children, 62
relevance, horizontal *vs.* vertical, 4, 6
reminders,
  choice opportunities and 81–82
  respect for tools and materials, 152
representational knowledge, 28–30
  project planning and, 99
representational strategies, 75, 138
research, 2–3, 75
  see also data; investigation; field work
resources
  assessing, 100–101
  drawing in the classroom, 152
  natural materials, 185–189
  project ideas and information, 67
  scarcity and responsibility, 152
responsibility, learners' perception of and
    rewards, 39
revision, 17
  displays as motivation for, 124
  drawing, 138

rewards
    decrease of interest and, 38–41
    performance goals and, 43
rocks and stones used in teaching, 186
roleplay, 57–58, 122
    see also dramatic play
roles of teacher
    advisor or guide in project work, 76
    during concluding phase (III), 73
    debriefing learners, 49–50, 130
    in discussions, 108, 113
    dispositions, strengthening, 41
    as ethnographer, 108
    evaluation of progress, 135, 149
    as interested listener, 117
    in knowledge construction, 27–28
    modeling inquiring disposition, 101
    during planning phase (I) of projects, 70–71
    during progress phase (II) of projects, 72,
        125–126
    in project work, 81–82
    social competence, fostering, 32
    in structuring project, 70–71, 73–74, 91–103
    in topic selection, 84, 88–89
routines, optimal informality, 48–50
rules, safety, 110

S
scaffolding, constructivist theory, 27
schemata, representational knowledge, 29
school, attitudes toward, 8–9
science
    competencies, 196–197
    natural objects used to teach, 186–189
scripts
    defined and described, 30–31
    learning through dramatic play, 122
    script knowledge, 30–31, 72
seasons, 63–64
    time of year and topics, 102
secondary sources, 31, 101, 117
self-directed learning. *See* interest, capacity for
self-esteem, 53
    confidence and skills application, 42–46, 98
    damage to, 42–46
    displays of accomplishments, 131–134
    drawing and, 139
self-evaluation, 49, 130–131
seriation, 186, 188
shade and shadow studies, 62
shapes, 188
shopping projects, 55–59, 179

short term *vs.* long term outcomes, 36–38
skills
    acquisition of, 13, 31–34
    application of, 12, 13, 97–100, 127
    defined as learning goal, 25
    documenting improvement for learner, 136
    drawing, 138
    mini-projects and development of, 162
    as planning criterion, 97–100
    practice and proficiency, 31–32
    social competence and, 32, 161
    see also basic skills
social competencies
    choosing co-workers, 80–81
    interaction and development of, 47–48
    skills required for, 32, 161
    social dispositions and, 44
social dispositions, 44
social studies, competencies, 197–198
socialization/play approach, 6–7
sorting, 188
space, classroom, 79–80
spontaneous play
    vs. academically oriented curriculum, 6
    vs. projects, 3
    scripts in, 30–31
standards
    accountability and, 17
    for children's drawing, 154
    inappropriate comparisons, 152
    setting and communicating, 81–82
sticks as teaching materials, 188–189
stones and rocks used in teaching, 186
subject areas
    interdisciplinary work, 8–9
    as project topics, 95
    see also specific subjects
symbolic drawing, 146
synthesizing, disposition toward, 35
systematic instruction
    in art *vs.* drawing in project context, 139
    in balanced curricula, 20, 160
    contrasted to project work, 12–17, 126
    developmental appropriateness of, 8
    teacher's expectations in, 81

T
tape recording, 56
task goals, performance *vs.* learning, 42–44
tasks
    choosing, 77–78
    mismatched to abilities, 45–46

providing range of complexity, 122–123
teachers
    assessment and diagnostic responsibilities, 14
    dispositional development of children, 37–38
    drawing ability of, 154
    engagement and work satisfaction, 10–11
    experiences with projects, 162–163
    journal excerpt, 165–169
    personal interest in topic, 101
    pressures from parents and administrators, 19
    social competence encouraged by, 32
    see also roles of teacher
teaching
    methods, 47–48, 50–53, 91
    overcoming challenges, 10–11
    resources for, 67
    styles, 3
team teaching, 91
temperature studies, 60–61
textbooks as sources of knowledge, 31
theme work. See project work
themes, defined and described, 4–5
time management
    choosing when to work, 78–79
    optimal use of school time, 86
tools, stones as, 187
topic work. See project work
topics
    accountability and, 89
    age ranges and, 18
    animals, 63, 71
    appropriateness of, 83–86
    clinical considerations, 88–89
    community awareness and democracy, 87
    construction sites, 64–66, 165–169
    content of interaction, 48
    criteria for evaluation of, 89–90
    culture and diversity, 86–87
    curriculum areas and, 95
    distant in time or space, 101
    evaluative criteria for, 89–90
    fanciful or exotic topics, 85
    hierarchical classification and, 96
    learning goals and, 87–88
    mandated by administration, 159
    plants, 171–172
    potential delicacy or offensiveness of, 88
    predication of, 96
    project planning and selection of, 91–95,
        159–160
    scope of, 95–96
    seasons, 63–64

seedpods, 171–172
selection of, 83–90
shopping, 55–59
subsequent learning and, 87–88
teacher's interest as criterion for selection,
    101
themes as sources for, 5
weather, 59–64, 180
webs or graphic maps of, 92–95
"zooming in" on, 95–96
traditional education
    abstract representational knowledge empha-
        sized in, 29
    nursery/kindergarten, 6–7, 52–53
A Trail Through Leaves, 154
tributes, 40

U
units, defined and described, 5

V
Venn diagrams, 118–119, 124
vertical vs. horizontal relevance, 4, 6
visual texts, 148
vocabulary
    describing stones, 187–188
    displays as glossary, 123
    drawing terms, 154–156
    growth and project work, 58

W
walks, 185–189
water and rocks, 186
weather
    animals and seasons, 63
    climate, 63
    rain studies, 62
    sayings and myths, 63–64
    shade and shadows, 62
    temperature studies, 60–61
    weather forecast projects, 60
    webs, graphic maps, 180
    wind studies, 61
webs, graphic maps
    in concluding phase, 135
    construction site project, 180
    fish project example, 191
    "Houses: How are They Built," 135
    school bus examples, 181–182
    shopping project, 179
    teacher's topic webs, 92–95
    weather project, 180

"zooming" example, 183
websites, 67, *xvi*
weighing, 186, 188
wildlife, 63
wind studies, 61
wondering in discussions, 113
work products
    of activities, 131–134
    displays of, 75–76, 122, 127, 131–133
World Wide Web, resources available, 67, *xvi*
writing
    choices of form, 77
    communication through displays, 124

competencies, 196
drawing and expression, 148
literacy, preschool interest in, 35–36
in planning phase of project, 110–111
play or pretend, 98
revision of, 17

Z
zone of proximal development (ZPD), 14, 27
    feelings and task difficulty, 45
"zooming in," 95–96
    using webs, graphic maps, 183